XXXIX

KT-432-857

DESERT OF DEATH

LEO DOCHERTY

Desert of Death

A Soldier's Journey from Iraq to Afghanistan

faber and faber

First published in 2007
by Faber and Faber Limited
3 Queen Square London WC1N 3AU

Typeset by Faber and Faber Ltd
Printed in England by Mackays of Chatham plc,
Chatham, Kent

A CIP record for this book
is available from the British Library

ISBN 978–0–571–23688–6

10 9 8 7 6 5 4 3 2 1

This book is dedicated
to the soldiers still serving in Iraq and Afghanistan

My sincere thanks to Bob and Margaret Docherty, Abi Docherty, Paddy Docherty, Susie Hyde-Smith, Bessie Kelaart, Hannah and Billy Woollen, Thierry Kelaart, Henry Volans and Neil Belton. – L.D.

Contents

Afghanistan and Helmand Province

International frontier
Frontier of Helmand province
Land over 1000m (in Helmand province)
Land over 2000m (in Helmand province)

G H O W R

Baghran valley

F A R A H

U R U Z G A N

to Herat

R. Helmand

National Ring
Road (Route 1)

Now Zad

Musa
Qalah

Kijaki

Route 611

Sangin

FOB Robinson

N

Camp Bastion
and Tombstone

Gereshk

to Kandahar

Lashkar Gah

A F G H A N I S T A N

K A N D A H A R

H
E
L
M
A
N
D

Desert of Death
(Dasht-e-Margo)

R. Helmand

PAKISTAN

0   km   100

Illustrations

All photographs courtesy of the author.

Preface

Hurriedly striding out of Wellington Barracks, I check my watch again.

'Fuck!' I exclaim in a whisper. I'd better get a move on; I'm due to the see the Major General in ten minutes, and must be there at least five minutes beforehand.

Cutting a diagonal through the gaudy flower beds of St James's Park, I reset my tie knot, button my suit jacket and draw my shirt cuffs over my wrists. Despite my haste I'm feeling pretty smart in my favourite grey suit, cut like an hourglass, with ultra-sharp trouser creases, and – thanks to my old orderly, Guardsman Lambe – my shoes are like black glass. The finishing touch is a couple of inches of pink silk handkerchief floating out of my breast pocket; a bit of dash will go down well with the Major General.

Darting out of the path of a black cab, I cross the road, onto the gravel of Horse Guards Parade, heading towards the main building: a great white stone edifice, ancient and solid. This is the headquarters of the Major General, commander of all the troops in London. Crunching across the vast parade ground I survey its fringes: the nondescript rear of

Downing Street, Mountbatten's bronze effigy clutching binoculars, and a pair of mounted stone generals, rigidly upright on each flank of the empty square.

As I walk under the archway in the centre of the vast building, I pause beside a cavalry trooper, ceremoniously guarding the entrance in a blue cape and white-plumed metal helmet, and press the door buzzer. The trooper looks a bit peeved to be dismounted, unlike his mate on the White-hall side of the archway who's getting all the attention on his colossal 'cavalry black' war horse.

In the Aide-de-Camp's cramped office I'm ushered to a sofa, to wait for the call to see the Major General in the adjoining room, behind a tall oak door. I struggle to dry my sweat-sodden palms on the sofa cushion, not that I'm expecting to be shaking hands. Having already been formal-ly charged with misconduct I'm about to find out what my punishment will be; the best-case scenario is that I get a ver-bal reprimand, the worst case that I'm court-martialled, fined and dishonourably discharged without pension. How-ever, as I'm leaving the Army anyway, if the Major General kicks me out I wouldn't much care. My greatest worry is that he'll deprive me of my leave by ordering me to do duties in London for the next couple of months.

The ADC, an earnest Irish Guards officer, answers inces-sant phone calls at a desk littered with paper. He's basically a diary assistant to the Major General. It's his first day in the job and he's flustered but resolutely good humoured. The atmosphere is a little awkward; he's junior to me but I'm here for a bollocking, which seems unnatural for us both.

'Could you get Captain Docherty a cup of tea please?' he

asks the secretary in between phone calls. She agrees cheerfully, perhaps glad for the chance of a fag break.

Drinking my tea and sweating into the sofa, I wait to see
the General.

I used to be a soldier: a Captain in the Scots Guards, a traditional, blue-blooded Foot Guards regiment. Late last year,
having served in Afghanistan, I publicly expressed my opinion of the campaign and caused an almighty furore in the
media. As a serving officer, I was punished by the Army for
breaking the rules. But now I'm out; I'm a civilian, at liberty
to speak, to look back on the journey that's led me via Iraq,
London and Afghanistan to the Major General's door.

I'm not a journalist or a writer. Unlike TV news and print
media this is a *soldier*'s true account of being on the ground at
the very centre of the British campaign in Helmand at its
inception. This is a version of events that hasn't yet been told.
It does not seek praise; better stories will come of heroic bravery and courageous endurance, and also greater understanding. This, the first word, will surely be followed by a deluge.

I never imagined that I'd speak publicly or write about my
time in the Army. The military culture of reticence and obe-
dience stifles honest, reflective expression. Leaving the Army
doesn't make it any more natural, because in a way, you *never*
leave; military culture doesn't get removed with the uniform.
I would therefore deny any charge of disloyalty. It would be
disloyal to those still serving in Iraq and Afghanistan *not* to
speak. Only silence would be contemptible.

I was in Afghanistan at the beginning of the new war. This
is my story.

CHAPTER 1

In the Desert

Fumbling, I unclip the torch from my webbing vest and wave the little red light frantically towards the Chinook beating down onto the helicopter landing site before me. Ideally I'd have it on a bit of string and whirl it around my head, spinning a red 'O' for the pilot to see, but I've been crashed out for this operation, without time to prepare properly, so I just wave it optimistically back and forth.

The Chinook looms down, huge and black. Grains of sand deflect off the tips of the giant twin rotors and burst into green sparks, generating a pair of vast fiery halos, bristling in the darkness.

The loadmaster replies to my light with his own red torch, waving me onboard. I run through the deafening storm of the downdraught, up the tailgate and into the helicopter. I flop down on the canvas seats and buckle in as we pull up hard, my chin forced into my chest. Craning my head, I can see the lights of Sha'iba Logistics Base fading as we make a rapid ascent.

I'm chuffed to bits to be getting out of camp. All I know is that I'm needed as an interpreter for an operation being carried out by 45 Commando Royal Marines. The normal interpreter is on leave, so I've been offered up as a stand-in.

Within a few minutes we descend into the Az Zubayr Port complex, a few kilometres south-east of Sha'iba, on the Shatt Al Arab waterway, where the Marines are based. I'm picked up on the landing site and taken straight into the Orders Group – a meeting in which a commander gives his men their orders for an operation and on a map or model explains how the plan will work.

The company commander, a Major in his late thirties, has the officers and senior non-commissioned officers gathered around him. They've already done rehearsals so these orders are for just for confirmation. The Major has a tough, angular face, deep brown, and dark thinning hair. He runs through the plan in a conversational manner: 'As you already know we're out early doors tomorrow to arrest some people connected with the transit of suicide bombers into Iraq from Saudi ... They have a Thuraya satellite phone ... Intelligence has picked up the signal, so this is the key to locating them ... It's also what we need to find on the objective, which will probably be a Bedouin tent ...'

The company will be in three main groups: a break-in group, an inner cordon and an outer cordon. The break-in group will go directly to the tent and arrest and search its occupants, while the cordon groups will prevent anyone escaping. I'm to go with the Major in his little command group and be ready to move to the break-in group when called forward.

'This is Captain Docherty. He's the 'terp,' the Major says, nodding in my direction.

I blurt a greeting and add, 'I've done a *short* course,' trying to indicate that I'm not exactly qualified for this, but no one really seems bothered. This op sounds like more of a linguistic challenge than I had anticipated. It is a potential interrogation, not a 'meet and greet'. I now realise why it's too sensitive a mission to use a local interpreter.

After the Major has finished and answered a couple of questions, the wiry Company Sergeant-Major (CSM) gives a few admin details. We're to carry our morphine in the left-hand trouser pocket, so that everyone knows where it is if we take casualties; Zap numbers (the first two characters of your last name and the last four digits of your Army number) are to be marked on the front of body armour, and we're to carry a twenty-four-hour ration pack and as much water as possible.

The men assembled around the map-covered table, with well-worn notebooks, bronzed faces and battered combats, exude the sanguine confidence of those constantly on operations. This is the most exciting thing that I've done so far in Iraq but they're all very used to it; some of the 'bootnecks' – the Marine private soldiers – have done three or four operational tours already in as many years of service. This is my first tour, and I'm delighted to be on operations at last. When I left Sandhurst almost three years ago my regiment, the Scots Guards, had just returned to London from Northern Ireland. Bursting with physical fitness and enthusiasm, I was gutted to find myself marching around in a bearskin and tunic outside Buckingham Palace while my contemporaries in other regiments were in the Balkans, Afghanistan and Sierra Leone. After more than a year inside the M25 the low point came with missing out on Operation Telic 1: the invasion of Iraq in March 2003. With disgusted envy I watched events unfold on the Officers' Mess television.

Now on Operation Telic 5 I've finally got my chance to do something interesting. I did a ten-week basic Arabic course in the spring and I'm pleased this seems to be opening doors. I'm really hoping to get out and about and see some action. I especially like the idea of working closely with the Iraqis, and secretly want to become fluent in their language. I know it makes me unusual as a soldier but I'm passionate about Arabic. During the course I ventured into a Lebanese music shop in London's Edgware Road and bought a cassette of narrated Holy Qur'anic verses. Though ignorant of their meaning, I found the words beguiling and wanted to know more.

Onboard a pair of Chinooks we depart just after dawn the following morning. We make a brief touchdown at the main British headquarters in Basra to collect a couple of Americans – a short pale Sergeant, wearing gloves and wraparound sunglasses, runs up the tailgate, followed by a tall black Major. They're jammed in among the Marines opposite me. The Sergeant's got proper ear-defenders while the Major, like me, has spongy little yellow earplugs which must be compressed and jammed into the ear canal. The visceral turbo-whining and shaking of the engines numb us. The Marines are well used to it, most sleeping over their weapons, rested barrel-down onto the floor. Corporal Fox next to me dozes open-mouthed.

After two hours we make a smooth descent onto the tarmac of an Italian-run Forward Air Refuelling Point (FARP).

Because of the fuel hazard, we have to disembark on the hot gravel next to the runway. The Marines sit listlessly on their patrol packs. The sky is a cloudless pale blue and the sun is ferocious; we're truly in the middle of the desert now.

The American Sergeant is the arresting officer; this operation must have been of US origin in Baghdad. He's come personally for the sake of sound evidence: the same arresting officer must be present with any arrestee from the point of arrest to the courtroom. He gives me the official line that I must tell anyone being arrested the legal jargon about 'being detained for questioning . . . you're not a prisoner'. I reckon I can probably get the gist across, and the Sergeant doesn't seem fussy anyway.

The Major is an artilleryman currently working in the US intelligence department. As a bureaucratic staff officer he rarely gets out of camp: 'I can't believe I'm doin' this shit . . . I'm from an Air Defence unit, they won't believe it when I tell them.'

He makes notes in tiny writing on a square pad; he needs to recall everything in chronological order in case it's required as evidence. I ask him when the Falluja offensive is going to start; I've heard rumours of a massive US operation to rid the northern town of its Sunni insurgents, who've held sway there and across the 'Sunni Triangle' since the spring.

'Today, man. That place gonna be levelled.'

Back on board I look up a couple of words from the official statement in my mini Arabic dictionary. It fits neatly into one of the smaller pouches on my webbing vest – a waistcoat of small pouches. My mind wanders to the memory of purchasing it in Damascus during my recent summer leave: three weeks spent practising my newly learnt Arabic, drinking tea amid a cacophony of backgammon dice, and exploring the bazaars around the Umayyad Mosque.

I'm shaken from my daydreaming as the 'five minutes to go' signal – an open raised palm with fingers splayed – is passed down our seated line. Helmets are replaced and weapons cradled more firmly. I loop my rifle sling over my head and draw a gulp of water from my water satchel, trapping the mini-tap carefully in a zip-up pocket. The 'one minute to go' signal comes. Out of the porthole I can see the desert floor race past, a flat beige blur no more than twenty metres below.

A bump rocks us in unison towards the pilot: we're on the ground, trundling forward, the tailgate lowering into a swirl of dust. Belts are flung off as the helicopter shudders to a halt. Springing to life, we haul ourselves upright and run towards the light and dust at the tailgate. The sand whips my face as I follow the lumbering figure in front of me. The Chinook rotors fade. I can hear my own panting breath, amplified until I extract my yellow ear plugs.

Coming to a halt, we go down on one knee. We're surrounded by hard, flat desert, featureless except for a low black tent about a hundred metres away towards which the break-in group are now sprinting. In front of me is the company commander and Corporal Fox, his signaller. He swings his backpack off his shoulder and extracts an antenna. As he folds out its spiky arms it takes form like a short black metallic Christmas tree. It's the secure VHF radio link back to headquarters in Basra. He's got another radio with a short fat antenna, like a truncheon; this is the UHF set which he uses to speak to the helicopter.

Over the Personal Role Radio (PRR) jammed to my left ear, the break-in group asks for me. I run forward towards the tent.

Outside, a few metres apart from one another, two small men in long white shirts sit cross-legged with their hands on their heads. Wispy black beards and tousled hair poke out from under broad blindfolds. Their small dark bodies and thin limbs look almost fragile. Their tent is a long, low construction of scruffy black cloth, open along one side. Inside, two women huddle with a pair of young children and a baby among a ramshackle collection of cooking implements, grimy bundles of cloth, sacks of flour and a couple of dusty carpets. The Marine searchers are steadily working through it, wearing plastic gloves as a forensic precaution.

'Ask them if they've any weapons, would you, boss,' says the Sergeant in charge of the searching team.

Kneeling down, I ask one of the men, speaking close to his ear.

'Yes,' he replies, shaking with fright. 'We have guns in the tent, for protection.'

At the same moment one of the Marines finds a weapon under one of the carpets. The bundles of cloth and the possessions around them are quickly scattered. The stash of weapons consists of a new but slightly rusty Kalashnikov, a replica of a German G3 rifle, a rusted old Lee Enfield of Second World War vintage and a little pistol. There's also a plastic bag of mixed ammunition: it's clearly just for their personal protection.

'Ask if they have a Thuraya phone,' says the American Major, pausing from his furious note-taking. Unsurprisingly, they say they don't.

While the searchers get really busy dismembering the tent's contents I continue the interrogation, relaying questions from the American Major. Agitated with fear, they garble their replies: they're brothers, their father's dead, their mother and a wife are in the tent, they don't know of any satellite phone . . .

The American Sergeant grows impatient: 'Ask him if he knows about Abu Ghrayb prison,' he says, keen to shock out something incriminating.

I relay the question but it falls flat. It holds no meaning. A silence follows, and the steam has gone out of the interrogation. It seems our detainees are a poor Bedouin family unrelated to the trafficking of suicide bombers. It's baffling because we've been specifically targeted onto this location by the intelligence people in headquarters. Perhaps whoever it was using the Thuraya has already packed up and left.

Sensing that we're onto the wrong people, the American Major has the two detainees moved into a slim band of shade skirting the tent. The Marines half-heartedly start re-constituting its contents, silently watched by the two women. The wife, wearing a tatty party dress, jogs the baby on her arm, her face partly hidden under a head scarf. The old woman, her mother-in-law, is swaddled in a large black gown, tight about her head, that leaves her face exposed. Tiny tattoo dots are just visible amongst the deep lines of her face. Like faded blue tear drops they dot her chin, forehead, cheeks and nose in rough symmetry. The other children burrow silently into her side. On their little shirts, rows of sequins and embroidery glint out from under a layer of grime.

We've now been here for a good hour. Some of the Marines get a photo with the weapons. The American Sergeant joins them. 'This is nothing,' he says, now resigned to not making an arrest. 'I got more weapons 'n that in my house anyway.'

The Chinook beats across the sky and comes down nearby. The two men are helped to stand and have their blindfolds removed. Blinking, they smile fearfully, still uncertain if the ordeal is over.

'We're very sorry to have troubled you,' I shout over the helicopter's roar, feeling a complete shit.

'Thank you, thank you,' they stammer, shaking my hand repeatedly.

As we retreat towards the helicopter, the old woman gains confidence and berates me. I can't understand her words. The men try to calm her.

'I'm sorry,' I shout, turning away and running for the Chinook. I plunge again through a wall of face-stinging dust, heat and noise, and sprawl onto the metal floor as we power upwards.

I'm dehydrated and nauseated by the helicopter's turbo engine whining. I've already drained my water satchel and have lost my yellow earplugs. The heli is packed with blokes now. I'm in a tangled mass of sweating Marines on the floor. Exhausted, we're quietly tolerant of one another.

I'm feeling a bit guilty about the last hour or so, especially as the unfortunate Bedouin were so magnanimous. It was clearly an intelligence cock-up. In a way, though, I'm relieved that it was the wrong target, as a deeper interrogation would have been beyond my linguistic means. Using my fingers I struggle to keep the noise out, shut my eyes and submit to a piercing headache.

Landing again at the Italian base, we're disgorged onto the gravel at the runway's edge as the Chinook is refuelled. I'm now desperate for water. Running over to a group of huts near the runway, I find a group of off-duty Italian aircrew lounging in deckchairs. They're delighted to give me a couple of big bottles of mineral water from a tall fridge behind a home-made bar. I drain them into my camel back, thank them and with a '*Ciao*' dash away, envious of their neat little beards, deep tans and cushy set-up.

After dropping off the Americans at Divisional Headquarters we have a quick de-brief at the Marines' base. No one is too worried about the fact that our mission has been a failure. The Major is still relaxed. I get a thank you. For the assembled NCOs, sweat-stained and weary, it's just another day's work. They're unexcited about the outcome. Perhaps I'm naive but I feel let down by our failure; I hope my next meeting with an Iraqi is less confrontational.

Two days later I'm back in Shai'ba Logistics Base, waiting outside the Commanding Officer's Portakabin. My ultra-short 'high and tight' haircut has not met with his approval. I had it done in an American camp just over the border in Kuwait while coming back from Az Zubayr with the Marines; they have a small guard force there which checks the passports of British Forces personnel crossing the border.

Marching into the office, I come to a formal halt just in

front of the Commanding Officer's desk. The rapid left-right slamming of my heels shakes the entire frame of the flimsy Portakabin.

The CO is displeased. 'The problem, Leo, is that you have shown yourself as wanting to be different to all the other officers . . .'

'God, what bullshit!' I shout inwardly, while nodding contritely. I knew it might cause some mirth among my colleagues but I can't believe that he's bothered by it, given that we're on operations in Iraq, not on parade in London.

'I have no choice but to reflect this in your report as a "lapse of judgement". The adjutant will award you extras.'

'Yes, sir,' I reply, taking my leave with a salute and a sharp turn to my right, slamming my left heel into the floor, again shaking the Portakabin.

'What a load of nonsense,' I think, continuing my unspoken defiance as I walk out into the warm evening. I'm bemused by the fact that in the middle of a counter-insurgency campaign my regiment is under the command of someone who seems more interested in the haircuts of his officers than their operational activity; he didn't even mention the failed arrest operation. Getting 'extras' means I'll have to do extra duties as Picquet Officer – the duty officer – when we're back at our home base in Germany.

The bollocking has touched a nerve because I'm frustrated by the CO's refusal to let me be attached to another unit in Iraq. At the moment I'm often at a loose end because the Scots Guards are in reserve, sitting in Shai'ba Logistics Base. I'm desperate to get out of camp and do something constructive, make some sort of difference, however small. In other regiments – especially those that have a geographical area of responsibility like Basra and Al Amarah – there's plenty going on. Operation Bracken is under way: the Black Watch are up in Babel, in the north, towards the Sunni Triangle, making a show of supporting the US Marine Corps. It's purely political window-dressing in anticipation of the US Presidential election the following month, meant to show the American electorate that the Coalition is rock solid, but it seems exciting. Despite the fact that five Black Watch boys have been blown up by suicide bombs I'd like to go up there. It's the biggest thing going on at the moment for British Forces and we've sent a couple of Scots Guards Captains to be liaison officers. More are required, but ironically because of my Arabic I'm not allowed to go, the CO says, just in case I'm required by him in Shai'ba Logistics Base. I can't help feeling I won't contribute much to the rebuilding of Iraq from here.

To keep me busy the CO takes me as his aide to a series of negotiations between two conflicting tribes in Basra: the Halaf and the Garamsha. In a cold conference room in the Governor of Basra's office we wait by a long table. We've met each side separately already so we're hoping that today they'll agree a truce, mediated by the Tribal Council, a supposedly impartial body of pan-tribal leaders.

The council members, a dozen old men, wander gracefully into the room, resplendent in their flowing *abeyya* gowns (finely spun white or black cloth with broad gold trim, worn over ankle-length *dish-dasha* shirts). Their white-and-black headdresses are kept in place with fat black ropes. Next, the two opposing delegations trickle in and sit down around the long table. The Governor enters and everyone stands, returning his greeting in near unison. He's a handsome forty-something with a neat black beard and smart suit. Supported by the Coalition, he's got the unenviable job of running a city where the electricity supply is more off than on, the police and army are corrupt and a bloody insurgency continues to escalate. He thanks everyone around the table for their attendance and appeals for reconciliation and settlement between the two sides. I get the gist of most of what he says but for the fast bits I strain my ear towards the CO's interpreter.

The Governor leaves soon after his speech. He probably has more important things to do. The mullah, who's from the Iranian-sponsored Supreme Council for Islamic Revolution in Iraq (SCIRI), takes over as chairman when the Governor's tribal-affairs officer, a small man in an ill-fitting suit, fails to get a grip of proceedings.

Both sides make their representations. The Halaf spokesman's resonant voice is accompanied by emphatic hand movements. His anger is sincere but controlled and channelled into frequent rhetorical questions. The Garamsha representative, in an old suit jacket rather than costly *abeyya* gown, is equally passionate but less articulate. His voice reflects the grief of the man sitting next to him – he wears his white headdress without a head-rope as a mark of mourning for his dead son, murdered by the tribal kin of those facing him at the far end of the table.

This death is the latest event in a prolonged feud caused ultimately by the devastation of the marshes. The Garamsha, as marsh dwellers, were deprived of their traditional lifestyle when the vast marshes of Southern Iraq were drained by Saddam after the first Gulf War, in retribution for the failed Shi'a uprising against him. Without water the rich flora and fauna of the marshes' reed beds – which nourished their inhabitants – ceased to exist almost overnight. Destitute, the Garamsha sought refuge in Basra, where the Halaf, as the established tribe, took exception to the sudden incursion of marsh Arab country bumpkins. Both tribes were Shi'a Muslims and had no religious disagreement, but economic competition created animosity and personal feuds, which developed into full-blown tribal conflict involving theft, kidnap and murder. This escalation was fuelled by the unavoidable demands of their tribal code of blood feud, in which blood must be spilled to avenge a death.

After the initial speeches other members of each delegation speak, sometimes at great length. The man whose son has been killed does not speak, but, head bowed, chain-smokes cigarettes. The council members listen while fiddling with prayer beads, talking quietly to one another, answering their phones and snoozing.

The meeting is jolted back to life by a sudden burst of shouting: 'You dog, you have my vehicles!'

'How dare you? You're the thief, unclean bastard!'

Two old men, both of the Garamsha delegation, are chin to chin, gesticulating wildly, their voices rising to incoherent screams. Their peers pull them apart but one breaks free and slaps the face of the other man – who in turn, yelling with blind rage, pulls off his headrope and beats his opponent with it. They enmesh in a thrashing contest before being quickly manhandled apart by members of the Tribal Council.

Sitting apart, the old men look quite feeble, exhausted by their efforts. Breathing hard, they restore their headdresses and wipe specs of saliva from their beards. A few minutes later they're forced to embrace briefly as a formal gesture of reconciliation. I'm thrilled by the sudden burst of activity: they have incredible fire in their bellies for such old men, and though they look spent now, I can't but admire their passionate, ferocious pride.

The excitement seems to reinvigorate the Tribal Council and encourages them, with the mullah's help, to wrap up proceedings. A truce between the two tribes is agreed with a symbolic gesture: the head of each delegation makes a knot in a headdress tied to a walking stick. The mullah announces that the Tribal Council will meet again at a later date to set the amount of blood money to be paid, the crucial element in making the truce last. His words are quickly drowned out as the delegations rise, break into chatter and leave, each side studiously avoiding the other. The members of the Tribal Council are in less of a hurry; after four hours of discussion they continue to converse as the CO and I depart.

Bouncing through Basra in the back of the CO's Snatch (armoured Land-Rover), returning to Shai'ba Logistics Base, I reflect that although the tribal feud is the result of Saddam's draining of the marshes, they're only fighting because the police in Basra are corrupt and ineffectual. Chaos has allowed this tribal violence to escalate, the chaos that filled the vacuum left in Basra after the invasion eighteen months ago. More sinister than the tribal violence is the anti-Coalition insurgency that exploded in the spring. Over the winter it has cooled down but it's bound to kick off again when the weather improves and I'm not sure we're able really to deal with it. We're trying to improve the police and the army but perhaps our very presence is part of the problem and the Iraqis themselves would be better off sorting things out on their own, like they did at the meeting. Our military presence is propping up the local government, but they're almost certainly just as corrupt as anyone else. We're vain if we think we're having a great, morally superior impact.

CHAPTER 2

'What's Arabic for Hello?'

December 2004: Basra, Iraq

It's not long before I meet another tribal sheikh. His house, flat-roofed and low, nestles under a clutch of date palms arching into the clear winter sky. Its white exterior is dulled by a rash of black mould. A rusting footbridge leads over a deep channel of green water and rubbish to the front door. A chorus of croaking toads echoes upwards.

'Welcome,' wheezes the Sheikh, as we enter his reception room in our socks, having stacked our kit inside the door. I'm here because the Sheikh is an ardent supporter of the Coalition and we've got a Scots Guards company doing an operation near his part of town; they're securing the area around a conference centre in Basra where the Iraqi judiciary are deciding on the judicial system for the new Iraq. As the leader of the Basra branch of his tribe the Sheikh is reputed to hold considerable influence over 15,000 subordinate tribesmen. He might be useful in calming any kind of civil disorder we may face. It's my task to be with him for the duration of the operation. I met him yesterday when we devised a plan for him to show me a munitions dump containing explosives that might be used by insurgents.

17

'Welcome, Captain Loin,' he splutters in English, pleased with his rendition of 'Lion' – the nickname he bestowed on me during yesterday's lunch. 'This house is your house,' he continues, pumping my hand with both of his, a cigarette jammed deep in his fingers.

'This is your house,' he repeats, embracing the man standing next to me.

'Hi, how you doin'?' says Terry, an American officer who's come with me for today's outing.

'What's Arabic for hello?' Terry asks me quietly as we sit down next to our host, pulling our feet under our legs on the thick red carpet. Terry's a Navy Seal Captain who's brought a team up from Kuwait to help with the surveillance of the conference centre. He's interested in seeing a bit of Basra; they've been stuck on their aircraft carrier anchored in the Persian Gulf a great deal lately.

Lowering his chubby frame onto the carpet, the Sheikh beams a broad smile, revealing a small collection of blackish tooth stubs. Wheezing, he ignites a new cigarette from the stub of his old one and inhales deeply. He's clean-shaven and double-chinned under a short moustache and cropped black hair. The bulge of his belly strains the cloth of his black *dishdasha* shirt, protruding through the open front of a dark suit jacket.

'Abbas!' he roars over his shoulder. A boy's face quickly emerges from a door behind us.

'Bring Bebsi,' the Sheikh instructs, substituting the 'P' unfamiliar to the Arab tongue with a similar sound.

'My eldest son,' he says, turning back to us, beaming again with pride.

'It is an honour to be here, O Sheikh,' I say solemnly as cold cans of Pepsi are placed before us.

'This house is your house, a Coalition house,' the Sheikh repeats in automatic obsequy.

The drinks are soon followed by large dishes of rice, roasted chicken, yoghurt and bananas carried in by Abbas, smiling deferentially.

'Abbas!' the Sheikh roars every few moments, sprinkling fragments of masticated rice and chicken. The young boy shuttles back and forth, bringing more food, Pepsi, cigarettes and, finally, tea. The Sheikh answers his mobile repeatedly, barking and wheezing.

I'm happy to allow the Sheikh to think that we have US Special Forces with us especially for his protection, but really they're here because their Unmanned Aerial Vehicle (UAV) – a radio-controlled spy plane – is helping with the surveillance of the conference centre. It's being operated by the rest of Terry's team, who are currently with our company headquarters – a little knot of Warrior armoured vehicles parked up in a muddy field just outside the edge of the city.

After lunch the Sheikh eagerly changes into the set of combats – my own – which I've brought for him, dons my helmet and a radio and climbs into my Snatch wagon, standing up through the hatch in the roof. As we depart, the Sheikh is on top of my vehicle, unrecognised by his own people, guiding us through the streets of suburban Basra. He's delighted and jubilant, as am I, at this mischievous deception.

We head east, out of town and towards the Iranian border. The close-knit dwellings of Basra's outskirts quickly give way to scruffy, rock-strewn desert, interrupted by the sudden green of little irrigated farmsteads. Near a deserted, broken-down farm-dwelling the Sheikh shows us a munitions dump, but it's old debris of the Iran–Iraq war, more than twenty years old. Dozens of mortar rounds, full of explosive, lie in rusty stacks. I mark the location on my GPS (global positioning system); I'll report it later to the intelligence cell. Terry films it with a camcorder.

'These are used by insurgents for making bombs,' says the Sheikh, wheezing.

'You are very kind to show us this place,' I reply. I can't help thinking that the insurgents have probably got much better sources of explosives and wouldn't risk blowing them-selves up with this dodgy ordnance. However, it would be churlish to tell the Sheikh this.

I pick up an old helmet. A piece of shrapnel has passed through it, splaying its glass fibres. The inside is dust-ridden, holding no trace of its unfortunate wearer's gore. Nearby, the Sheikh rests cross-legged on a rock and lights up another cigarette.

Returning to town, we take a different route. Near the Sheikh's house we pass rows of small mud dwellings. A power cable above the road catches in the 'cheese-cutter' on my wagon – a defensive bar holding an angled blade to pro-tect the two top-cover guys from electrical cables or mali-ciously placed wires. The cable falls limply to the road, sliced through.

A man emerges from the house and enquires quietly what we're going to do about it. The Sheikh hides in the vehicle, terrified of his ruse being uncovered.

'We fix it later,' he rasps from behind the wagon door.

I relay this to the man at the side of the road. He accepts it, silently nodding.

The following day the Sheikh is emboldened by the success of his deception, and during lunch is keen to enhance my opinion of his status.

'I have been in Moscow two years ago,' he reveals, eyes glinting. 'For shopping.'

'You are very well travelled, O Sheikh,' I reply with false credulity.

'Also I was invite to Prince Charles' wedding with Camilla ... I was sorry not to go. He's a good guy.'

I say nothing, silently acknowledging that shameless ego-massaging comes with this sort of territory: I won't burst his bubble. Inwardly, however, I can't help wincing at his desperation to impress. Siding wholeheartedly with the Coalition has raised his status and brought fawning British officers to his door, but in the long term he may have backed the wrong horse. As he waves me farewell I ponder what will become of him when the Coalition withdraws.

Back in camp, I'm called to see the CO. He's been sorting out officers' jobs for the coming year.

'When we get back to Germany, Leo,' he says, unsmiling, 'you're to be the Intelligence Officer.' This is not what I'd been expecting; we previously agreed that I'd go on the long Arabic course after the tour and eventually return to Iraq as a proper interpreter.

'What about the Arabic, sir?' I ask, trying to be upbeat. 'I was expecting to continue ...'

'Well, you can do, you'll just have to wait a bit,' he replies, frowning.

This is bad news; it means at least eighteen months back in Germany doing repetitive, tedious training exercises without, crucially, any operational tours. The prospect is terrifyingly dull and, having started the Arabic, it's the last place I want to be. Perhaps I'd be better off leaving and doing my own thing? I could travel for a year and learn Arabic on my own, and maybe go back to Damascus. I didn't join the Army to waste my youth training in Germany, and having waited so long for this tour I really don't like being told to 'wait a bit' again.

The good news, however, is that I'm allowed to join a Scots Guards company that has deployed to Maysan Province, far to the north of Basra. It's a desolate place of muddy plains and salt flats interrupted by oil pipelines, smoking stacks of brick kilns, clumps of date palms and ramshackle pylon lines.

On 30 January 2005 I'm in an operations room in Maymunah, a small town north of Al Amarah, Maysan Province's volatile capital. I'm with a platoon securing the police station during the first national elections of the new Iraq. We're supposed to be discreet, to allow the whole process to be presented as Iraqi-led, but our Warrior Armoured Fighting Vehicles (AFVs) are parked menacingly outside the front gate, surrounded by barbed wire. We give the police some credibility. In our absence they're ineffective due to corruption; poorly paid, they're susceptible to bribes, and their loyalty is multi-faceted to an extent that we can only begin to fathom.

It's a pleasure to get away from the mud and stinking Portaloos of camp. The police station is a solid flat-roofed building which encloses a large grubby courtyard bustling with blue-shirted policemen. They tout Kalashnikovs and shout into walkie-talkies. I'm on the radio most of the time, speaking to another team in a neighbouring town. I share the operations room with a police Major, the district and station commander.

He's an engaging man, with striking black-lined eyes, a swarthy face pitted with pox scars, and an untidy moustache. He wears a sports sweater under his blue shirt against the biting cold. A subordinate Iraqi policeman listens to their radio – an American HF system – and simultaneously watches TV: Hollywood violence under flickering Arabic subtitles.

The Major shares his lunch with me – delicious kebabs of mutton still hot from the roadside stall. Picking up bits of meat with flat bread, we munch away, adding onion segments and nibbling slender green chillies with each mouthful.

'The Shi'a list will win,' he replies in answer to my question about the election. His answer is unsurprising, given the poster advocating the main Shi'a party on the wall outside.

'But of course most Sunnis cannot vote,' he whispers with a chuckle, sharing the humour with the radio operator.

'They will stay in their homes, it is too dangerous to go outside,' he says, referring to the Sunni Triangle far to our north, where the level of violence is much higher than here in the Shi'a heartland of southern Iraq. This fact, combined with fears of political domination by the Shi'a majority, has led some elements of the formerly powerful Sunni minority to boycott the election, hoping that a reduced Sunni participation might discredit the results and stall the Shi'a ascendancy.

Having lost political clout with the fall of Saddam, the Sunni minority are not only terrified of this political role-reversal but concerned also about their loss of control over the vast oil reserves that lie in the Shi'a south and Kurdish north; the Sunni lands of central Iraq hold none.

The Major's words are an ominous glimpse of the sectarian schism hanging over Iraq.

'Insh'allah here it will pass peacefully,' he says with a raised finger, encouraging me to share his prognosis.

His hand comes to rest conspicuously on the Glock pistol in a shiny brown leather holster on his hip – a prize possession and status guarantor supplied by the Coalition, and in consequence repeatedly asked for by all policemen and army officers.

From the police station's roof I can see the election in full swing. Voters wait in a ragged line to be searched before entering the polling station, a blue-painted school across the street. The women are searched by other veiled females behind a white hospital screen. Explanatory posters adorn the walls; a colourful cartoon flow chart starts with a ballot box and leads to three other stages, which my eyes cannot distinguish. The atmosphere is peaceful and almost festive.

Two police guards emerge from their watchtower, and join me in silently watching the polling station.

'Good,' I say, pointing towards the voters below.

'Good, very good,' replies one of them in English. Proudly, they both hold up ink-stained finger tips: they've voted.

It's a pleasing moment: democracy visibly in action in Iraq for the first time in half a century. But as my gaze moves from their blue-black fingertips to our Warrior AFVs at the police station's front gate, the illusion is abruptly punctured. The election is a fragile and almost false construct, well-meaning but self-defeating in its dependence on the presence of British troops and heavy armour.

Before coming to Iraq I dismissed the false basis for invasion. None of us in the Scots Guards officers' mess believed the Weapons of Mass Destruction nonsense; we knew it was a pretext for the toppling of a dictator, which surely must be good news. My overriding emotion was a desire to be there – this at last was action! After a long and arduous professional training, my desire to actually get involved in something real, dangerous and uncertain was overwhelming.

Up on this rooftop, however, I'm feeling a bit uneasy. The pseudo-democracy happening before our eyes surely doesn't justify the chaos and trauma that our invasion and occupation have brought to Iraq.

Descending from the roof, I realise that I'm sick of seeing Iraq from inside barbed-wire compounds, from armoured rooftops, from the turret of a Warrior. Even, simply, from inside a uniform.

From Maysan Province I'm called back to Shai'ba Logistics Base. I'm to be the second-in-command for one of the battalion's rifle companies. We're on constant standby to deploy into Basra at the behest of the brigade commander and arrest suspect individuals.

At about 2300 I'm woken by a call from the company commander:

'Crash the boys out in Snatch – there's something on.'

I wake Scotty, one of the platoon commanders, who shares my tent.

'We're going out . . . Stand to and get ready in Snatch.'

He dashes off to alert the other two platoon commanders and then his platoon sergeant. I jump onto my bicycle and burn round to the CSM's tent.

'We're on . . . I'm going over to the ops room.'

'Aye, nae bother, sir,' he replies in his confident Inverness-shire tone, promptly emerging from his mosquito net.

Peddling frantically, I head over to the operations room among the white-box cluster of Portakabins. I'm going there to get a brief from the company commander – all the stuff he can't tell me on the mobile phone:

'Right, Leo,' he says in an urgent whisper. 'We're going into Basra to help two-two grab a high-value target.' His eyes are wide with excitement: 'two-two' means the 22 SAS Regiment. Getting out our 'spot maps' of central Basra he marks where we're going: 'The target house is here . . . Seven Platoon will be the lead group with the blades [SAS soldiers] who'll blow the doors and identify the bravo [male target] . . . I'll be just behind Seven Platoon. Nine Platoon will be the inner cordon here with you, Eight Platoon will be the outer cordon here,' he says, drawing two concentric rings around the black pin-prick that marks the target house.

'Get the company here asap. The two-two blokes will brief us in detail before we go.'

I scream back to the company's line of tents to find everyone now frantically preparing, packing themselves and their kit into the wagons amid the dust-laden glare of headlights.

'This is gleaming,' I think. A huge jolt of electricity has been sent through the company; everyone's up for it.

A couple of minutes later the six commanders – three sergeants and three young platoon commanders – and the CSM are around me. Their bodies are cluttered with body armour, webbing vests and rifles, and trailing radio headsets. They're wearing head-torches and clutch their maps intently. I relay the outline plan with the help of a scrawled white-board sketch balanced on my vehicle bonnet. The commanders are deliberately calm, determined not to show any hint of excitement on behalf of the SAS.

Mounting up into our Snatch wagons, each team reports ready to me. We rattle over to the operations room. Lined up behind me are a dozen Snatch vehicles in column. It's been less than half an hour since the call so we've done well, it's been a fast crash-out. Calling the team commanders together, we go in to the Battalion Headquarters. Jammed into a tiny Porta-kabin, we crowd around a desk under a humming strip light.

Bob, the SAS bloke who's done the reconnaissance, takes us through the plan:

'I'm not teaching you guys to suck eggs but I'll run through it just so we're all happy ... Once the outer cordon is in place the lead group will dismount with me and move forward here.' He points on the map to a street running north towards the objective. 'If I could ask you to put one team on either side of the road that'll allow you to cover the rooftops of the houses on the opposite side of the road.'

Pointing to a black-and-white satellite photograph, he shows us the target house, a substantial flat-roofed building surrounded by a wall.

'I'll lead the break-in team to the front door and Kiwi'll blow 'em in.'

Kiwi, a rangy SAS bloke with a buck-toothed grin, nods. 'I'll make a bit of a bang on the door and might have to use the twelve-gauge if it stays on its hinges,' he says, dangling a black pump-action shotgun under his arm.

Bob continues: 'When we're in you can do your bit – you know how. But get everyone down asap, I'll have a look to ID 'em. When you're searching, show everything to me. I speak the lingo. On the way out, if we get any bother we'll get the top cover (helicopter support) down to give us a bit of rat-ta-ta-tatt.'

Wiry and slight, with a neat brown beard (he's trimmed it and clean-shaved his cheeks in the smart, typically Iraqi fashion) and clear blue eyes, Bob strikes me as intensely able and unforgiving. He's wearing a standard-issue set of chest webbing but his green (not desert) combat jacket and civilian walking boots make him, in contrast to us, exotic and intriguing. As we leave the room, he chats to his colleague Kevin. Stocky, with a dyed-black beard, a hint of ginger in his eyebrows and hair that is too black against his fair skin, his chest is festooned with green canvas ammunition pouches.

None of the three wears rank but I can tell from their age and demeanour that they're senior NCOs, probably staff sergeants or warrant officers. They're a breath of utterly exciting fresh air, a wonderful contrast to the grim ortho-doxy of the Scots Guards. The staff officers in the headquar-ters who aren't deploying onto the ground sniff slightly, trying to show they really aren't impressed, they've seen this all before – which of course they haven't.

At 0100 we race into Basra. The streets are deserted. The moonlight reflects off the brimming roadside gutters. The target house is in an upmarket part of town: the streets are broad and the roads properly paved with tarmac. On either side of us high-walled compounds, with the upper boughs of trees spilling over, screen large houses.

Bringing up the rear of the convoy, I've got Corporal Montgomery driving and a couple of signallers in the back. We glide to a halt on the right-hand side of the road, as described in our orders. The lead team and company commander's group are ahead of us. Their shadowy figures emerge to the right of their wagons, making a hurried, hushed dismount.

They disappear off to our right in a tightly packed caterpillar huddle. I pass all the empty wagons and stop at the corner of a street branching away to the right. The target house is down there somewhere on the right-hand side. Left with my team, I send Monty to turn around some of the wagons left without drivers, so they're all facing the right way for our extraction. I also put one of the top-cover blokes at the corner to keep an eye on the target, and leave the other on top of the wagon. I stand next to my door, near the radio, although we're on radio silence until the break-in team enter the house.

The night is silent. My mental picture of the break-in team creeping towards the front door is interrupted as *bumph!* – a huge explosive thud shatters the air, seemingly much closer than it is. A ripple of dog-barking spreads around us. The radio crackles into life as the company commander's signaller starts relaying events back to headquarters: 'First team inside . . . We're inside . . . Two bravoes, one echo . . . We're searching.'

I listen in; this means that they've found two men and a woman.

Out of a door in the compound wall beside us, two faces peer timorously. I greet them. A man in his twenties, with a short moustache and yellow tracksuit, steps cautiously out of the door.

'Why the explosion?' he asks, smiling nervously, with an inquisitory inwards spin-flick of the opened fingers typical to Iraqis.

'We're arresting terrorists,' I reply solemnly, glad that my answer carries weight.

'Good, very good.' He speaks in English, accompanied by a raised thumb. 'God be with you,' he says, slipping back into his compound and closing the metal door.

The company commander comes up on the radio. 'We're coming out with one echo.' So the detainee is female.

I send two wagons round the corner and warn the helicopter that's circling unheard above us that we're about to extract to the pick-up point. The convoy, simultaneously starting engines, roars into life. A brief flurry of excitement flickers through my stomach.

The pair of wagons shortly re-emerges, wobbling with top-heaviness, chased by the break-in team scurrying along, their faces shiny with streams of sweat, wide-eyed and jubilant. They jump into their wagons with breathless, whispered instructions.

We get a 'follow on' from the company commander over the radio as our convoy grinds forward, going back the way we came. At a large junction the teams providing the inner and outer cordons arrive simultaneously to rejoin us; this is good timing. I count all the wagons in, telling the company commander over the radio:

'We're all in – good to go.'

We zoom south out of the city, triumphant at our success and exhilarated by the sudden speed.

In the city's outskirts we pull up by the roadside. A Chinook comes down on a patch of wasteland, to the bewilderment of the few passing drivers. A cluster of bodies scuttles across towards it; it's the SAS guys bundling away the prisoner. They disappear up the tailgate, and the Chinook rises up and vanishes noisily into the black sky.

Back in my tent with Scotty, it's past dawn before we sleep. He commanded the break-in team and is still wired with excitement.

'It was a bird . . . Behind a brick wall on the stairs. Said she was a judge, can you believe it? They ID'd her and took a load of documents. Man, that was fucking gleaming!'

Forty-eight hours later, we're told something's wrong. The company commander is summoned to headquarters. He calls me:

'This is direct from the CO. Go and get a load of white paint from the Quartermaster. It turns out that the echo we grabbed really *was* a High Court Judge . . . The brigade commander's making an apology to the Governor and we're on stand-by to fix the door and repaint her house.'

'You're fucking joking!' I blurt back, the laughter rising in my voice.

'No, I'm deadly serious,' he replies. 'Anyway, the company

did a bloody good job, so it's a success from our point of view.'

Returning from the Quartermaster, I stack four six-gallon tins of white paint and a load of brushes in my tent and wonder who cocked up. Was it the SAS? Was it higher up, whoever feeds them their intelligence? Perhaps it was the right person and she's just exploiting her position to be released. I simply don't know.

Soon afterwards I submit a letter resigning my commission to the CO. I'm disillusioned and frustrated. If I stay in the Army, I'll be stuck in the tedious rut of regimental life for more than a year, after which the best chance of excitement will be coming back out to Iraq. I've come to realise over the past few months that our presence here is at best misguided and clumsy, at worst deceptive and immoral.

I've been struggling reluctantly to work it out. I know the Weapons of Mass Destruction issue was a pretext, but if we came here to replace a brutal dictator with democracy then we're making a terrible hash of it. The facade of democracy we've created doesn't justify the chaos and sectarian bloodshed unleashed by our invasion and unresolved by our continued occupation.

I've got an unpleasant feeling that ultimately, behind the layers of pretext, we're here because of the oil in the ground beneath us, in a botched attempt to secure a dependable supply to fuel our economy. I dismissed as left-wing nonsense the 'no blood for oil' rhetoric that appeared in much of the press during the time of the invasion but now I'm not so sure. Oil infrastructure is ever-present throughout Basra and

Maysan Provinces. Wire-fenced refineries house vast tangles of metal piping. Flare pipes spew out great plumes of orange flame, burning the by-product gas that's uneconomic to bottle. Dirty pipelines criss-cross the desert. It's all part of Iraq's scenery, ubiquitous and hardly noticed, yet if it wasn't here, would we be?

I'm disillusioned, but at the same time I'm not angry – I simply don't want to face it. There are nearly 10,000 British troops here just getting on with the job, taking terrible risks and dying for the sake of a doomed project, and yet *crack on* they do, like it's inevitable, reasonable and sensible to be here. The error of our presence in Iraq is so fundamental, so enormous that it's invisible, beyond analysis, and best avoided. I just want to break free from the crushing futility of serving here to explore the Middle East and Asia on my own terms.

My resignation is accepted without hesitation, as is normal in the Scots Guards; there's no shortage of new officers keen to join this ancient and prestigious regiment.

The last weeks in Iraq drag slowly past. We're on constant standby, ready for more nocturnal arrests, but the call never comes.

My tent-mate's collection of paperbacks is a welcome diversion. Rummaging in his trunk I find a book written by a Victorian member of the Household Division: *A Ride to Khiva* by Captain Fred Burnaby. It's a compelling account of a journey made in 1875 through Imperial Russia to the last independent Central Asian Khanate, now in Uzbekistan. Burnaby was obsessed by the extent to which the Czar's influence had advanced towards British India. This issue was at the core of the Great Game, the covert and intrigue-filled struggle between the Russian and British empires for dominance of the remote yet strategically invaluable parts of Central Asia just beyond their borders. Thirsting for adventure and without the sanction of his superiors, Burnaby set off during his winter leave to play the Great Game for all he was worth. Racing through the pages of antiquated typescript, my imagination is fired. It seems that, like Burnaby, my surest route to adventure is to do my own thing. I crave the limitless freedom of travelling alone, beholden to nobody. The ridiculous paradox is that I'm *leaving* the Army to pursue excitement abroad. Counting down the last turgid days before quitting our sterile camp, I give my imagination free rein; it takes me east, riding through central Asia. I make daydream plans to retrace Burnaby's journey on my departure from the Army.

Before this, however, I must do my time; I still have one year to serve according to the terms of my engagement. It seems I might avoid the extra duties awarded for my incongruous haircut as I'm to be posted, after our return from Iraq, to our ceremonial company in London.

CHAPTER 3

'Nothing like Iraq'

August 2005: London

Facing forward, but glancing right, I draw breath. The column of marching Guardsmen, their scarlet tunics shaded by my black bearskin fringe, wheels to the left.

'Buckingham Palace detachment,' I roar, watching the column move past, right to left. The regimental colour flag, carried at the head of the column, draws opposite. This is my cue:

'Pre-seeeeent arms!'

Three palm-slapping cracks ring out in unison as the dozen Guardsmen behind me strike their weapons into a position of symbolic deference, held out to the front, bayonets uppermost. Simultaneously I move my sword upwards, pressing the hilt to my chin, and then down to my right side, tucked in behind my thigh, the shiny blade tip hovering just above the forecourt's red gravel. I stand stock-still. I'm sweating profusely into my thick tunic, still faithful to a centuries-old pattern designed to deflect musket-balls. It's made even heavier by the gold cuffs and collar, with silver sequins fashioned into a thistle, my regimental emblem. My thick woollen trousers – blue with fat red stripes down the sides of

35

the legs – further insulate me, sending rivulets of sweat trickling down my shins and into my boots.

The column disappears through the forecourt's heavy ornamental gates, heading for the Mall.

'Slooooope arms!' I roar again, stretching and bellowing the order. I return my sword to its position of carriage: held out to my front, the blade vertical. Turning about, I see the Guardsmen in three ranks before me. I position myself at their head and we march over to the guardroom at the side of the Palace, accompanied only by the rhythmic crunching of our heels on the gravel.

Entering the guardroom, I breathe a sigh of relief. That's another Guard mount done, or 'Changing of the Guard' as it's commonly known. I'm commanding the Buckingham Palace half of the new Guard, who'll stand outside the palace for the next twenty-four hours. The column that's just marched down the Mall will provide the Guard at St James's Palace, the London home of Prince Charles and his sons.

Leaving the Palace forecourt I wander through the park to St James's, or *Jimmy's* as we know it. I'm plagued by a throng of tourists taking turns to trot excitedly alongside me and snap one another's photograph. I've now been back in London for a month doing 'public duties'. My morale is high. I'm delighted to be here. I've got bags of time off in between Guards to really get about town, ride out in Hyde Park, see my friends and prepare for life after the Army. I'm also very excited about the prospect of five weeks of summer leave starting in a couple of days.

I walk into the Queen's Guard mess, where the table, set for a large lunch, is laden with gleaming silver, countless crys-

tal glasses and immaculate napkins. The room is encrusted
with military oil paintings, ornamental silver, walnut furniture and chandeliers. I feel deep in the womb of martial privilege. At the gilded epicentre of the establishment, this really
is the last untouched bastion of the old-school Army. There
are two other officers on Guard with me and we'll stay here
for the next two days. We can have guests up to dine but,
finding long dinners tedious, I have guests infrequently, and
focus more on doing long runs around the parks.

Public duties are fun while being purely superficial. We're
here to look good, to represent the majesty of the Queen.
The security of the Royal palaces depends on the high-tech
monitoring of the Metropolitan Police, not the Guardsmen
on sentry. The officers, whose social lives tend to thrive in
London, generally have an absolute hoot, but for the young
Guardsmen it's tedious; they're prone to becoming fat and
poor while drinking away their wages in the city's fleshpots.

Coming off Guard, we finish the parade in Wellington
Barracks, where I live. In my rooms on the third floor –
which overlook Buckingham Palace and St James's park – I
pull off my tunic with the help of Lambe, my orderly, a bid-
dable eighteen-year-old from Lanarkshire with orange hair
and spectacles. I've appointed him because he's keen to learn
and seems loyal. His predecessor, an excellent orderly, is now
doing time in Colchester Military Correction Centre prior to
being discharged from the Army for absence without leave;
he was gone for almost three years, during which time he was
an unsuccessful landscape gardener.

Putting on a suit, I take the Tube – a form of transport
officially deemed beneath the dignity of a Foot Guards offi-

cer, but these Standing Orders are sensibly ignored – to Sloane Square. Emerging, I stroll down to Chelsea Barracks, a mishmash of near-derelict 1960s architecture. I'm told the architect defrauded the MoD, went to jail and was a suicide. Perhaps he felt remorse for the state of the Guardsmen's accommodation: the damp, cramped four-man rooms are a travesty. Nothing's done about it because the Barracks have been on the verge of demolition for the last decade. There's a plan afoot now to sell the entire site.

I meet one of my fellow platoon commanders. He's been recently bruised by a scandalous encounter with a pair of hookers: he stupidly brought them into Wellington Barracks and, as a result of their camera phones, ended up with his face splashed across the *Sun* newspaper, to much regimental outrage and secret mirth. He needs cheering up, so, with him explaining his side of the story, we wander down the King's Road to find lunch.

A month later I'm wearing a grimy knee-length shirt and baggy trousers (*shalwar qamiz*), an itchy woollen flat hat and a cheap cotton scarf. I've got a short scruffy beard, and am utterly thrilled to be in Afghanistan.

Indulging my passionate interest in Pakistan and its Urdu language, I spent the early weeks of my leave riding and playing rustic polo in a village beyond Chitral, high in the remote and mountainous Northern Areas of Pakistan. Returning towards Islamabad, I paused in Peshawar, and couldn't resist the temptation to dash through the Khyber Pass to Kabul and onwards to the Panjshir valley.

I've been completely drawn in by the intoxicating brand

of heroism and danger that the North Western Frontier Province and Afghanistan represent. I'm as far from London as I possibly can be in every sense and loving it.

In front of me stands a green-domed and whitewashed mausoleum, the tomb of Ahmed Shah Masood, the iconic former leader of the Northern Alliance Mujahideen. Intriguing and charismatic, Commander Masood, as he's called in Afghanistan, was the Taliban's most bitter and enduring enemy. With his fellow Tajiks, he held out in the Panjshir valley, where I stand now, which never fell to the Taliban. The Northern Alliance, allied with the US-led Coalition, eventually swept the Taliban from power in the wake of 9/11. But it did so without Masood: he was murdered by Al Qaeda suicide bombers just three days before September 11. The bombers, posing as Moroccan television journalists, were sent by Osama Bin Laden as a means of repaying his Taliban host's hospitality. Since his expulsion from Sudan in the late nineties, Bin Laden had based himself in Afghanistan as a guest and benefactor of his fellow Sunni fundamentalists.

Inside the mausoleum a marble slab lies flat, hidden by a green velvet cover richly embroidered with Qur'anic verses in silver and gold. A Mujahid in camouflage trousers sits unarmed and cross-legged at the side, his flat woollen pakol cap worn at the very back of his head in the unmistakeable style of his dead leader.

Hesitantly, I pull out my camera. The pair of young men who've brought me here in their car smile delightedly: it seems that photographing the grave will honour it. Leaving the mausoleum, I want to ask them about their lives, about the Panjshir valley and Masood. But I know neither Dari nor

39

Tajik, and they speak only a few words of Urdu. In silence we move to a little wooden kiosk, the only other building in the mausoleum's vicinity. It's selling Masood paraphernalia, and I choose a poster with his smiling face set under the inscription 'The Martyr and Mujahid Commander Ahmed Shah Masood'. Resigned to it being squashed, I slide it into my dusty satchel.

Beside the shack lies a derelict Sherman tank. I can't imagine what bizarre route this particular piece of hardware, of American manufacture during the Second World War, took to its final resting place. Almost all of the ubiquitous defunct war materiel littering the valley is of Soviet origin. Armoured hulks are often adapted as components in domestic construction or lie half-covered by dust, claimed by the barren earth as part of the landscape.

Returning to the nearest village, Rokha, just five kilometres from the tomb, I'm approached by the local policeman, who beckons me into a chair on the police station's veranda. Surrounded by a knot of curious villagers, he scrutinises my passport, for much of the time upside-down. Surrounded by villagers in *shalwar qamiz*, he seems more incongruous than I, in his khaki uniform and outsized Soviet cap – looking like a fancy-dress parody, a fat grimy meringue. After an hour of repeated assurances that I'm an Australian student, the policeman is content. The fact that, as a serving British Army officer, I'm forbidden to be in Afghanistan unofficially during my leave makes this minor deception entertaining rather than nerve-racking. I'm not fearful; I trust their hospitality and am convinced that my trust will be reciprocated. The policeman shakes my hand and directs me to a shared cab, in which I can head back down the valley towards Kabul.

The road hugs the valley side, high above the blue-green torrent of the Panjshir river. The valley sides themselves are of dry earth disturbed by a shock of verdure at the water's edge. Stopping off at a roadside eating-house, we piss behind its concrete walls and wash our hands and faces. Inside, we tuck into plates of Uzbeki pilau – a mound of steaming rice, cooked with ghee, raisins, shards of carrot and almonds, piled over a fatty lump of mutton. Imitating the cab driver's actions, I compact a little ball of hot rice with the fingertips of my right hand and flick it into my mouth. It's delicious. A poster of Masood, similar to the one I've just bought, watches over us. There's also a rug woven in his image hanging by the cashier's wooden table. One of my co-travellers pays for my lunch, and while refusing repayment mentions a Dari word I do know: '*mehman*', meaning 'guest'.

Out of the valley, closer to Kabul, we're passed by a column of Dutch armoured vehicles heading for the nearby Bagram Air Base. A pair of Black Hawk helicopters zip past, scanning the road ahead of another convoy which soon thunders past. It's made up of huge trucks packed with dusty soldiers, their faces hidden by helmets and goggles. A 'SEMPER FI' ('always faithful') sticker on a door reveals they're US Marines.

A veterinary doctor who we've picked up at Charikar, a small town at the mouth of the valley, shares the front passenger seat with me. He's astonished by my presence.

'It's too dangerous for you. Why are you here?' he asks in English.

'To see Afghanistan,' I reply, secretly amused at his reaction.

'Do not travel at night, and if you have any problem, call me; here is my number.'

Folding the small square of paper, I thank him sincerely, touched by his kindness.

Back in Kabul I stroll about with perfect ease; it's such an ethnic and sartorial hotchpotch that I'm not out of place. Fair hair and blue eyes are not uncommon, and my clothes are local. I'm stopped by a man with a laden cart, asking me to read an address for him. Though familiar with the Persian script, I can't decipher the scrawl; and not knowing Dari, Kabul's predominant language, I hand it back with a shrug of my shoulders, silently claiming illiteracy.

This is thrilling! I'm delighted that I'm generally taken as Afghan until I speak, when my bad Urdu exposes me as a Chitrali perhaps, from northern Pakistan. I love the deceptive mischief involved in playing this role. But more, I love the sensation of seeing things without them being altered by my presence; it's the absolute reverse of experiencing Iraq in a uniform.

At a roadside juice stall I drink cold, sweet mango pulp. Having become a frequent customer in the last couple of days, I'm greeted by Hamood the Pashtun stall owner. He's keen to express his preference for the Afghan parliamentary elections, due next month.

'I will not vote for anyone with a beard: the Mujahideen killed my father and my two brothers. Dr Najibullah [the Soviet puppet premier brutally murdered by the Taliban on their capture of Kabul in 1996] was the best president,' he says in Urdu.

'How's business? It's good, since the end of the Taliban . . .'

In the busy traffic, a black Land Cruiser with opaque windows pulls up, escorted by a beige US Army Humvee. Dismounting, a couple of soldiers in unusual greyish camouflage walk up the street. One of them walks right past me; he's wearing a helmet and sunglasses, with his rifle slung to his side. An eagle's-head badge is Velcroed to his left arm. He looks bizarre and fairly lethal but also vulnerably incongruous. Watching him sideways, I finish my juice, silently triumphant at going unnoticed in an Afghan crowd.

Leaving the stall, I reflect again on the strand of interest that brought me here in the first place: learning Urdu in Lahore, before joining the Army. I relished the cultural submersion involved in throwing myself, anonymous and humble, into a society: adopting its dress, eating its food, and striving to learn its poetic and beautiful language. I was drenched, drawn in, intoxicated by the culture and hospitality of those around me.

Now, here in Afghanistan, this passion has returned, more strongly. I feel a glorious sensation of being in the thick of it, absorbed, alert, all excess concerns stripped away. I've attained a simplicity of form and intent which allows a greater appreciation of my surroundings. I'm in awe of these people who, often despite terrible poverty, still live their lives by social tenets of honour and hospitality, long forgotten by my own society. I feel privileged to have received their generosity, and each successful conversation in Urdu gives me a surge of joy.

But my Urdu is imperfect and I know neither Dari nor Pashtu. The satisfaction is fleeting. I want to get closer to the Afghans, to live absolutely on their terms. I'm gripped by a

desire not only to pass through a crowd of Afghans unnoticed, like a latter-day Great Gamer, but to be able to par-
ticipate and engage with them in their own language. I know
that I must return.

Back in London, I'm clean-shaven and in a greatcoat. Public
duties continue in winter order. I've got another few months
to do before my departure from the Army in the spring. On
Queen's Guard, I unfold my map of Asia on the billiard table.
I'm planning to retrace Burnaby's ride to Khiva, and then keep
going. With growing excitement, I study place names along his
route from Russia to Central Asia: St Petersburg, Moscow,
Orenburg, the Aral Sea and Khiva. From there I want to go
even further: on to Bokhara, Samarqand and Afghanistan.

My finger comes to a halt at Peshawar; my memories of
this chaotic Pashtun frontier town at the foot of the Khyber
Pass are still fresh from my autumn travels. On returning
through the Pass to Peshawar, I saw its university, a splendid
red sandstone monument of Imperial gothic-orientalism.
Why not go to Peshawar to study Pashtu? Guardsman
Lambe's arrival jolts me back to current reality; I must prepare for the guard dismount.

Later, in Wellington Barracks, I get a call from James, a Scots
Guards contemporary.

'I've just spoken to the Adjutant [officer in charge of disci-
pline and manning] at 3 Para. They're after Captains who've
got their wings to go on Operation Herrick, to Afghanistan . . .
I know you're leaving but just thought it might interest you.'

He's right. My interest *is* pricked. A phone call to a friend in 3 Para reveals that they've been 'warned off' to deploy in the spring to Helmand Province, in the lawless, opium-growing south of Afghanistan, as part of a big counter-narcotics and 'nation-building' effort. They need a Captain to act as a company second-in-command. Having passed the 'P Coy' pre-parachute selection and the 'Jumps' course, I've got my Para 'wings' and I'm therefore qualified to serve with a Para battalion. Tantalisingly, there are Army Pashtu courses being run specifically for the deployment.

Before I speak to the 3 Para Adjutant, it occurs to me that my experience of travelling in that region and my knowledge of Urdu would perhaps make me more useful outside a battalion; and in any case I've already experienced the frustration of being tied to my own unit in Iraq. Surely I could do the Pashtu course and go along as some sort of liaison officer? There's been a minor British presence in Afghanistan since 2001, with troops in Kabul as part of the International Security Assistance Force (ISAF), and in the northern city of Mazar-e-Sharif as a 'Provincial Reconstruction Team', but this big deployment to Helmand is a new operation. Despite not knowing any details, I'm drawn to the idea of going to the Pashtun south of Afghanistan and intrigued by the intent: 'nation-building' sounds fascinating and very honourable. I imagine myself speaking Pashtu and cutting deals with Pashtun tribal elders while drinking tea in the Hindu Kush. What an awesome prospect! It's exactly the sort of experience I'm leaving the Army to pursue. Ironically it seems that, on the verge of my leaving the Army, the ideal opportunity to play a new version of the Great Game has presented itself. Perhaps I should stay for a bit longer?

45

Another phone call to the headquarters of 16 Air Assault Brigade, the unit deploying, is conclusive.

'I'm being posted to 3 Para,' I say to the Chief of Staff, using a white lie. 'But I thought as I've been around that part of the world and speak a bit of the lingo that I might be more use to you as a liaison officer . . . Getting involved with the local population is what I love,' I say, eagerly recounting my previous travels, including my illegal foray into Afghanistan.

'I think we might have something for you . . . Do you speak Pashtu?'

'No, but I'll get myself on the course, so I'll be ready by March,' I reply, the decision to stay having flashed through my head – unthinking, automatic almost.

'OK, you're onboard. See you then.'

That's it! I'm staying in and going to Afghanistan! This is amazing! I can't believe that a senior officer can be so positive and decisive. Hurriedly picking up the phone again, I book myself on the Pashtu course. Another phone call to the Army manning department in Glasgow reverses my resignation. It's immediate, because it's for operational reasons. I'm thrilled by the executive urgency of all of this; it's so unlike the stultifying protocol and negativity that smothers enthusiasm in the regiment. Luckily, this should make it past the Scots Guards Adjutant: only when the official posting order gets faxed from Glasgow to 16 Air Assault Brigade and copied to the Scots Guards will he find out, and faced with an officially sanctioned fait accompli, be powerless to change it.

At the Cenotaph a few days later, I'm at the head of a detachment of Guardsmen at the Remembrance ceremony. Standing still, in bearskin and greatcoat with my sword resting tip-down on the road, I strain to see any movement from Downing Street: our cue to brace up. Around the sandstone memorial thick ranks of soldiers, sailors and airmen are drawn up. The band plays soft contemplative music as we wait for the wreath-laying to begin. I've got woollen skiing socks on but I can feel the cold of Whitehall's tarmac through my boot soles. I had a drop of port before coming out but that was three hours ago. Anyway, I wouldn't dare complain about the cold or the tedium of standing still for three hours when our purpose is to commemorate the dead and honour the surviving veterans of all wars.

Standing unmoving, I reflect on my recent change of plan. Though I've nothing more than a general idea of what I might be doing, I'm completely certain it'll be interesting. I feel lucky to be going; the couple of friends that I've told about it in confidence, still serving in the battalion, are outraged with jealousy.

'You jammy sod!' cried Scotty down the phone line from Germany. He knew what I was talking about because the deployment hit the headlines last week: 'I read about it today, sounds like the wild west!'

'I know. The locals call it the Desert of Death.' I chuckled, entertained by the comic gloominess of the name. Like Scotty, I'd also read that morning's papers and seen the 'Dasht-e-Margo', as it's known in the Persian vernacular, sweeping across Afghanistan's southern border, covering an area greater than Wales and swallowing the bottom half of Helmand Province.

*

Poring over the increasing press coverage, I'm increasingly thrilled at my coming involvement in an important cutting-edge project. I'm mustard keen on the idea of 'nation-building' and getting really involved with the Afghans. I consume as much background information as I can on the region.

I attend a lecture in the cosy library of the Royal Society for Asian Affairs, where a noted scholar and Afghan expert narrates, to much amusement, chunks of an Imperial mem-sahib's diary. Full of dry wit and stoicism, it relates the dreadful hardships and tragedies of the British retreat from Kabul towards Jalalabad in 1842. As I listen I'm grateful that we won't make such foolish errors this time around. Indeed, it reinforces my secret self-image as a new Great Game player, serving NATO, not the Empire.

At the fringe of the suited, mostly geriatric audience sits a girl with a strikingly elegant neck and dark skin. She's been living in Kazakhstan, she tells me after the lecture. She's nearly as tall as my 6 feet 4 inches, with brown eyes that flash when she emphasises her words. Intrigued, I ask for her card, determined to get in touch and e-mail her some queries I have about riding in that part of the world.

My last Guard is in December at Windsor Castle. It involves a mini Changing of the Guard, followed by two glorious days spent visiting the Guardsmen on 'stag' (standing on sentry), running in the Great Park, and relaxing in the perfect solitude of the officer's flat. Its ancient oak panelling bears the epigrams, sketches, names and initials of the countless Guards officers who've captained the Guard and entertained in the flat over the last two hundred years.

Having enjoyed a festive evensong in the chapel, I despatch Guardsman Lambe to get a box of mince pies from the high street. The girl I met at the lecture is coming to tea.

'Are your boots made of plastic?' asks Lucy, picking up one of my gleaming black Wellingtons.

'No,' I reply, quickly taking it from her to avoid more fingerprints, 'but Guardsman Lambe is a bulling genius.'

Like a boot alchemist, Guardsman Lambe can change dull leather to reflective glass, 'bulling' the leather with beeswax and polish.

Replacing the boot with a mince pie, I listen with increasing fascination as she recounts her travels: an epic nine-month journey along the ancient Silk Road on horse and camel, and years spent living, working and travelling across Central Asia and Iran. Her Kazakh riding boots, of soft leather in a traditional pattern, catch my eye as she speaks.

In the New Year I'm on the Pashtu course. I devour the daily lessons and learn new words in the evening. Our charming Afghan teacher devises the curriculum on a week-by-week basis (the most recent textbook was produced in 1880, at the time of the second Anglo-Afghan war). I'm chuffed to be learning Pashtu, and excited about the coming deployment. I can't believe I haven't done this earlier during my time in the Army. As the deployment draws closer I make plans to attend a longer, eighteen-month Pashtu course on my return from Operation Herrick, the Afghanistan deployment, and afterwards to spend maybe a couple of years with the Army as an interpreter in Afghanistan.

*

'Prepare for action!' hollers the jumpmaster.

I'm in a Hercules above Salisbury Plain, deafened by the drone of the engines and pulled into the canvas troop seats by the weight of the parachute on my back. Though qualified as a military parachutist, I haven't jumped for a couple of years. Before deploying I need to do a couple of refresher jumps in order to get an extra few pounds of daily 'Para pay'.

Standing up with a slight wobble, I fasten the chin strap of my para helmet and attach my rucksack to the pair of quick-release hooks on my chest harness. The jumpmaster, a small lean man in a tight grey jumpsuit, clips a line from the back of my parachute onto the static line that will initiate my 'chute approximately four seconds after I jump. I'm number one on the port side. We number off with a shoulder slap passed down the line of eight men, ending with me.

'One OK, port stick OK,' I shout to the jumpmaster, with a thumb up.

I'm beckoned forward to the jump door. My stomach lurches. I take position: left foot forward, left arm holding the side of the door, right arm across the reserve 'chute on my chest. The wet greenness of Salisbury Plain whizzes past below me, incredibly close. Forcing the hint of a smile onto my face, I strive to appear utterly unafraid, knowing that the jumpmaster is watching for a flicker. Waves of adrenalin sweep up from my stomach. All my instincts are screaming at me to back away from the door. The red cautionary light comes on: jumping is imminent. The green above it flashes.

'GO!' screams the jumpmaster.

Launching myself out of the jump-door, I'm falling and

twisting, battered and wrenched from the aircraft by a screaming barrage of wind. Suddenly my chin is smashed onto my chest as my whole body is wracked upwards by the drag of my parachute and downwards by gravity. My 'chute is open. 'Thank fuck!' I garble in the floating stillness. Above me, my canopy is huge and green: 'Big, round and sound!' I shout in delighted repetition of the training mantra. Checking my air space, I look left, right and below. I steer away from the parachutist above me, gathering the canvas rigging lines and heaving them down into my chest. A slight twitch in the canopy pulls it forward and left. Looking down, I pull my rucksack quick-release strap; it falls for a couple of seconds, then jolts as the connecting rope takes the strain. I'm drifting forward and right; I take the rear risers and pull them down, squeezing them into my midriff. I'm still going forward, squeezing my legs and ankles tight together, and now I'm shooting sideways and the ground rushes up.

'*Umph!*' I'm bounced onto the ground, still moving; the wind's got my chute. Dragged bumping over the grass I fumble for the quick release: I break a rigging line and grind to a halt. My deflated canopy swirls around me.

'Thank fuck!' I gasp, genuinely grateful that I haven't broken my legs, and jubilant and exhilarated at having survived the mad risk of the last forty-five seconds. This mad risk, shared as a common experience, is the glue that holds the airborne forces together. Though I'm a Scots Guards officer, Para 'Toms' – private soldiers – that I've never met before will automatically make positive assumptions about me (and vice versa) on seeing the set of blue Para 'wings' on my shoulder.

Gathering up my 'chute, I run for the vehicle at the side of the drop zone. I need to get back to load up for the second jump of the day.

In the late afternoon, elated by two successful jumps, I drive away from RAF Lyneham. Stopping off at Lucy's for tea, my green combats (striped with Salisbury Plain's mud) and maroon beret take a verbal battering from her all-female household. But the doughnuts and lardy cake I've brought win some sympathy, and before departing Lucy and I make plans to go the cinema on the following evening.

Later that night, my euphoria at the jumping is cut short by a phone call from an Army friend.

'Leo, it's Chris . . . I've got some bad news – Rich Holmes has been killed. He was blown up in Al Amarah.'

Richard was our friend at Sandhurst. Deeply gentle and humane, he was the lynchpin of our platoon. His kindness, modesty and ability allowed him to never once be riled during our year of frequently exhausting and tedious training. He showed particular patience with the often-confused foreign Officer Cadets.

A week later the church, bathed in clear winter sunshine, is packed out. Mourners spill onto the grass outside, following the service on a video screen. I stand at the edge of the throng with other former platoon-mates. His closest friend from the platoon is in the church and with admirable composure does a short reading.

It's an accidental reunion of good friends, long unseen. We've not been together like this since the passing-out parade. We've all changed – a testament to the last four years. Some, dressed in suits, have recently left the Army; some are in Regimental Service dress with two or three medals; a couple, conspicuous with longer hair and lamb-chop side-burns, are now in the SAS. All of us have been in Iraq. Some will go again soon, for their second or third tour.

The professional devotion of our group allows us to focus on the comforting fact that Richard was killed doing a job he loved, among men he led with mutual respect and admiration. Such a good man, so selfless, so brave: surely his death is a reflection, a confirmation, of these qualities? We're soldiers, dedicated to soldiering and bound together by a simple ideal: the acceptance, pursuit even, of risk. We're loyal to our profession of choice and loyal beyond our own knowledge to our fellow soldiers. Moralising about the rights and wrongs of the Iraq war would at this moment be unthinkable, irrelevant. The fact that our friend was a victim of what we all know to be a disastrous and dishonest campaign lies dormant, unspoken. There is no outrage at his death, just a sad acceptance.

Outside on the grass, at the periphery of the mourners, I cannot begin to conceive what measure of grief his widow and family must be suffering at this moment inside the church, sitting next to the flag-draped coffin. I stick to small talk, in vain trying to avoid the horrible truth that our friend is being buried in the very place where he was married six months previously.

'So what's happening in Afghanistan?' Chris asks as we disperse from the church.

'Well, it's reconstruction really, you know, nation-building ...' I answer, vacantly.

'So not like Iraq then?'

'No, thank god, nothing like Iraq.'

*

On the wet square of Goojerat Barracks in Colchester figures slowly gather in the chilly darkness, exchanging excited banter, hands thrust deep in the pockets of pale desert smocks. We're waiting for the bus to take us to Brize Norton in Oxfordshire, to catch a flight to Kabul and onwards. I feel good, really good. The lean simplicity of my previous travels in Afghanistan has returned: it's just me, my rucksack and my weapon, in the desert combats I'll wear constantly for the next few months.

CHAPTER 4

The Comprehensive Approach

April 2006: Southern Afghanistan

I sit just behind the Helmand Task Force Commander on the flight out to Kabul. I'm to be his Aide-de-Camp. I'm like an assistant, but I'm pleased as involvement at this senior level and the responsibility it brings should prove interesting. The Commander is a very likeable senior officer, unusually down to earth for his senior rank. He's in a tricky position: in addition to commanding an incredibly complex operation at its inception he's a newcomer to 16 Air Assault Brigade, of which the Task Force is mainly composed. The loyalty of most of the senior officers in the headquarters is bound to lie still with the Brigadier who's overseeing the whole thing at a higher level in Kabul.

The Commander hands me his copy of the Operational Order – the set of orders for the entire Task Force. 'Fuck me,' I think. 'This is it – these pages will determine the future of Helmand!' Our deployment is all over the press now and I can't help feeling excited to be at the epicentre of something so huge, important, maybe even historic, at its very beginning.

Signed off by the Commander, it's essentially the product of the precociously bright Chief of Staff, effectively his second-in-command. I take notes in order to remember the complex sequence of phases that it stipulates.

At the tactical level – for the troops on the ground – the plan is to use something called 'the Mosaic'. It demands that all British units be aware of all facets of Afghan society – the tribes, the economy and local politics – while working within it. There's a neat illustration resembling a Tudor rose.

Strategically, the plan for Helmand Province as a whole is based on 'the Comprehensive Approach'. This means the problems in Helmand – like opium production and lawlessness – will be dealt with in a comprehensive manner, from all angles.

I'm familiar with this jargon because in Colchester the headquarters personnel participated in 'joint' planning days, a chance for the military to get to know the representatives of the Foreign and Commonwealth Office (FCO) and the Department for International Development (DfID) who'll be working with us on the ground in Afghanistan. In outline, our intent is to improve security in Lashkar Gah, the provincial capital, allowing DfID to start practical development projects, while the FCO will focus on counter-narcotics and improving governance. An 'inkspot' – a security haven – will therefore be established in which life can return to normal. If all goes to plan security, development and governance will go hand-in-hand in the push to reconstruct civil society. Success lies ultimately in depriving opium barons and insurgents of their basis of support by winning the hearts and minds of the civil population. As success is consolidated, the inkspot will grow.

While a frequent practical term of reference for this sort of campaign is the successful British counter-insurgency conducted in Malaya in the 1950s, the doctrine behind the Comprehensive Approach is contained in a little glossy manual produced by the Ministry of Defence: *Operations other than War*. In Colchester the bookish Colonel in charge of its production dished out copies and gave us a slide-show of vivid diagrams illustrating its content. My favourite was a colourful multi-stranded rope representing the simultaneity and interdependence of each 'Line of Operation'.

Some of our partners in the Comprehensive Approach struck me as unlikely Afghan operators but seemed to have hidden depths. The DfID woman in charge of development in Helmand, with her fake plastic fingernails glued on wonkily, had spent the previous eight years sinking wells in Nigeria.

'Improving livelihoods is the key,' she told me over a vol-au-vent during our lunch break. The statistics were shocking. Afghanistan is one of the least developed countries in the world, where a majority of the population lacks access to electricity and clean drinking water, 20 per cent of children die before the age of five, and more than 70 per cent of the population are illiterate. Despite this she was optimistic.

'We've got ninety million pounds this year to spend on the National Development Strategy so we should make progress . . .'

As she detailed how livelihoods might be improved through 'microfinance lending' and 'Quick Impact Projects', I shared her enthusiasm.

The counter-narcotics part of the plan was also upbeat despite the colossal challenge: Afghanistan's economy depends on poppy-growing, producing 90 per cent of the world's opium.

'We won't be too hasty, we'll promote alternatives,' said the representative from the Foreign Office. He couldn't name the alternative crop to poppy but the plan seemed pretty sensible: 'an eight-strand strategy,' he said, starting with 'public information' leading to 'alternative livelihoods' and 'eventual eradication'. I found this fascinating and left the planning day sharing the earnest optimism of our 'Joint' partners.

Handing back the orders to the Commander, I accept a smoked-salmon sandwich, which he kindly offers from his lunchbox. The fact that he's prepared to divvy-up his packed lunch is a good sign.

Landing in Kabul, we're greeted by the sparkling white tops of the surrounding mountains. It's April, so the morning is cool and the air is clear, almost crisp. An abundance of multinational fighter jets and helicopters are lined up on the tarmac. In the cookhouse there are thirty different signing-in books: one for each nationality in the Coalition. I wonder what it is the Bulgarians do, and am entertained to see a solitary Icelandic soldier guarding the front gate alongside some Italians. The French seem especially ornamental and pose absurdly in their too-short combat trousers. These over-clean staff officers are the physical opposite of the Afghans whose city they live in. As a body they are bloated and ineffectual. Their only value lies in the veneer of international inclusivity which they lend the Coalition. They represent the worst aspect of the international force. Thankfully I'll be getting well away from them; there's no room for their sort in Helmand.

In a Hercules transport plane to Kandahar, we're crammed into the hammock-like canvas seats by the RAF crew. The recollection of doing parachute jumps inspires a brief surge of exhilaration as we file in through the tailgate. I imagine myself as a paratrooper in some heroic Second World War operation and wonder if the rumours of there being a 'lob-on' – a para jump – in Helmand will materialise. The RAF loadmasters hand out squashy yellow earplugs and try to look cool in their flying suits. As we make a grinding ascent over Kabul the G-force drives our bodies downwards. Dazed by the deafening noise and vibration of the turbo propellers, some of us sleep, some read, others try to look nonchalant. I crane my neck to see out of the circular window. Distinct among the mass of ramshackle buildings closeted by sudden, sheer hills is the bombed-out shell of King Zahir Shah's old palace, Dar-ul-Aman. Surely this is a symbol, related to the reconstructive nature of our mission? I spend a few moments trying to concoct an appropriate metaphor before my mind wanders.

Seeing Kabul from the air brings to my mind's eye the aerial photograph that two weeks previously my Pashtu teacher in Beaconsfield had laid out before me. Homesick, he had acquired the photo from a friend in the MoD so that he might locate his home. On the floor of his office the map drew us in as he showed me his home, his school and where he used to eat ice cream and go to the cinema. I was intrigued to locate, with his help, Hotel Spinzar – a crumbling pre-Soviet pseudo-European tower where I'd stayed the previous autumn. I wonder if what I'd seen on his map is still standing below me, or if it's become sadly fictitious under the horrific rocket barrages fired by the Mujahideen factions as they turned against one another after their capture of the city from the Soviet puppet government in 1993.

Descending into Kandahar, the beige monotony of the ground is dotted with crooked verdant rectangles of agricultural land gathered about glistening irrigation channels. Everything else is barren, flat and dusty. The distant jagged mountains are devoid of the softening snow-caps seen around Kabul.

In Kandahar Air Field (known as KAF) the phenomenal scale of the US war machine announces itself with an array of hardware that easily dwarfs that in Kabul. A single row of USAF Black Hawk, Chinook or Apache helicopters outnumbers the entire British complement.

Away from the asphalt of the runway, a mini-America has been spookily recreated. KFC, Subway, Pizza Hut and Tim Horton's peddle their junk food to the homesick. The Green Bean Café sells Frappucinos for four dollars a go. The PX (military supermarket) is crammed with everything one might want for a comfortable and productive war-on-terror: pistol holsters (I opt for a black leather leg holster as used by NYPD), chewing tobacco, and T-shirts publicising the wearer's participation in 'Operation Enduring Freedom' with the reverse side advocating the opening of a can of 'whoop ass'.

The inhabitants of this bizarre mini-city are its greatest fascination. Hundreds of civilians are employed by the vast administrative machine that is required to feed, clean, wash the laundry of and process the shit of every soldier. For this task the American mega-corporation Kellogg Brown and Root employs the purest rednecks and poorest blacks and

Hispanics. Many have been in KAF since its inception as a US base of operations five years ago, and are looking forward to owning their own homes or sending their children to college on the back of it.

Numerous cavernous DFACs (dining facilities) churn out lobster and T-bone steaks, cheeseburgers and cookies with ice cream. Fridges hold free soft drinks and M&Ms. This is an unimagined luxury for the British soldier, sustained on 'one choice only' – probably curry or shepherd's pie and polystyrene sponge cake. The British troops staying at Kandahar before deploying to Helmand will briefly enjoy this catering at a cost of 44 dollars per day per soldier to the MoD.

The welfare facilities provided for the US military also come as a revelation to the Brits arriving in Kandahar. The Morale, Welfare and Relaxation centre (MWR) offers a cinema, a dance hall, dozens of computer play-stations, pool tables and free coffee and popcorn. In the evenings groups of blacks play dominoes, while the Hispanics dance salsa. Everyone else munches popcorn or chewing tobacco, watching noisy Hollywood violence. Men and women are both dressed in combats or identical grey Army sports shirts and shorts, some with a yellow reflector band clipped about their waist to ensure a safe walk back to their tent at the evening's close. Over the road in the vast gymnasium great heavy-limbed, lumbering, jar-headed men pump iron. Outside, next to the gym, is an immaculate floodlit basketball court, spoilt only by the dust and sewerage stench whipped up by an incessant south-westerly wind.

The MWR provides its users with a taste of the US homeland. It's a monument to a collective attempt to forget that the nearest town is Kandahar and not Kansas. Everyone, however, even those in sports kit, carries a perpetual reminder of the reality. Their weapon, probably a 9mm pistol, long M16 rifle or stocky M4, slung under a shoulder or leaning intimately on a leg, is never more than an arm's reach away.

The following day we set out with the new headquarters staff to 'recce' Lashkar Gah, where the HQ will eventually be located. We're on a pair of Chinooks (they always work in twos). The door gunner trails his legs off the back of the rear ramp and waves to the pilot of the second 'bird'. I think of the Americans offending Muslim sensibilities in Mogadishu with their dangling footsoles, but the desert whizzing past fifty feet below seems bereft of inhabitants.

The camp at Lashkar Gah is a muddled building site of yellow half-cylindrical Temporarily Deployable Accommodation (TDA) tents clustered around a few flat-roofed concrete buildings. There's a small US Provincial Reconstruction Team (PRT) here who'll shortly hand over to British troops. Portakabin accommodation is also being constructed for the FCO and DfID staff that will be part of the Helmand Task Force. Unlike the Army, for some reason, they'll not live in the TDA. It's perhaps not up to their required standard of comfort. The camp is protected by the Texas National Guard.

Moving away from the gaggle of the headquarters, I'm drawn to the vivid colours of a patch of floral garden. The gardener, a wizened man with a white beard and faded prayer cap on the back of his head, stands upright from the flowerbeds as I approach. We have a stilted Pashtu conversation. Delighted to be able to share his passion, he names each type of flower, which I forget immediately on hearing. He asks me if I'm coming back, and I hope I will if only to enjoy the garden further. Asking him to repeat his name, I write it in my notebook: Sayyid Shah. Later I wonder why he had not grown kitchen vegetables as a source of a little extra income or nourishment. This Afghan devotion to flowers (*Gul*) is widespread and sincere. In Afghanistan the previous autumn I'd seen men wearing flowers behind their ears, and floral decorations ubiquitous in restaurants and vehicles.

Back in Kandahar I take advantage of the fact that the Commander is away in Kabul for the day to zero my rifle. In the Commander's four-wheel drive I turn up at the range to find three US Special Forces and an FBI agent. The Special Forces have neatly groomed beards, climbing boots and mixed clothes, some civilian beige, some old issue US cam-ouflage – the stuff with wavy brown and beige lines rather than the new greyish computer-generated 'visual white noise' kit. I like the old stuff better. The FBI guy gives me some ammo, as I'm concerned about having to account for my own (this range is closed by the Brits to their own troops for not meeting petty MoD health and safety regulations, so none of the HQ have zeroed their weapons yet). The mag from his M4 fits my SA80 A2 – 'Yay for NATO,' he chuckles. The senior SF guy, who quickly introduces himself, lends me his binoculars. I expend three mags correcting my sight and then accept their offer to fire the M4. I like it more than my weapon; it's lighter, has a better scope and less recoil. They fire mine and take photos. The FBI guy shows me his lead-tipped 5.56 rounds. With a soft nose they have the dum-dum effect of a small entry, large exit wound. Luckily, he says, though forbidden for use by conventional troops, they're legal for him. The senior SF bloke gives me his business card before leaving and asks if they can come along if there's an operational parachute jump. 'Just gimme me a call, Leo. I'd love to hop and pop with you guys.'

While I'm cleaning my rifle five minutes later their four-wheel drive returns and one of the SF guys jumps out. Embarrassed at his carelessness, he picks up a rifle magazine he's left on the firing point.

On his return from Kabul the Commander is summoned by the Governor of Helmand. The Pathfinder Platoon, a reconnaissance unit, have had a contact (live rounds being fired) involving the police near Now Zad, a small town in the north of the Province. This is a 'blue-on-blue' – friendly forces shooting at each other by mistake – and the Governor wants an explanation. We jump onto a Chinook, overfly the site of the contact and then land at FOB (Forward Operating Base) Price, the Pathfinder base near Gereshk.

In a blacked-out operations room housed in a low concrete building the Commander is briefed by the platoon sergeant, a weather-beaten man in a faded green T-shirt. Over a map board, he explains that the contact was superficially the result of the police mistaking the British for a Taliban convoy: 'The patrol went into an overnight lie-up position here,' he says, pointing with a pencil to a blue pin in the map, near Now Zad.

'In the morning they were approaching the town and were fired on by the police. They returned fire, and one of the wagons rolled when it swerved during the initial contact so they fired the Milan [anti-tank missile] into it to prevent the ECM [Electronic Counter Measure: used to prevent hostile detonation of improvised bombs by remote radio control] equipment getting nicked.' He pauses, rubbing his bald repeatedly sunburnt head, then continues: 'There was a bit of a stand-off, then everyone realised what was happening and things calmed down. We had no casualties but two police-men were injured so our guys helped patch them up.'

'So, mistaken identity was the cause, was it?' asks the Commander pensively.

'Well, boss, ICOM hits [intercepted radio communica-tions] indicated that the police thought the patrol was after their opium stash. I reckon they opened fire as a delaying tactic.'

'Jesus,' I think, 'this is a serious can of worms.' The depth of narco-corruption in Helmand Province must be catas-trophic if even those charged with upholding the law are complicit in the opium industry. It's a daunting revelation of the enormity of the task facing us, especially as we're sup-posed to be working jointly with the Afghan police. How on earth can we make them un-corrupt? Probably the answer lies in retraining and improved salaries, but given that Hel-mand's entire economy is opium-reliant, an alternative to poppy is badly needed. Whatever the solution, it's going to involve a massive, fundamental change in Helmand's econo-my and government and, crucially, the loyalty of its people. It's something that'll take years, not months, to put right. However, I'm intrigued rather than exasperated by the prob-lem; after all, we've got the Comprehensive Approach.

This is the first contact for British troops in Helmand Province and the platoon sergeant seems chuffed by all the attention. Outside, we bid farewell and scurry towards the waiting Chinook. He gives us a wave, shading his eyes from the afternoon sun, then draws on a cigarette.

Onboard the Chinook I guzzle a few half-litre bottles of mineral water, trying to stay hydrated. The water is warm and the air, already hot, is heated more by the Chinook engines. I feel slightly sick.

Landing in Lashkar Gah, we're met by a British Major, a softly spoken northerner who commands the troops due to take over the Provincial Reconstruction Team role from the Americans. He tells us that they're patrolling the town to a limited extent and yesterday suffered a suicide-vehicle bombing at the front gate in which two soldiers were injured. One has a minor arm wound; the other had part of his ear blown off.

After bundling into a convoy of three Snatch wagons, we head out of camp towards the Governor's compound. Keen to see the town, I get up on 'top-cover' (this involves standing out of a trapdoor in the roof of the vehicle). Next to me, revealed by the hair bun under her helmet, is a young woman. I'm surprised at this, given that Afghan women are invisible to us except for the odd glimpse of a burqa scurrying away, or stepping quickly back behind a door, after scooping up a child or two. I wonder how the locals of Lashkar Gah feel about it. Driving through the town, though, no one seems perturbed and my top-cover buddy gets stuck in to giving lots of 'steer away' hand signals to passing cars.

The men and children of Lashkar Gah are a deeply strik-ing bunch, fulfilling every stereotype of hawk-nosed, swarthy, handsome Pashtuns. Brightly clothed, barefooted children wave happily, their kohl-lined eyes flashing under thick black hair. The streets are broad and well maintained and the town has a solid feel to it. Much of this is the legacy of capital injected in the 1960s from an American-sponsored cotton cultivation programme.

At the Governor's headquarters, a large rambling pile right on the edge of the Helmand River, the Commander and I dismount. Just in our combats, without weapons, we're ushered into a waiting room by a lean, ugly British bloke with beige fatigues and a stubby little machine gun. He's an employee of the private military company protecting the Governor. The waiting room has a high ceiling and is adorned with painted panels depicting renowned highlights of Afghanistan: the Shrine at Mazar-e-Sharif, the Salang Tunnel, the minaret of Djam and others. They have a naive charm about them, probably unintended by the artist.

Tom Tugendhat arrives: a Brit in his early thirties, he's the Governor's special adviser. He's surprisingly dapper in a blue gingham shirt. With unconvincing gravitas he says that the Governor has now calmed down, having earlier been furious about the Pathfinder contact. Still, this is definitely a bol-locking; our host has not yet arrived, we are standing and have not been offered any refreshment. According to the Afghan concept of hospitality, such treatment, in normal cir-cumstances, would be unthinkable and shameful.

Finally the Governor, Engineer Daoud, arrives. We all shake hands and sit down. Like his townsmen outside, the

Governor is a striking individual with a long, elegant nose, neatly clipped beard and a calm countenance.

'Let me start with a proverb,' he says slowly. His English is well pronounced and deliberate. He pauses often, considering his next sentence. 'Only those who are working make mistakes. I was angry when I heard of this incident but I know those involved were acting in good faith.'

The Commander relates his version of events, omitting the bit about the police deliberately firing on the British patrol and the fact that it's a vivid illustration of police corruption.

The Governor nods his head. 'I would like to request an investigation into the causes of the incident.'

He's no fool and is bound to be aware that events were a bit more complicated than described.

'. . . Also I need more police.'

Given that the police force is involved in the opium business, it's hardly surprising their impact is limited and he feels he needs more. The Commander agrees that this would be sensible. The Governor then makes his final and most ambitious request of the Commander.

'The Taliban have occupied a village and closed its school in Baghran. We must try to re-establish law and order and re-open the school . . .' The Governor continues calmly: 'Could you send your troops?'

At the furthest northern part of Helmand, the rugged Baghran valley lies high in the foothills of the Kindu Kush.

The Commander says he'll look into it and assures the Governor that we're here to support him. By the end of the meeting the atmosphere, having become increasingly amicable, is hearty and friendly.

Back in camp I phone through the message about Baghran, but the Operations Officer – in charge of controlling current operations – is vexed. He's busy producing computer slides for the daily evening update in the headquarters, and says reluctantly that he'll look into it.

Later in the afternoon, the Commander is determined to come up with a solution to the policing problem in Helmand. It's clear they're untrustworthy and ineffectual. We need to sort it out because the military will need to work alongside them. On a whiteboard, the Commander brainstorms the problem with the help of Tom Tugendhat, the Major commanding the Provincial Reconstruction Team and the FCO police adviser. I take notes. It's an overwhelming prospect: a new police force will require selection and training and a huge amount of resources to clothe, equip, feed and accommodate them.

'Let's have an *auxiliary* police force!' declares the Commander, scribbling feverishly onto the whiteboard. 'Something for the interim, until a proper force is ready to take over.'

'There should be enough money in the FCO budget,' says Tugendhat, nodding, 'for, let's say, twenty-four men per district? They can be casual auxiliaries at first and get special training later on . . . Like the seed of a new force.'

'But they *must* be selected by the community,' continues the Commander, 'so they have the trust of the people. In fact they'd be *Community Police*,' he concludes with a flourish of his pen.

A list of required kit is hastily drawn up on the whiteboard. The plan is concluded.

'I'll present it to the Governor,' says Tugendhat, 'but I'm sure he'll be happy.'

'This is the way to do it,' I think. 'Action this Day!'

The FCO police adviser has been quiet. Perhaps it's an apt reflection of the FCO's practically non-existent police strategy up until now. The Germans are supposed to be sorting out policing at a national level, and at the provincial level in Helmand it's the FCO's bag, but nothing seems to have been achieved. Having said that, maybe this new plan is folly and we're blundering after a solution emboldened by our ignorance. There've been no Afghans at the meeting and it's probably too complex a problem to solve in half an hour in front of a whiteboard. But at least the Commander's doing something practical, which is more than the FCO have even tried.

That evening at supper in the DFAC I sit with Tom Tugendhat, who's living in the camp until he gets a safe house in town. He takes monumental pleasure in devouring a pair of Snickers ice-cream bars- a luxury available only in American DFACs, which won't be there when the Brits formally take over the camp and run the catering in a couple of weeks' time.

Tugendhat's role in Lashkar Gah harks back to the days of political officers or 'Residents' in British Colonial India – experts who, having spent probably their entire lives in the region, resided with the local ruler in order to advise, coerce and persuade in accordance with the central government's intent. The ability of a single confident Brit to discreetly control the reins of local governance was the necessary foundation of the entire imperial project. In his unique position, Tugendhat is paid by the FCO and wields considerable influ-

ence with the Governor, whom he previously knew by asso-
ciation in Kabul where the Governor (an engineer by profession) was working for the United Nations. On accepting the
governorship of Helmand from President Karzai, Engineer
Daoud (professional titles are assiduously used in Afghanistan as a status marker) requested that the bright young ori-
entalist come with him. The current situation is of course
very different to the imperial project, but Tugendhat's influence is immeasurably more efficient, discreet and beneficial
than that of any number of conventional troops trying to
have a political effect.

'If I'm to maintain such a high standard of cuisine in my
new house,' he says, scrunching up his ice-cream wrapper
with a grin, 'I'll have to employ a Hazara chef!'

From the high Hindu Kush, such people with their repu-
tation for good cooking are a rarity in the remote Pashtun
south.

That night, the Commander gamely accepts an invitation
from the 'other agencies' to an illicit glass of wine that's been
brought from the UK, secreted deep in the luggage of an
overconfident FCO girl. We sit in a group between their new
Portakabins on a circle of plastic garden chairs. A pallid, sincere Finnish girl from DfID describes her experiences of
having amoebic dysentery in Sarajevo. The FCO police
adviser tells me he's sad to be leaving soon. The likelihood of
the Governor receiving an armoured car from the FCO is
also discussed. With no thirst for the wine I go to find a brew.

In the DFAC the troops are having a quiz night. Being
Artillery, rather than Infantry, there are girls present and
they're all in civilian clothing: shiny tracksuit trousers or

jeans, football tops or trendy T-shirts. They're healthily sun-burnt and defiantly good-humoured. I can sense a collective feeling of relief and elation that no one was killed in yester-day's attack. A close shave having passed, morale is surging. As they huddle around the plastic tables, conferring in their teams and drinking cans of soda, I immediately feel a deep liking for them all. I make a cup of tea and leave them to it.

The following morning we're due to return to KAF. The Governor's coming with us – he's got an appointment to have his back seen to at the excellent Dutch hospital there. Waiting for the helicopter, I climb up into one of the corner guard-towers on the perimeter.

The inside smells of urine and has Spanish graffiti scrawled across the grey walls. A Texas National Guardsman sits on a plastic garden chair in the middle of the concrete floor, facing a heavy machine gun pointing ominously out of the narrow window, wrapped in a belt of bullets. His rifle leans in the corner.

'I've been in this tower for the last four hours,' Ramez tells me. With eight more hours to go, I assume he's bored out of his mind, but he loves it.

Eager to talk, he joins me at the window. 'I'm glad to be serving in Afghanistan; I lost weight and learnt a lot. I want to help these people,' he says, pointing a chubby finger through the small window. 'I'll tell my children about it when they're older. I'll tell them that they shot at us and we had to shoot back. I dunno . . . It's maybe hard for them to understand.'

Wishing him a safe tour, I shake his hand and climb down the stepladder.

On the Chinook the Governor and his two Afghan secretaries are thrilled by the experience and take numerous photos. In camp I organise lunch in the vast main American DFAC. After chatting up the Filipino table-clearer I manage to get a bunch of grapes put in the middle of the table, but this improvement cannot mask the incongruity of the situation: the Governor gingerly chewing a cheeseburger next to the Commander and the Chief of Staff. In an odd reversal of roles, the Governor looks much less awesome than yesterday. Despite being of local origin, he's spent a lot of time in Kabul so in Helmand his power base – his ability to exploit personal connections to achieve things – is limited. In a country where family, kin and tribe are of paramount importance in political affairs, it's suddenly very clear that he's relying on us to support his position. He's a bit like the Iraqi Sheikh I met eighteen months ago but on a grander scale. It's hardly surprising, then, that he wants us to bolster his authority in the chaotic north of Helmand. Giving up with the cheeseburger, the Governor pops a grape into his mouth, his countenance remaining serene.

With the north emerging as an area of interest, the Commander and I go on a recce to FOB Robinson (named after a US fatality). It's a ramshackle collection of mud buildings, metal storage containers and vehicles, encircled by a vast wall of earth-filled barrier blocks. We drop off at around midnight from a US Chinook crammed with re-supplies, and with a crouching half-run find our way out of the biting wall of dust kicked up by the Chinook's twin rotors.

We get a brief from a Canadian company commander. He

says they've recently done an operation which failed to find a local opium baron. The good news, however, is that he's since been killed by an American Hellfire missile. In the last month they've done some patrolling near the town in their Light Armoured Vehicles (LAVs), and have had two KIA (killed in action): one was a result of blue-on-blue, the other was an officer who got a hatchet in the head, having taken his helmet off while in a local village. The attacker was shot dead. Significantly, in March there was a full-on frontal assault on the FOB from two directions simultaneously, initiated by RPGs (rocket-propelled grenades) fired in a volley. This is clearly serious stuff and says a great deal about the level of skill and commitment of the Taliban – if that's who the enemy is. He explains that the US Special Forces team working from the FOB have been twitchy as hell since losing two guys a couple of weeks ago in an ambush. During their retreat, under enemy fire, they called in air strikes which dropped a total of thirteen 500 lb J-DAM bombs – an incredible amount of destructive ordnance. Consequently they now stay mainly in the FOB, sometimes going out for unambitious local operations such as searching the nearest villages.

A few hours later, following a freezing night of broken sleep in my jungle sleeping bag next to a Canadian armoured vehicle, I head over to the Afghan National Army (ANA) compound with the Commander. As we walk towards the watchtowers overlooking the Helmand River a gaggle of grubby, smiling ANA greet us. They wear soiled green camouflage fatigues donated by the US and plastic sandals or inferior black leather boots. I ask them in Urdu how they are.

'We're fine,' replies the most confident, advancing slightly from the group. 'But we want to be relieved and return to Herat, our base.'

In the very north-west of Afghanistan, this ancient city with a great poetic and artistic tradition has long been renowned for its pleasant climate.

'We don't mind living here,' he says, pointing at the ramshackle watchtowers where they eat and sleep, 'and the river is pleasant for bathing, but we miss our home.'

Declining tea, we move over to a small mud-walled compound, home to the American Training Team. They're from the Alabama National Guard and their role is to mentor the ANA and facilitate joint operations with the other troops in the FOB. Two of them are on the flat roof glumly watching the fat orange sun come up. They say they've been pretty much stuck in the FOB since the Special Forces suffered the two fatalities. They seem pretty disappointed to be here, but one of them immediately perks up when I ask him about the .38 sporting rifle slung under his arm, giving him the air of a professional hunter. He flicks off the scope cap and puts it up to my shoulder. I gain a sight picture and scan the glistening green edges of the Helmand River. I imagine him sniping an Afghan in the head with it but can't bring myself to ask the question.

Back at the Canadian armoured vehicles, an athletic black guy brings over some pop-tarts for breakfast. He's the commander of the US Special Forces team. He's clearly rattled by recent events and is keen to leave. He hates the Afghans.

'I just wanna get away from these people. You never know what they're thinking . . .'

As we wait for the helicopter just outside the FOB, the Commander muses on how to deal with Sangin. He's thinking out loud: 'We'll not get sucked in to Sangin, I'll tell the Paras to contain it and not get sucked in . . .'

Beside us, adjacent to the FOB's defensive tangle of razor wire and earthen wall, is a field of poppy plants, their white and purple flowers quivering in the slight wind. In the field two bodies are bent double, busily weeding. The crop smells sweet and in a few days will be harvested of its opiate gum.

CHAPTER 5

With the Afghans

Three weeks later I'm already bored with being based in the headquarters. Doing recces with the Commander is fun but I spend a lot of time hanging onto his coat-tails in the vast air-conditioned headquarters tent, under ghastly yellow tube lighting and among ranks of computers manned by diligent but very dull staff officers. I physically detest it and know that I'll never be able to cut around on the ground in this job. It represents the absolute opposite of what I want to experience in Afghanistan. Luckily, there's an empty slot in the team that'll be embedded with the ANA (Afghan National Army) and if I play the language card I reckon I've a good chance of being allowed to go. The Commander doesn't really need an ADC anyway. There's no shortage of brown-nosing staff officers willing to make his cups of tea.

As we leave the Dutch hospital in Kandahar after visiting two Pathfinder casualties injured by a land mine, the Commander seems in reflective mood. I reckon it's a good time to ask to be moved, and I'm quietly delighted when he agrees to my request without hesitation.

Feeling optimistic, I lug my kit from the headquarters

tents (eight men in each tent with air-con) to a vast hundred-man transit tent. Like gigantic budget marquees, these tents are designed to accommodate all new arrivals during their brief stay in KAF before they deploy 'forward'. I dump my kit on an empty bunk. There are some Dutch troops on one side and female nurses on the other. Most of these nurses won't deploy forward at all. As some joker points out, Kandahar for them should more suitably be renamed 'Kandaraki' in homage to the type of Club 18–30 destinations of which they're fond.

Among a gaggle of T-shirted troops sitting on a crooked square of metal bunk-beds I meet Company Sergeant-Major Johnstone. He's an Edinburgh man in his early thirties with greying temples. With cropped hair and a broad grin, there's a whiff of the violent jock about him. A confident sparkle in his eyes seems to say, 'I'm happy with discomfort, squalor and violence, I've lived through them all and have no fear of them.' Although he's from the Army Air Corps he's an Infantry specialist and has just completed a six-month tour instructing Iraqi Officer Cadets at the Al Rustamiyah Officer Training Academy, known as the 'Baghdad Sandhurst'. During frequent patrols into the city – the epicentre of Iraq's insurgent, sectarian and all other types of violence – he saw a great deal of action, firing six hundred rounds in six months. The CSM and I will mentor a company (approximately sixty men) of ANA soldiers. Our purpose will be to further train and conduct operations with these freshly trained troops newly arrived from Kabul Military Training Centre, where they complete a basic six-month infantry course.

Johnstone tells me that the Mentoring Team has been in

theatre a couple of weeks and is composed of volunteers who responded to a trawl across the Army, including the Territorial Army. It's the MoD's clever way of dealing with an over-stretched Army: an additional unit is effectively created by borrowing men from those already established. The benefit, however, is that the Mentoring Team's range of experience is diverse: some, like Johnstone himself, have returned recently from Iraq, while others left the regular Army a dozen years ago. There's about thirty men in all. Because the team is not a normal unit there's been a cock-up with equipment. The usual operational stuff that any unit would take for granted has not been allocated and there's simply no extra materiel in theatre. Consequently the team currently has no radios, no night-vision equipment, no heavy machine guns and no medical supplies. I assure him someone in HQ is bound to be dealing with this problem.

The Afghan battalion which we'll mentor has not yet arrived from Kabul, so we make use of the time to conduct our own training. The medic, Sergeant Stoddart, a TA Geordie whose last operational tour was 'Gulf War One', gives us first-aid lessons in the shade of the concrete bomb shelters outside our tents. After the lesson I blag a load of plasti-cuffs for use as tourniquets from a sympathetic engineer who has a few extra packets.

An unwelcome return to the bomb shelters is made in the horribly early hours of the following morning. A double bang reverberates through the tent, shaking me awake.

'Oh God,' I groan, disgusted at the prospect of having to get out of bed.

The siren cranks up. It's either a mortar or a rocket attack.

Sliding out of bed, I put my helmet on and make for the hard cover, pulling on my body armour. Inside the shelter the Dutch are smoking excitedly, looking ridiculous in the pyjamas/body-armour/helmet combination. I happily deprive myself of the full benefit of the shelter to avoid their cigarette smoke. Returning to the tent after the all-clear has sounded, I'm piqued to see that others have slept through the whole thing.

In the morning the nurses sunbathe and flaunt their ill-advised tattoos, while the advance party of 3 Para ride around on their quad bikes. The nurses have gained sudden desirability purely due to their location. There's a least one hundred blokes to every one girl in KAF.

The Kandak ('battalion' in Dari) having arrived from Kabul, we go to meet them in Camp Shirzai, about a kilometre away from KAF. The troops are mustered into a hollow square, more than four hundred of them, waiting for General Raufi, the Commander of 205 Corps, which has been assigned to Helmand Province. We stand to the flanks. The Afghan officers at this distance are indistinguishable from the men, all massed together in their dark green camouflage fatigues and green berets. As the General approaches, a grey-beard Sergeant Major brings them to attention; they slide their left heels together with their right, Soviet style.

The General, saluting, goose-steps into the middle of the hollow square and begins a speech. He says every sentence twice, once in Pashtu and once in Dari, my interpreter relaying the meaning. The troops are congratulated on the completion of their training and told to expect a hard campaign against the enemies of Afghanistan. Those who have gone absent – apparently more than a hundred in the last four days – are savagely belittled. This harangue has been going for ten minutes when my interpreter goes silent. I don't bother to prompt a restart. After a further ten minutes attention among the troops has diminished and those in the rear ranks, who can't be seen by the General, rest on their haunches. I'm eager to get among these ranks of scruffy troops and make an impact. We've clearly got our work cut out, with deserters leaving in droves, and our team like a rag-tag Afghan version of *The Wild Geese*. Despite this, however, I'm optimistic; a good bit of British Army banter should be able to turn their morale around.

Unable to find the HQ company commander (whom I'll mentor), I depart for KAF with Will, another Captain, driving the Ford Ranger which we've borrowed from the ANA. There seems to be an abundance of these US-supplied pick-up trucks in Shirzai – which is lucky, as ours are (hopefully) waiting for us in Helmand. Unconcerned about the short distance we have to travel, we chuck our kit onto the back seat – but then, as we're approaching the front gate of KAF, a huge whooshing wall of flame suddenly explodes directly to our front.

'Fucking hell! Get your kit on!' I shout, as Will slams on the brakes.

Jumping out, I scramble on my webbing vest, ram on my helmet, cock my weapon and look around in case a further attack is imminent. Apart from the shouting of the soldiers at the gate, there's nothing unusual apparent. I feel danger-ously exposed.

'Let's get back in the wire!'

We leap back into the Ranger and scream towards the gate, now suddenly more concerned at the prospect of being shot as suicide bombers in our beige ANA wagon by the terrified Canadian gate guard.

A few days later we've moved to Helmand. We're in Camp Tombstone, a tiny Amercan-run compound that accommodates the engineers building Shoraback, a sprawling brigade-sized camp for five thousand men, next door. Tombstone is a cushy little camp: there's a pukka American DFAC, and cabins for accommodation rather than tents. The officers have their own dormitories, as do the sergeants and private soldiers. We're packed in like sardines but the air-con blower keeps it cool, and an array of home-made furniture, constructed from plywood salvaged from a half-constructed cabin next door, gives it a homely atmosphere. I'm on a top bunk above Will and next to Jim.

At 0500 I slide off my bunk and use my newly purchased shelving unit as a step down. I paid 20 dollars to one of the carpenters working next door for the lavish unit – designed to hold a TV and stereo system, it's currently housing our webbing vests, helmets and body armour. It reminds me that Will hasn't yet repaid me his half of the 20 dollars. Having silently put on my trainers and PT kit, I leave the sleeping dorm and run laps around the absurdly small inner perimeter of Tombstone. The sun is already on the rise and after about 0600 running is intolerable due to the heat and the dust carried on the wind from Camp Bastion, being built to house the main British contingent and still under construction five hundred metres away. Half an hour later, drenched

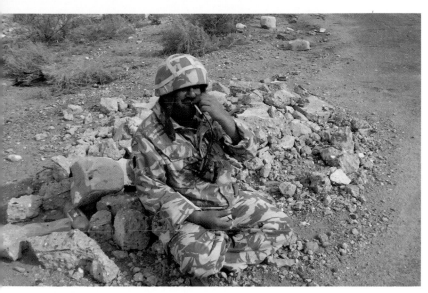

1. Pleased with my combats, the Sheikh takes a fag break.

1. With elders of Basra's Tribal Council, who gather to resolve disputes by
lying traditional tribal law.

London. At the gilded epicentre of the establishment: the Officers' Mess at 'Jimmy's' – St James's Palace.

London. The Changing of the Guard: I'm very smart but very bored.

kistan. In the far north, near the Afghan border, my guide pegs down his horse
r the night.

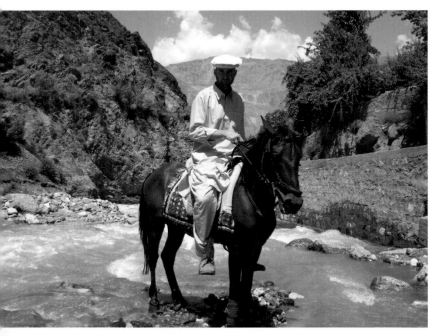

kistan. A brief taste of the frontier.

A Hazara man (left) and a Pashtun man crippled by one of the millions of land-mines scattered across Afghanistan (right) seek alms outside the mausoleum of Ali (the Prophet Mohammad's son-in-law) in Mazar-e-Sharif, northern Afghanistan.

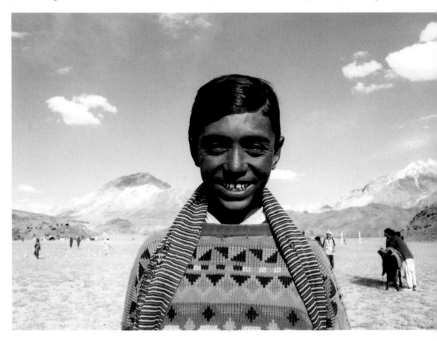

A Wakhi shepherd boy, near the Wakhan Corridor, northern Pakistan. Parcels of cloth-ing from international relief agencies often result in colourful incongruity.

bedded in the Afghan National Army (ANA). The faces of Captain Hameed's
illustrate the pan-ethnic mix of Tajik, Pashtun, and Uzbek designed to make
ANA non-sectarian and representative of the Afghan nation.

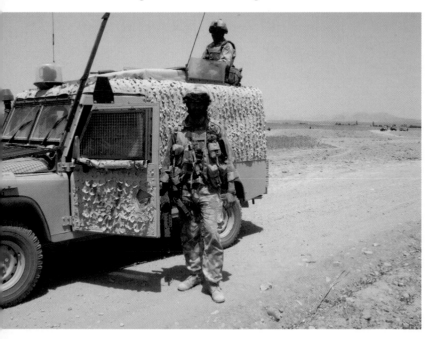

he 'Desert of Death'. Advancing to seize and occupy Sangin, with my 'Snatch'
on – an armoured Land-Rover hopelessly ill-suited to desert conditions.

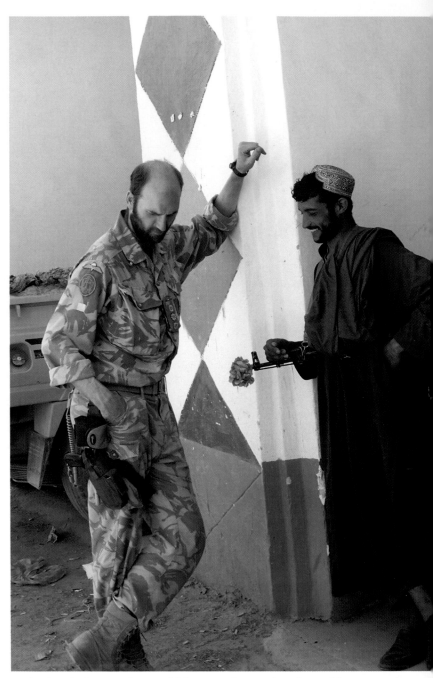

In the Sangin District Centre. Afghan men have a deep love of flowers, and use th[em]
frequently for decoration.

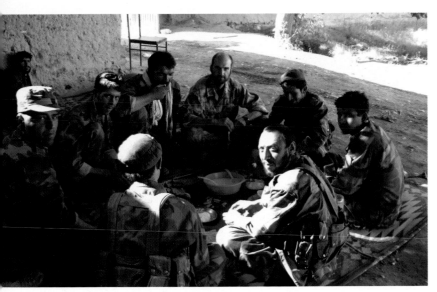

e calm before the storm: breakfast (milk whey and naan bread) with the ANA in
e Sangin District Centre.

1 impromptu tea party during a lull in operations. The ANA vehicle behind us (a
painted Ford Ranger pick-up truck) and the uniforms are donations from the
5A.

On patrol in Sangin: determined to win hearts and minds, we've removed our sun glasses and helmets.

in sweat, I take a proper plumbed-in American shower, throw on my combats and, buckling my pistol onto my leg, head for the DFAC. Forgoing the pancakes, crispy bacon and grits option, I tuck into a bunch of fat red grapes and half a dozen green melon slices. My breakfast has, remarkably, been flown in from Dubai. It is a logistical wonder of the developed world that American soldiers in the Afghan desert can eat the same breakfast as those in the middle of the United States.

My next meal is of reassuringly local origin. Our Afghan company is now installed in Camp Shoraback next door, where I meet its commander. Captain Hameed is stocky, smooth-skinned and very clean. He has short, thick black hair and a neat, close beard. His combats, which are pressed, are tucked into new American desert boots which, I note, are in better repair than my own. Sitting cross-legged in his office we await the reappearance of Ramadan, the elfin tea boy, sent scurrying away with the metal teapot and a volley of shouted instructions. The Captain's office is a small room at the end of a long semi-cylindrical metal cabin which also serves as accommodation. It's essentially the same as ours, but without air conditioning. He seems fairly mystified by my presence, yet unwilling to summon the energy required to be fully inquisitive. He speaks Dari and via Tamim, my interpreter, assures me that he knows what he's doing.

'I've been fighting all my grown life with the Shura-i-Nazar [the Northern Alliance]. We fought the Taliban when no one else did.'

'I'm here purely to advise if necessary and will surely learn a great deal from you,' I reply, determined to be humble.

Thankfully, Ramadan reappears and serves glasses of boiling green tea and little Pakistani toffees. Captain Hameed is a Tajik from the Panjshir valley. Portraits of Ahmed Shah Masood furnish the office walls above me.

'Captain Hameed, I visited the mausoleum of the great Commander Masood while travelling in the Panjshir valley last year,' I reveal, hoping to impress.

He is unmoved, and does not respond. He seems to be taking it silently for granted, perhaps thinking, 'Hasn't everyone?'

His deputy, Abdul Qadir, and Company Sergeant-Major, Pir Ahmed, enter and shake my hand warmly. Both lithe, fine-featured Panjshiris, they settle beside us in anticipation of lunch. Ramadan places metal lunch trays before us, brought from the cookhouse. Each contains a little mutton stewed with potato, yoghurt, a mound of dark rice, and a thick, foot-long naan bread, crispy brown at the edges. Invoking the name of God with a whispered 'Bismillah!', my hosts and I break our bread and eat in silence. When my portion is finished, Captain Hameed places pieces of his own mutton on my tray until I am stuffed full. Reclining slightly, we have another round of tea, and conversation resumes. I broach the idea of doing some training which would be useful if the rumoured deployment to FOB Robinson occurs. Captain Hameed assures me that HQ Company isn't going anywhere as its duties are to guard the camp perimeter only. Less ambitiously, I suggest taking mugshots of his troops, for his records, to which he agrees. With Abdul Qadir and Pir Ahmed now fully reclined, I take my leave and, thanking him for lunch, leave them to sleep.

Tamim and I emerge blinking into the afternoon sun. It's

now almost 50 degrees and after our heavy lunch sleep is inevitable. Leaving Tamim at the interpreter's hut, I trudge back through the dust. Tombstone's rows of cabins appear like a little prisoner-of-war camp, a mini Afghan stalag-luft, but with great scoff and hot showers.

While CSM Johnstone and his opposite number Pir Ahmed muster the troops into a hollow square for the photo-parade, I sit next to Captain Hameed at a table which reflects a solar glare. We work from left to right, each man marching into a formal halt and saluting in front of the company comman-der – an action they've just learnt in Kabul. I take each one's photograph and record their name, age, Province of origin and specialist training. Mostly young, small, grubby and dishevelled, they are not the Afghan tribesmen of Western stereotype and their appearance belies their heroically beau-tiful Persian names: Hafizullah (divine guardian), Hakim Khan (great judge), Jehangir (world ruler). The troops enjoy the attention, and CSM Johnstone gets some banter going by getting them to learn his name: 'Sergeant Major Tommy,' they cry in unison.

Unfortunately there's a serious mismatch between the names I've recorded and those on Captain Hameed's nomi-nal roll.

'Where are the other men on your list?' I enquire

'They are absent, they left without permission after the graduation ceremony in Kabul last month . . . They will not return,' he says matter-of-factly.

We're left with about thirty men, including NCOs and officers.

Retreating from the fierce sun for tea with Captain Hameed, I broach the subject of what training we might do. He's interested only in driving training and says we can train all those not involved in guarding the perimeter, including, of course, himself. Disappointed by Captain Hameed's lack of enthusiasm and the fact that his company is turning out to be more like a platoon, I decide against discussing the idea of taking a patrol out around the local area. Sipping our tea silently, we chew sweet Panjshiri raisins.

In the innumerable brief pauses between his interpreting for other people, I listen intently to Tamim's gentle voice as he tells me about himself.

'My grandfather's family was from Kandahar, but left for Kabul in the 1960s when my grandfather became a General in King Zahir Shah's army . . .'

His family's good fortunes had not survived the last forty years intact.

'My father was employed in the Defence Ministry and was killed by the Mujahideen in 1993, so I fled with my mother and sister to Peshawar. I was fifteen years old. I worked in a matches factory, it was a very difficult time but I worked as hard as I could . . .'

Sacrificing any spare time and money available to take English lessons, Tamim eventually returned to Kabul after the fall of the Taliban. Using his knowledge of Pashtu, Dari and English, he got a job interpreting for the US Army, with whom he worked in Kabul and Paktia Province. Money was still tight, however.

'My grandfather was very angry that we had gone to Peshawar and did not forgive us for leaving Kabul. He still refuses to allow us back into his house, so we have to rent an apartment in Macrorayon [vast Soviet housing blocks in Kabul]. My sister is still in school and mother is too ill to work, so I need my wages for the rent and other things.'

I'm touched by his calm honesty. Like me he's in his late twenties, but has already seen a lifetime's worth of trauma. A gentle man, he's sick of violence:

'I'm glad to be away from the Americans. I like them but it was too dangerous. I hope this mission can be safe, soon I want to return to Kabul to marry my girlfriend. The remainder of my wages I'm saving for the celebrations.'

A few days later, I'm sitting in Captain Hameed's office – which now has a metal table and three chairs – drinking the inevitable green tea. Our training has started but is so far limited to some driving with a few of the soldiers, and Captain Hameed instantly dismisses any idea of a patrol whenever I suggest it. He's whinging to Pir Ahmed about the fact that Colonel Shirdil, the battalion commander, has ordered him to remove the photograph of Commander Masood that was fixed to the windscreen of one of HQ Company's Ford Rangers. This has been done to guard against factionalism, which so far seems to be happily absent from the Kandak.

Unannounced, a junior NCO brings in a filthy, sullen soldier and, pulling him by the shoulder, places him before Captain Hameed's desk. The NCO says something to Captain Hameed, who stands up and asks the soldier a question, to which he receives a mumbled reply and a shake of the head. The Captain then harangues the soldier, growing angrier and louder until, advancing around the table, he punches the soldier full in the face. The soldier falls onto his knees and clutches his nose. Kicked in the chest, he falls backwards and crawls for the door, sent on his way by a left and a right kick from Captain Hameed. All this has started and finished so quickly that Tamim can only now interpret the meaning of the conversation. The soldier, Hafizullah, had been found smoking hashish in the lines. Captain Hameed, smoothing his combats, settles back down on his chair and resumes his glass of tea.

Tramping back through the dust to Tombstone, I reflect that the beating I've just witnessed makes me realise how little I know of the ANA from spending a few hours with them each morning. I'm desperate to be properly 'embedded' with the Afghans, to truly get to know them and turn the company into a slick, effective unit. But they're not really interested in doing any serious training, so we end up wasting a lot of time and just drinking gallons of green tea. Perhaps when we start patrolling and go up to FOB Robinson the relationship will feel a bit more meaningful? Each time I return from Shoraback to the clean sterility of Tombstone I feel mildly fraudulent and self-compromised. I'm also annoyed with myself for my enjoyment of the Afghan-free DFAC. As a remedy to this disappointing double-sided existence I spend time with the interpreters as a compromise, a sort of cultural halfway house.

I'm intrigued to be invited by Tamim to take tea after the Friday prayer meeting in Shoraback. The prayers are still under way when I arrive, and I'm about to retreat through the door when Tamim spots me, jumps up and insists that it is appropriate for me to join him. Sliding off my boots, which I've loosened in anticipation, I settle cross-legged next to Tamim as he resumes his devotions. The room has been cleared of all furniture; all that remains is a hollow square of mattresses, full of bodies turned inwards towards a large young man with a full beard and shaven top lip, absorbed in reading silently to himself. This is the mullah, on his weekly visit. Those around him are reading the holy Qur'anic booklets he's brought. They read in whispers, lips moving in vigorous enunciation. Some rock back and forth slightly, in union with the rhythm of the sacred text. At its conclusion the reader kisses the text, holds it to his forehead and replaces it on the stack in the middle of the room, taking another. Some, who cannot read, sit with a friend and listen to a hushed narration. These men have momentarily given up their rank at this prayer meeting. Officers sit by soldiers, with no regard to their distance from the door – unthinkable in any other situation, when a person's status diminishes the closer he is to it. As the prayers end and the tea-drinking begins I feel humbled to be included.

The following day I'm determined to plan a patrol with Captain Hameed. We've done bags of driving training with the small group of guys we get each day and I want to move onto something a bit more meaningful. Surprisingly, perhaps because he's bored with my pestering, he immediately agrees that we should take out a patrol in the local area in a couple of days' time. After this is agreed and we've finished our tea, a small crumpled plastic bag is offered to me by the Captain with a mischievous grin. This is naswar, an ultra-strong mixture of dark pungent tobacco and god-knows-what-else. Its name in Pashtu literally means 'brown'. Having observed him taking it on a daily basis, my curiosity wins over and I accept the little bag, take out a pinch and place it under my tongue. Taking care not to swallow any saliva, I settle on my chair. Within moments my body is beset by a rush of tingling and simultaneously becomes very, very heavy. I sink further into my chair, wanting to roll off and sleep on the floor. I'm briefly amused by this sensation when it's suddenly superseded by a nauseous urge; I struggle off the chair and go outside.

As I leave the office, Major Sayyid, a company commander known as 'the Russian' for his fair complexion, is in the corridor energetically beating a soldier's upturned foot soles. The soldier is held on his back by two assistants. Major Sayyid seems to be expending more energy than necessary due to the fact that his weapon is a broom handle and devoid of the flex appropriate to a whip.

Back in Tombstone, I wander vacuously into the operations room to check for mail. Getting a 'bluey' – an MoD airmail letter free to the families of serving personnel – is absurdly exciting, out of all proportion to its content. A parcel therefore is even more thrilling – pure morale gold dust.

On the TV screen at the back of the operations room a friend's face flashes up. It's Dobson from Sandhurst, a shiny blond grinning face. He's in the Army Air Corps. His brother was in the Scots Guards with me. As I'm drawn to the screen, his image is replaced by a pall of smoke over urban rooftops; this is Basra on the BBC News. His Lynx was shot down. Dobson's dead.

Seconds later the news item changes. Stunned, I check my

post: nothing. I'm very glad to be here; we're detached, far away, which makes his death simple, avoidable. My mourning for Dobson will last for as long as it takes me to turn away from the TV screen and leave the operations room.

Two days later we head over to Shoraback for the patrol. We've got two vehicles; I'm in one with Private Finau – 'Finny', my Fijian driver – and following in the other is CSM Johnstone with Sergeant Stoddart. We've borrowed two extra bodies: one to man the 'Jimpy' (General Purpose Machine Gun) mounted on my wagon and a signaller to monitor the radios.

On our arrival Captain Hameed is in his office wearing flip-flops – not a good 'combat indicator'.

'Captain Leo, let's maybe do the patrol tomorrow,' he says, wincing, clearly intent on having the day off.

At this point, from my recent exposure to the Afghans, I know that 'face' is extremely important. I must get him to change his mind but make it look like his own idea, thus allowing him to avoid appearing work-shy, keep his honour unblemished and save his 'face'.

'I must commend you for your well-judged postponement,' I say, sitting down uneasily on a flimsy metal office chair, encumbered with my body armour and webbing vest, 'but hadn't we better clear this with Colonel Shirdil? He's expecting us to depart immediately, and it would be a shame if your admirable concern about overworking your men were construed as disorganisation or even worse, idleness . . .'

Flip-flops replaced by desert boots, we finally depart after the two hours of chaos required to get three ANA wagons, filled with fuel and each complete with a commander, driver, signaller and as many men as possible (each with an AK) clinging onto the open back, out of the gate.

Thrilled to be out of the cramped monotony of the camp, we bomb around the lunar-desert landscape that surrounds us. It's uninhabited and pancake-flat for miles in all directions, contained only by the summit spikes of the distant Hindu Kush. Kicking up furious dust clouds, we thrash the wagons as fast as possible and practise changing formation on the move, exhilarated by the space, the speed, and the heat.

The Afghans love it. The following day, our rapport is markedly humorous. Even Captain Hameed can't help admitting that he enjoyed it. Interestingly, I felt a little bit of pride when we all parked up outside the headquarters in Camp Bastion and I went inside to tell the operations desk that we were departing; my beard raised numerous eyebrows and I was reminded how glad I was not to be spending my tour in a tent full of computers. I was pleased too that my Afghans could see what a rancid dusty shit-hole Camp Bastion is and that the Brits are living in worse conditions than they are.

I'm also pleased we've got our Afghans out the gate, as our deployment to FOB Robinson is impending. With this departure in mind Colonel Shirdil has ordered that a party be thrown. The Brits provide a PA system (borrowed from the Americans, naturally), the Afghans provide the dancing and the enthusiasm. A Pashtu pop tune is blasted out repeatedly, and a circle of dancers grows. ANA soldiers in grubby green combats and flip-flops move in a rhythmic train, hands in the air with palms raised and backs straight. They kick their heels forward for each step and turn repeatedly inwards then outwards. A cup is produced and balanced on the crown of the finest dancer until with renewed bravado he outdoes himself, the cup tumbles and is passed on . . .

Away from the dancing a football match is played, Brits versus ANA with an interpreter refereeing. The Afghans win on penalties. The ANA doctor, really a male nurse trained thirty years ago in India, is drunk on medicinal spirit and after unsuccessfully picking a fight with a British sergeant, spends the night locked in his own clinic. Later, some wag among the British plays 'I wanna take you to a gay bar' through the PA system. The jest goes unacknowledged by the Afghans and some of their more committed dancers struggle valiantly to maintain a rhythm.

Had they known the song's meaning some of the Afghans might have reflected discreetly that its being played in an ANA camp is not without relevance. Due to the complete absence of any female company, intimate male relation-ships, sometimes homosexual, commonly develop. It is, however, a temporary diversion for the participants while they're deprived of their normal lives rather than anything with long-term meaning. The exact role performed by the tea-boy doting on every ANA officer is consequently a source of endless banter amongst the Brits working with the Afghans.

With the move to FOB Robinson just days ahead, I suggest to Captain Hameed that we take HQ Company to test-fire their rifles. True to form, he suggests an excellent counter-plan which involves staying in camp, definitely drinking tea and probably sleeping. However, Major Sayyid is also present, and says it's a good idea. Captain Hameed agrees, chuckling at my constant enthusiasm for training, which to him seems baffling, misguided and unnecessary. On the range near the camp the soldiers, under the control of CSM Johnstone and Pir Ahmed, fire twenty rounds from their AK47s into wooden targets a hundred metres distant. The troops are keen and are fairly good shots. Before departing, Captain Hameed and I fire off some excess rounds, each taking a turn on the same weapon. I shoot a couple of mags. The AK47 is far louder and has a greater kick than my normal weapon, due to its larger 7.62 cartridge. I hand the AK and a magazine to Captain Hameed. He holds the magazine up to the weapon and struggles with the locking mechanism, approaching it from the wrong end, before clicking it into place. For a former Northern Alliance Mujahid, he's surprisingly unfamiliar with Afghanistan's most common weapon.

The Orders Group the night before the move to FOB Robinson drags on for two hours, mainly because of the interpreting between our commanding officer (a Colonel) and Colonel Shirdil. The 3 Para Patrols (reconnaissance) Platoon will observe the ground five kilometres ahead of us and an American unit will lead our convoy, taking advantage of their aggressive rules of engagement and superior firepower. The appropriately named Sergeant Triggs says they'll happily shoot anyone they don't like the look of with their .50-calibre heavy machine guns and will carry a world's worth of ammunition.

After the main Orders Group I give my own set of orders to my little team in the DFAC: CSM Johnstone, Finny,

Sergeant Stoddart and a signaller who's with us just for the move. I keep it brief, focusing on the route on my map, and what we'll do if we're 'contacted'. We've practised our reaction drills repeatedly so everyone knows it backwards, while also knowing that it'll never be that neat when it's for real.

Exhilarated to be leaving Tombstone, I'm in high spirits as I stitch the ANA badge (crossed swords and delicate Dari script on a green oval) on to my left shirt sleeve, the final piece of preparation before some half-sleep and departure in a couple of hours' time.

CHAPTER 6

Seizing Sangin

May 2006: Helmand Province, Afghanistan

At 0100 we're roaring out of the Tombstone gate in a great column, forty vehicles long, over-revving through the sand, dust billowing into our headlights. I'm thrilled that we're finally leaving after all the waiting around and sluggish preparation. We're fully expecting to be 'contacted' because our impending departure has been a poorly kept secret; everyone, including all the ANA troops, has known about it for the last few days. This anticipation only adds to our excitement.

I'm jammed into the commander's seat (front left-hand side) of my Snatch wagon, which barely accommodates my 6-foot 4-inch frame combined with my body armour, webbing vest, three-litre water-pouch on my back and 9mm pistol strapped to my left leg. I've got my helmet on and my PRR (Personal Role Radio) is strapped onto my left ear. It's for short-distance tactical use, but doesn't work well from inside the vehicle. My rifle is muzzle down, resting between my knees. My own personal GPS (global positioning system) is balanced up against the window on the dashboard in front of me to ensure a continuous signal. Alongside it are my map case and binoculars, which I managed to get in Colchester before deploying. In between Finny and me is a box of a dozen bottles of mineral water which Finny, quietly cheerful as ever, loaded up just before departure. He also had the presence of mind to pop into the DFAC before we left for a last-minute goodies-grab, and has got us two Snickers ice-cream bars each – the most prized of DFAC treasures. I can't face one at the moment, and don't have the heart to suggest that perhaps he might have got something a bit more durable.

It's not long before our convoy comes to a grinding halt: one of the ANA four-tonners is bogged down. Two US Humvees from the rear of the column whizz past to the rescue, bumping effortlessly over the sand that surrounds our dirt track. Twenty minutes later we shudder forward. It's not just the Afghans who get bogged down. Our Snatch wagons are woefully underpowered and ill-suited to cross-country driving. Designed for 'snatching' individuals from a crowd of rioters on Northern Ireland's streets, the inadequacy of the Snatch has been a notorious bugbear for British troops since the invasion of Iraq. Their thin little wheels cut into the patches of sand which cover parts of the road, becoming hopelessly stuck. The British vehicles are repeatedly pulled free by the Americans.

After hitting the tarmac of Route 1 – Afghanistan's national ring-road – the pace quickens and we're relieved to pass through the small town of Gereshk and cross the Helmand River still under the cover of darkness. Shortly, we turn north onto a mud track heading towards the Sangin Valley.

Static again, as we wait for another wagon to be dragged

free, the rising sun keeps us entertained. Tamim and Finny take pictures of each other posing. The expectation of being contacted has, at least momentarily, disappeared. Despite the wasteland appearance, there are occasional signs of life: poppy fields cluster around the irrigation channels that nourish them and lead to small mud-hut farm dwellings. The poppy stalks are now flowerless, brown and shrivelled, having been recently bled of their opium. They'll soon be cut down and have their seeds replanted. A more fleeting spectacle are distant black dots on the horizon – the tents of Koochi shepherds, a nomadic herding tribe of Pashtuns.

Our Snatch wagon has got inch-thick windows for ballistic protection. They don't open, so there's an air-conditioning blower to compensate. Unfortunately ours doesn't work, despite Finny's efforts at checking the fuse. By mid-morning the heat is fierce. I keep the door open to get a through draught, which drops the temperature to the high 40s. Our bodies, baking in body armour, are soon rancid with sweat.

Stopped yet again, we stretch our legs and refill our water satchels from the stack of mineral water bottles between our seats. I share out a four-pack of Del Monte diced peaches, my own DFAC steal. One each for me, Finny, Tamim and the signaller who's with us just for the convoy. Unsated, I sit and wait. Finny dozes. The Snickers ice-cream bars are now liquid.

Finally we crawl forward, and after a total of fourteen hours of stop-start frustration arrive at FOB Robinson to find the US Special Forces team leaving. They're 'bugging out' – making a hurried exit, delighted to be returning to

Kandahar. The little camp, half-familiar to me from the earlier recce, has all (excepting the outer wall) been ripped
down or taken away in an effort to salvage some of the re-
useable fittings. I wouldn't expect such a budgetary con-
straint for the US Special Forces. The Helmand Task Force
headquarters has clearly been unable to negotiate with the
American command to keep this crucial infrastructure in
place, which means we'll be sleeping in the sand. A new
watchtower, completed just days previously, lists precariously against the perimeter, its legs sheared off. All that
remains is a wooden shack and a couple of metal shipping
containers, doors open, spilling out crushed boxes of American rations. The deep sand is cluttered with rubbish – food
packaging, Coke cans, metal ammunition boxes and hundreds of spent .50-calibre brass cases. The Special Forces
team, muscular and bearded, jubilantly mount up onto
their Humvees, adjust their sunglasses and settle behind
their weapons. As they leave the gate they test-fire their
weapons into the side of the road, and a frantic rattling
echoes up the valley.

We 'bivi-up' at the corners of the perimeter, stretching our
plastic ponchos between the earthen perimeter wall and the
sand and foraging among the remnants of the smashed-up
camp for sheets of plywood on which to unroll our sleeping
bags. The left-over ammo boxes make excellent seats and
mini-tables. The challenge of creating a little living space has
refreshed our enthusiasm after the tedium of the convoy and
the disappointment of finding the camp in a shit state. The
ANA are adjacent to us, in another large perimeter towards
the river. Their Kandak HQ is in a walled compound with

brick rooms and they live in their watchtowers, so they're better off than we are.

The sun disappears beyond the Helmand River below us, but we're too absorbed in our new activity to take photos. We 'stag on' – mount guard – in pairs next to our bivi positions. Two hours each in rotation, spent staring into the night through the green glow of a Common Weapon Sight (night-viewing aid). We've got one in our team. Each man should really have night-vision goggles (NVGs) but the kit shortage has not yet been sorted. Erratically the night's silence is smashed by the pounding, ear-splitting boom of artillery, the ANA firing their howitzers at Taliban targets – maybe real, probably imagined.

Coming off my second stag as dawn breaks, I tumble exhausted onto my dust-laden sleeping bag. I'm woken about an hour later by a signaller from HQ: there's something on. The officers and senior NCOs gather round our Colonel's vehicle. An order has come from Helmand Task Force headquarters: we are to 'seize Sangin and re-establish governance'. The town is apparently overrun with Taliban; we must immediately carry out a planned attack, kill or disperse any Taliban, and allow the Afghan authorities to govern. Full details will follow at a bigger Orders Group in two hours. 'Holy shit!' I think, taking in the Colonel's words. It's incredibly sudden and unexpected but I'm game!

Electrified, I pace back to our bivi position and relay the message to CSM Johnstone, Finny and Sergeant Stoddart. They accept it without question. Frantic with excitement we start cramming our two Snatch wagons with ammunition, water and rations scavenged from the American leftovers.

We need a third wagon, so Sergeant Stoddart heads off to the ANA compound to see what he can find. As I make my way over to the O-group my stomach swirls with adrenalin.

'Fucking hell!' I think. 'This is it for real, a deliberate attack!'

The Orders Group takes place in the shade of a parachute canopy suspended from the mud walls of the American Training Team's compound. The officers and some senior NCOs of the British mentoring team are crowded around a map pinned to the mud wall. Its scale is 1:10,000, so individual buildings can be seen. I got my copy while ADC, which is just as well because we're short of these decent large-scale maps. Mixed in with us is the American training team: a dozen laconic National Guardsmen, who seem tired but utterly reliable. They're commanded by an unexcited but very willing black Colonel with powerful rounded shoulders and big hands. Some of these guys are probably nine months into their one-year tour, so they've seen it all before. It's their Kandak coming into town with us: the Heratis I met during the Commander's recce. We're meant to have relieved them, but they're better equipped and more prepared than our Kandak, which will stay at the FOB and guard the perimeter. The Kandak commander is the last to arrive. He's late, but only because he was the last to be told what's happening. He's a neat little Herati with a slight goatee beard and Mongol eyes. His second-in-command is with him, a suave Pashtun with his green beret clinging rakishly to his head.

Before this audience the Colonel sets out his plan of attack. He's what he himself would call 'a strapping cove', a broad-chested rugby player with sensible good looks who speaks with the confident ease of a man not interested in details. We'll enter the town from the east, approaching along a dry riverbed. The 3 Para Patrols Platoon (still here from yesterday) will guide the advance. The British teams will take an ANA company each, the order of march being 3 Company, 2 Company then 1 Company (with my team).

The Colonel's command group will be located just behind the lead company at all times. Half of the US team will go directly to the southern end of the town to block any enemy movement and be a diversion, the other half will travel in front of the lead company in order to provide extra firepower. (They've got .50-calibre machine guns on their Humvees, which pack more than twice the punch of a normal rifle.) We'll head for the District Chief's compound, as that's the seat of local government. We don't know where that is exactly; I mark three possible locations on my map. Apart from the fact that the town is apparently being overrun with Taliban, we've no more real information on the enemy.

The Colonel takes questions. One officer looks stricken.

'We're not equipped for this. We don't have night-vision goggles, or enough vehicles . . . We're a training team, this is not our job.'

'Don't be silly, it's perfectly within our means,' replies the Colonel, unmoved.

I agree with the Colonel. Let's do it! We could be better prepared and equipped but so what? This is a *real* deliberate, pre-planned attack. It's the most exciting thing that could possibly happen, and I'm up for it!

Lastly, the Colonel says our rules of engagement have been changed to war-fighting mode. This means that we can kill anyone we deem to be the enemy without them having to shoot at us first. Identifying the enemy may be tricky – the Taliban aren't going to be wearing uniforms – but common sense must prevail. The same officer again stands and asks for confirmation of whether this has been made officially legal by the Helmand Task Force headquarters. A hush falls on our group. This is almost insubordination, questioning the veracity of a commanding officer's orders.

The Colonel points at him with a karate-chop hand. 'Fucking shut up and get on with it.'

With only minutes to go before we have to meet up with our ANA company, I scurry back to our vehicles. I'm up for it, really up for it! I know we're doing the whole thing on a wing and a prayer but that just makes it more intoxicating; anything could happen! I also love the 're-establish gover-nance' bit. It's unclear exactly how we'll do this after seizing control of the town but I'm inherently comfortable with the notion of just 'cracking on' and exhilarated by the total uncertainty, reality and immediacy of this moment.

I have barely two minutes to give orders to my team. With cardboard tags hastily torn from a ration-pack box, I show them how the plan will work on my map. I tell them what our mission is, cover medical casualty evacuation (Sergeant Stoddart will apply first aid after which a helicopter should come if it's serious) and tell them about the war-fighting rules of engagement. They all accept this without question, quietly nodding. We mount up, now with a third vehicle – Stoddy has come up trumps with his scrounging. He's found a dented old ANA wagon, essentially a Ford pick-up truck spray-painted beige. It's hardly twenty-first-century war-fighting kit, but it's better than nothing.

Amid a chaos of dust and vehicles we meet Number 1 Company. They're in a column of eight pick-ups. I lead our three wagons to the front, ahead of the two belonging to the Kandak commander. He's oddly placed here; we're starting off as the reserve company at the rear, surely he should be further forward? From one of the trucks Hindi film music blares, its sweet soprano blurred by the volume. The Afghan soldiers clambering into their pick-up trucks shout excitedly at one another, thrilled by the sudden break in their mundane routine of watchtower duty. Wearing only berets or camouflage caps rather than helmets, without body armour and clutching their AKs, they seem sprightly compared to us, swaddled in cumbersome, hot but potentially life-saving personal equipment.

The company commander, Captain Birialay, steps forward. A smiling, fleshy-faced Pashtun from Jalalabad, he speaks Urdu and is delighted at my response in the same language. He's happy with the plan, or rather, happy to know it vaguely, unconcerned about its merits. He's a charming and jovial combination of careless optimism and fatalism, both enabled by a complete submission to divine providence. All will be well, 'insh'allah' – if God wills it.

Our convoy crawls through the FOB gate and then lurches forward, as if suddenly released, becoming a dusty snake of racing vehicles, all trying to keep up. I'm chasing the ANA wagons of Number 2 Company and being chased by Sergeant Stoddart and CSM Johnstone. The ANA following us keep dropping back. We're forced to pause, swearing and keeping one eye on the distant rising dust plume of the convoy ahead. The whole town will know we're coming at this rate. We're doing a big loop far into the hills to the northeast, for at least a dozen kilometres, to avoid being seen before we enter the town from the east, but we can hardly be going unnoticed . . .

Shortly before the dry riverbed that leads into town and behind a high, ragged ridge, the convoy stops. I get a quick brief from the Colonel: I'm to occupy the ridge to our front, for use as a helicopter landing site in case we take casualties that need evacuation. I'm also to be ready to move forward 'to echelon through' if the enemy opposition is strong. We get a section of eight Artillery soldiers to strengthen our team; with no space in our two Snatch, they pile into the back of Stoddy's knackered ANA wagon. I relay these orders to the Kandak Commander and Captain Birialay from the bonnet of the Commander's pick-up. From the map my eye is caught by the gaudy plastic flowers and red velvet covering the Commander's dashboard. A cluster of blue-bead charms dangle from the rear-view mirror, a ready defence against the evil eye.

Up on the ridge we spread out, observing in all directions in a defensive posture. We can see the centre of town about five kilometres away, but it's pretty miniature at this range, a low brown jumble of flat-roofed houses and mud compounds with the odd big house jutting up, clad in green and blue tiles. On its left-hand side, to the west, the brown drab merges into a shock of vivid green. This is the fertile ribbon accompanying the swollen Helmand River as it winds south.

From up here it looks peaceful, but really we're too far away to tell. I'd like to move further down to get a closer look but our priority is to secure the helicopter landing site until called forward.

Using my GPS I get a ten-figure grid reference of a our location and send it on the radio back to 'zero', our headquarters in FOB Robinson. We've got a secure high-frequency radio, part of the Army's new digital system, and it's working reasonably well so far. I've got a signaller in the back with the set, with a headset passed through to me in the front so we can both use it. The antenna has to poke through the hatch used by the top-cover bods as there's not one built into the vehicle itself. For a better signal, if we're stationary we put the set up on the roof. Sitting in my wagon I can see the ANA are still in good spirits; Capt Birialay's team is getting a brew on with a kerosene burner and a big steel teapot.

The radio crackles semi-coherent messages; it's the other companies talking to one another as they move into the town. From among this burble a terse voice is suddenly clear:

'Hello zero this is four one alpha . . . Contact wait out . . .'

'Fuck, it's kicked off,' I exclaim, keeping the headset jammed to my ear.

I order all engines turned off. The Hindi music drifting from the company commander's vehicle continues a defiant solo until I stifle that too. In the silence we wait for details. I'm half hoping it's a false alarm, half hoping something significant enough has occurred so that we too can get involved. The outcome is inconclusive: shots have been fired in both directions, but there's no enemy to be seen so it's not a decisive engagement. Accepting Captain Birialay's offer of tea I leave the signaller to man the radio and join him by his pick-up. I don't protest when the Hindi music restarts.

Sipping my tea, I notice that the Kandak commander, bored with hanging around, has headed off into the dry riverbed to our front with his two vehicles. From the mud-walled compound that he's just passed small figures are emerging and moving hurriedly to the east away from the town. They're clearly running away. I hope that we're not watching the first refugees from Sangin since the Soviet war of the 1980s.

Tea unfinished, we're ordered over the radio to move towards the town, staying on the high ground. We make a rapid descent into the dry riverbed and head for the next ridge. The track leading up is precipitous and fragmented. Finny grinds the gears and we crawl upwards, the Snatch engine straining frantically. The rear wheels begin to slide downhill, to our left. 'Top cover down!' I shout, anticipating a roll, the front wheels now also moving sideways. With Finny keeping the revs going the wheels finally bite and we remain upright, lurching precariously forward.

At the top of the ridge, we're surrounded by apparently empty mud-walled compounds, marking the start of the southern end of the town. These compounds are tight-knit and high-walled: easy cover for anyone approaching and not an ideal place for us to be. Entering a large broken-down compound, we get our vehicles in an awkward all-round defence and observe in all directions. The ANA follow on and spread out into the compounds around us.

I put my wagon behind a high wall, stand on the bonnet and scan the town with my binoculars. I can just about make out the main road in Sangin, the 611, running north into the bazaar, which seems to be marked by a tall blue building; perhaps that's the objective. I can't see any people but really I'm still too far away and the light is fading into dusk. Even so, it's still warm and we're dehydrated from sweating perpetually into our body armour and helmets. Finny hands me a big bottle of mineral water. Crouching on the bonnet, I take off my boiling helmet, rub my temples and drain the whole bottle straight down.

Shots crackle to our immediate left . . .

'FUCK! Get down!' I shout, tumbling off the bonnet and grabbing the radio handset dangling above my seat.

'Hello zero this is four one charlie contact wait out . . .' All I want is to know what's happening.

'Get yer helmet on, sir,' CSM Johnstone calmly shouts from his wagon. Having jammed my helmet on, I make a crouched run to the ruined wall to the left, throw myself over and crawl round a pile of bricks to see half a dozen ANA full of panicked fervour crouching and shouting, pointing their AKs at the next compound.

'Kya ho gaya hai . . . kya hua,' I shout, asking what has happened, but my Urdu makes no impression on them. I can't tell if we've been shot at or if the ANA were the ones shooting. Tamim's still in the wagon and I can't understand their Dari. There's nobody to be seen in the compound ahead and the ANA are now shouting at one another, getting stressed. We need to get out of these compounds and off this hillside. With a shout and a wave of my arm – standing in for a language we all understand – I tell the ANA soldiers, 'Let's go!'

In the gathering darkness we wind our way down towards

the main road through deserted, narrow lanes between high mud walls. This is *really* not a good place to be. Eventually the ground levels off, we hit a bigger road and are delighted to see a pair of Humvees parked up; this must be route 611 that runs north into town and the Americans must be the southern block, still in place. The black Colonel emerges and with a friendly 'How y'all doin?' points us in the direction of the British command group. They're at the petrol station in the middle of the bazaar, straight up the road. Leaving the ANA with the Humvees I go with my team to get orders. We have to give Stoddy a push to get started: his ANA cast-off wagon is just about dead.

At the Colonel's vehicle I neck another whole bottle of water. Little speakers rigged up on the roll bars crackle out a Dire Straits song. With the other company commanders I compare notes – there was some shooting when the lead company entered the town but it's uncertain who initiated it; it may have been the ANA shooting at civilians and/or Taliban, or vice versa. Certainly it's not been a decisive engagement and if the Taliban were occupying the town they've disappeared pretty sharply. Perhaps whoever supplied the original intelligence to the Helmand Task Force headquarters was misinformed, or deliberately misinformed us? Anyway an eleven-year-old boy was killed, shot in the head, probably by the ANA or the ANP (Afghan National Police), who had also joined the lead company. Nevertheless the Colonel is in good spirits: we've achieved our objective, Sangin has been seized, we're in the middle of town and we've got the run of the place. Again due to our lack of intelligence it's still unclear exactly where the 'District Centre' is, but the priority for now is to secure the town overnight. My team is to occupy the main police station on route 611 at the southern end of the town, Number 2 Company is to occupy the main bazaar and 3 Company is to watch over the bazaar from the ridge to the south-east (towards where we've just been). I leave the Orders Group and head back to my team on the main route. As the Dire Straits song fades, it occurs to me that I prefer the Hindi music.

The police station is easy to find, a high mud-walled compound with twin turrets at the entrance. A Soviet tank, a rusted trophy, serves as seating for a gaggle of men wearing dark shawls and clutching AKs who wave us in. The Kandak commander is already here and we're expected. The courtyard, though very broad, is half full with a cluster of old Soviet armoured vehicles. With a frightful gnashing of gears we squeeze our Snatch wagons in, facing them towards the gate in case we need to leave suddenly. The ANA follow us in.

Exhausted, our team spills from the back of the wagons. CSM Johnstone says he'll get some guys on the walls of the compound and get a 'stag' routine going. I need to find the Kandak commander to make sure he's happy with the overnight plan. Tamim reckons he's next door with the Chief of Police. Shattered, wretched with filth and stewed in stale sweat, I walk with Tamim through to the other half of the police station, an inner compound separated by a wall.

A clump of willows half-masks a low yellow light besieged by moths. I stoop under their branches and on righting myself see a multitude of richly bearded faces sitting around the edges of an inner square of dark red carpets. All are reclining, most with cushions, sipping tea. A small fountain to the rear trickles softly, beneath boughs of violet-pink blossom. The low murmur of voices pauses slightly on my arrival and then continues as I take off my boots and walk onto the carpet to greet the Kandak commander. He gestures me to sit. I put down my rifle, put my helmet on top and unbuckle my webbing vest. Wrenching open my body armour, a wave of heat rushes up from my slimy sweat-sodden shirt. Reclining cross-legged on a cushion, I heave a sigh of blissful relief. Bathed in soft light, we sip tea and crunch the white sugary sweets put in front of us, gobbling more as our hunger ignites. I'm stunned that such an exquisite little pleasure garden can exist here, a sanctuary of calm so closely adjacent to filth and chaos. Two courtyards in the same compound, each the perfect opposite of the other. This is Afghanistan's seductive, tragic paradox: beauty among brutality, terrible violence amid peerless hospitality.

The Kandak commander is flanked by his second-in-command and Captain Birialay. Before him, reclining in the middle of the carpets, is a great bear of a man swaddled in a black *shalwar qamiz* and waistcoat, leaning back, hands behind his head. This can only be the Chief of Police. Deep-set eyes blackened with kohl shine from his big beefy face. His hands nudge his jewelled prayer cap forward over thick black curls. He chats away with the Kandak commander, Tamim providing an intermittent interpretation; he says he needs more police and more weapons. He's asking for help to secure the police station.

I confirm with the Kandak commander that he's happy with the overnight plan and ask what he intends to do tomorrow. He just gives a 'we'll see' upwards turn of his head and resumes his chat with the Chief of Police. Shortly they both stand, then leave with Captain Birialay, to check on their men in the other parts of town. I briefly discuss the day's events with the Kandak second-in-command, and he tells me that the much-sought District Centre is just up the road at the top of the bazaar, near the river. Soon, he quietly unfolds his blanket, and offers me one. I decline and, keen to ensure that my team is happy, return to my wagon.

Finny is fast asleep in his seat. Only the signaller is awake, monitoring the radio next to two slumbering bodies. Beside the two other wagons at the foot of the wall, sleeping bodies are curled on ponchos spread out on the ground. The guards on the wall tops move slightly, silhouetted by the rising moonlight. I should sleep in my seat, in the front of my vehicle, where I can be easily found in an emergency, but I want really to accept the second-in-command's kind offer. After telling the signaller where I'll be, I return with Tamim to the other courtyard and stretch out beneath a pestilent blanket next to a row of still bodies. Under brilliant stars, I plummet into sleep, unbothered by the fluttering of moths' wings about my face.

Just before dawn the Afghans around me quickly fold their blankets and wash briskly in the fountain. I make my way to the front gate and climb up one of the watchtowers to survey the town, still silent and deserted, as it slowly emerges in the dawn's orange light. Turning, I look back across to the police station. The two courtyards lie side by side, one sprouting willow boughs and cherry blossom, the other a tangled mass of decaying tank hulls, pick-up trucks and filth.

A couple of hours later we make our way in convoy back

up to the middle of the bazaar. It's now full of people and normal daily life seems to be going ahead uninterrupted. On the Colonel's orders, we depart in convoy with the Americans and the ANA for FOB Robinson, leaving Sangin as it was before, in the charge of the police.

CHAPTER 7

The District Centre

May 2006: Sangin, Helmand Province, Afghanistan

Back in FOB Robinson we're dazed but happy, as the adrenalin and excitement of the last couple of days is superseded by relief and good humour. CSM Johnstone takes the piss out of Stoddy and his 'ANA taxi' and joshes Finny for nearly rolling the wagon. 'That was bonkers,' declares Stoddy, 'but we came through it – thank fuck!' Laughing, we get stuck into an 'admin phase': cleaning out our vehicles and restocking them with water and rations. We try to improve our rough shelters, seeking respite from the savage dust; a westerly wind races through the FOB and whips it up, throwing it into our little corner. CSM Johnstone and Stoddy peg their poncho sheets firmly to the ground, making mini-tents.

Finny gives up. 'I'd rather sleep in the wagon, boss, where I normally do.'

I erect a sheet of plywood against the perimeter wall as a windbreak and stretch my poncho over the top. Inside I put my issued mosquito net over my sleeping bag and arrange two metal tins, empty mortar containers, as a seat. With some more dedicated pilfering among the piles of American detritus I find a plywood box, which, when stood upright, makes an excellent wardrobe. The addition of some four-inch nails allows the convenient dust-free stowage of my weapon and headgear. Above all of this we string up a camouflage net of beige nylon foliage to provide shade and cover when we're on stag at night.

While the wind brings dust, a lucky gust has also brought a fleeting aroma of baking bread. Our neighbour on the perimeter, in the shack next to us, is the baker. Captivated by the scent, and offering salaams, I venture in. Sitting cross-legged on the lip of the tandoor that descends deep into the ground, the baker beams up a smile, asks his assistant to get some tea ready, and continues his working rhythm. On a low platform to his left he rolls a fist of dough into a flat oval, folds in the margins, prongs the surface with his arched fingers, stretches it onto a damp cushion and, leaning forward into the glowing tandoor, plants it onto the hot oven wall. Then, with a long steel rod in each hand, he again leans in, and skewers and carries out a fragrant naan, freshly baked after three or four minutes on the oven wall. His assistant takes the hot flat breads as they arrive in a steady rhythm, stacking them neatly by the door. The cycle continues until at least forty naan are in delectable warm lines. Resting his tools, the baker, Mohammad Qasim, wipes his glistening face and, handing me a bread, says I'm most welcome. He's a Pashtun, but having spent time across the Pakistan border in Quetta he's happy to speak Urdu. He has an earnest, wholesome and very cheerful face. Over tea he tells me that he's from Gereshk and has been employed by the Americans here for the last few months.

'I'm glad of the work, Captain Sahib, I make more money working here than in Gereshk, but the contract is just until the end of the month.'

The bread he makes feeds the security guards that the American Special Forces employed to guard the camp; they're leaving shortly, now that the American Special Forces have gone. With their departure Mohammad's contract will finish. As I bid him farewell he shakes my hand in both of his; they are soft but powerful.

'Perhaps you British might employ me?' he asks, still smiling.

'I'll ask my boss, but to be honest . . . we're not quite organised yet,' I reply glumly.

I know that, not having had the means to prevent the guts of the camp from being ripped out, it's rather unlikely that the Quartermaster in Helmand Task Force headquarters is going to stump up the cash to continue the loyal baker's contract.

The naan makes an ideal addition to our early evening meal. Stoddy's game but CSM Johnstone declines – if I'm eating local food he'd better not is his reckoning, so that we're not both ill at the same time. Under the camouflage net we sit on ammo tins and break out MREs – Meals Ready to Eat, American rations. Opening the brown plastic packet is like enjoying a bit of anonymous post. The main menu is printed on the outside but the little sundries always vary. What I covet most is peanut M&Ms, which sadly don't appear this time. I enjoy Mexican fajitas garnished with bright yellow cheese, squeezed from its packet like toxic toothpaste. CSM Johnstone has found some four-packs of

Del Monte tinned fruit in the American storage containers. I eat the diced pears, he tucks into the peaches, observing that they probably all taste the same anyway.

At about 1800 we're called together for an Orders Group – it's a 'well done' from the Colonel. He's pleased with the way it went in town. He goes on for a bit too long and we're shifting uncomfortably on our ammo tins and other makeshift seats when a signaller arrives with a scrap of paper. The Colonel reads it and digests it briefly before telling us its content. It's an order from Helmand Task Force headquarters: the police station in Sangin is under threat from a large Taliban force approaching the town, and we need to go back in and secure it. He'll send an ANA company and one British team with it – any volunteers?

My hand is straight up. I'm still up for it; besides, my team knows the police station and I'd much rather be out there in town than 'stagging on' in this dusty shit-hole of a camp. He agrees and, as the rest of the group disperses, we sort out the ORBAT (Order of Battle: who's doing what job). I'll take my team, in two Snatch wagons, and the same ANA company as last time. The Colonel will escort us in with his two vehicles. We'll also take with us the British platoon who came in yesterday by helicopter when the Helmand Task Force HQ realised that during the operation to seize the town there were no British troops left in the FOB. Our ANA battalion is, probably correctly, not yet trusted to hold the base alone.

In darkness, our convoy departs. I'm leading, with the ANA just behind me followed by the British platoon and then the Colonel's group. We're trying to do it in complete blackness, using night-vision goggles which we've borrowed at the last minute just before going out of the gate from the Artillery guys manning the 105mm light guns. They're damned tricky to use, however, and Finny's really struggling to see anything at all. We move slowly, straining to make out the road, relying on our top-cover blokes to help out. After I fail to see our turn-off in a dry riverbed, forcing the entire convoy to do a U-turn, the Colonel orders us over the radio to sack the goggles and get a move on with white light. Head-lights blazing, we race to the police station.

On arrival I leave CSM Johnstone and Tamim with Captain Birialay to give the British platoon a hand manning the compound, and go with the Kandak commander and some of Number 1 Company up to an over-watch position on a ridge to the south-east, near our route of the previous evening.

Up on the hill, we park up close to the Kandak commander, who's spread his men out. In my wagon I've got a signaller and top-cover bloke with Finny driving as usual. We take turns doing one hour standing up in the top-cover hatch and staring down into the town, which is completely dark but for a few compounds, including the police station, illuminated by their own generators. Nearer to us on the eastern side of town are silhouetted four squat tower-like houses in large compounds, perhaps the product of the narco-affluence that Sangin must possess as a trading post for the opium industry, where growers sell raw opiate gum to refiners and transporters. After my stag I sleep on the bonnet, reclining onto the windscreen, my rifle in my lap. It's a quiet night apart from an occasional rustling at the top of the wagon – Finny on stag, extracting a few nuts from his pocket.

Coming off the hill just after sun-up we meet the British Colonel in the police station. He's come for a meeting with the Chief of Police and the District Chief to try to find out what exactly is going on in Sangin.

Making our way through to the courtyard where I slept two nights previously, we find the Kandak commander and the Chief of Police breakfasting on a veranda abutting the outside wall. The British Colonel exchanges a brief 'salaam alaykum' and sits next to the Kandak commander, opposite the Chief of Police. I'm further down, next to Captain Biri-alay, with Tamim on my left. The rest of the space is taken by the police: beautiful thugs, non-uniformed, in brown and blue *shalwar qamiz*, shawls and jewelled caps, with AKs by their sides. We're cross-legged on a long carpet on which is stretched an elongated white cotton sheet. A gangly youth circulates with a large stack of naan on his left shoulder and places one in front of each person. Tea from a big boiling kettle follows in little glasses. The fresh naan combined with the hot sweet tea is especially delicious after the night up on the hill.

The Chief of Police immediately asks the British Colonel for more weapons and men. His force is insufficient, he says, to protect the town from the Taliban. The Colonel says he has no weapons to hand out, but that we'll make a plan to protect the town that'll involve the ANA. Shortly, another man joins the group, sitting down to the right of the Police Chief. A big man with a white *shalwar qamiz* and faded scarlet prayer cap, hawk-nosed and with long elegant moustaches combed into a great red-black beard, this is the District Chief, Haji Khan Mohammed, the Governor's representative in Sangin. He greets the Chief of Police in the traditional Pashtun manner, an extended series of reciprocal good wishes and repetitive polite questions: 'How are you? Are you well? Don't be tired, how are you? Be healthy . . .' Despite the greeting the two men show no real warmth for one another. The British Colonel asks him what is happening in Sangin. The District Chief rolls up a bit of naan, pops it into his mouth, chews deliberately, swallows it with a slurp of tea and says that perhaps it would be best if the Colonel came to the District Centre where he can be his guest and they can talk at length more comfortably. As he says this, the Chief of Police is silent and stony faced. The only thing that's clear about these two is that they dislike each other. I know that we're seeing only the tip of a very complex situation. The Colonel agrees and says we'll go there with him now.

Jumping into our wagons, we follow the District Chief to his compound. Bumping along the pot-holed road we chase his Toyota Land Cruiser, chock-full of his militia-men clinging onto the back. The bazaar, a continuous line of small shop fronts crammed together, right up against the road, is open and busy. Shop owners sit cross-legged, surrounded by produce: vegetables, meat, bread, shoes, clothes, pots and pans, umbrellas, bicycles . . . Those in the bazaar, dark and bearded, gaze at us passively. Toyota Corolla estate cars full of passengers edge to the roadside to let us pass. At a fork we turn left and head west towards the river. Out of the bazaar, buildings suddenly mingle with lush orchards, vivid green wheat fields and little farmsteads. Passing over a small bridge and along a track with tall trees on either side, we arrive at the long-sought-for District Centre: a big flat-roofed one-storey building, whitewashed and surrounded by fertile gardens. There's a veranda at its front with big square columns decorated with green and blue paint in a diamond pattern. A gang of militia men wave us in and we swiftly dismount. The Colonel, Tamim and I go with the District Chief into his small reception room, the *hijra*, the only contents of which are a well-worn dark carpet and some long cylindrical cushions.

As we sip our tea, the Colonel asks the Chief about the Taliban: where are they? The Chief says they come from villages like Jushalay, north of Sangin, and that he can help us find them. However, it's not really the Taliban that he wants to talk about.

'Colonel, the real problem in Sangin is the police. They're corrupt and violent. They harass and abuse the population and extort money from them.'

'Why don't you stop this?' the Colonel asks. 'You're the District Chief.'

'It would only lead to more bloodshed. The Chief of Police is the real problem. He himself is a criminal and a murderer – he killed a fourteen-year-old boy. But I cannot control him. If I try to, he'll start a feud which I couldn't win . . .'

The Colonel suggests a Shura, a meeting, to allow the elders of Sangin to discuss what's been happening and what should be done about it. They could also discuss the idea for a new 'auxiliary police force' that has been proposed, apparently by the Governor's office. The Chief agrees to call the elders together for the following morning. He also assures the Colonel disinterestedly that he's heard about the new police idea and, quickly moving on, suggests a more immediate solution to the problem.

'Colonel, if your troops were to stay here and patrol the town, the police would not be able to harass the civilians . . .'

The Colonel, with a karate chop of the hand, is decisive. 'You'll have troops here by this afternoon with Captain Docherty. My soldiers and the ANA will be all over the bazaar, we'll dominate this town.'

Smiling, he looks askance at me. 'Happy with that, Leo?'

'Delighted, sir. This place has got "platoon house" written all over it.'

As the Colonel bids farewell to the Chief I bound up a set of stone steps onto the roof of the District Centre. I quickly scan a 360; I've got excellent arcs of view all round. I can see most of the town, the other side of the Sangin valley, and northward up the Helmand River. The dry riverbed used as the axis of advance during our first entry into town joins the river basin from the east and we're on the corner of land between the two. There's a taller building under construction next door on the northern side, which would make an excellent observation post. The dry riverbed would make a good helicopter landing site and could be easily covered by troops on the roof of the new building. Overall it seems like an ideal place from which to conduct patrols.

As I descend from the roof, shiny red fruits in a tree catch my eye. 'Oh my God, pomegranates!'

Rejoicing inwardly, I mount up and our convoy departs, heading back to FOB Robinson.

Back at the base it becomes apparent that getting hold of sufficient Afghan troops to 'dominate' Sangin is going to be a problem. The Herati Kandak, who we've used on our two previous forays into town, are now demanding to be released to return to Herat. We came to the FOB in the first place in order to relieve them, so their demand is hardly unreasonable. Unfortunately the Kandak we brought with us is 60 per cent under strength. They've got a lot of men away on leave but the real problem is the desertion that occurred after they left Kabul Military Training Centre. The remainder totals fewer than two hundred men, all of whom are supposedly occupied with manning the watchtowers around FOB Robinson and guarding the vast perimeter.

With the British second-in-command, a Major, I go to see Colonel Shirdil in the Kandak headquarters – a courtyard busy with ANA vehicles and rubbish, enclosed by low brick buildings. Each of the five companies within the Kandak has an office here, as does Colonel Shirdil; it doubles up as his sleeping quarters. Sitting on his bed, the Major requests that some men are made available, to help man the platoon house.

Colonel Shirdil immediately launches into a lengthy complaint. 'Where are the heavy weapons I was promised before coming to Sangin? I can only just guard the perimeter, I haven't enough men to send any into town . . .'

His big square head nods up and down almost in rhythm with his speech, accompanied by his long hands: the right slapping the palm of the left. After an agitated few minutes he tails off into silence, white reservoirs of saliva having gathered at the corners of his mouth. Awkwardly we drink our tea.

'Maybe if I just took one or two men, it could be like a recce,' I suggest.

This would allow Shirdil to be seen to be making a clever

move, while also agreeing to our request and consequently saving face. Colonel Shirdil turns to speak to his second-in-command and, with a mute nod of his head, agrees. I'm hoping that it will snowball a little and, one officer having been given the go-ahead, he'll bring a few spare soldiers with him.

Emerging from Shirdil's room, I meet Captain Hameed outside the HQ Company office.

'Where have you been, Captain Leo?' he asks.

'In Sangin, Hameed Jaan [Dear Hameed]. In fact why don't you come back into town with me? Colonel Shirdil has ordered that one officer should come along.'

As Tamim interprets my response, the Captain rolls his eyes, half amused at my naive optimism. I clearly don't realise how impossible that would be.

'Sadly, Captain Leo, I'm far too busy. A spare officer will be found to come with you.'

Captain Ahmed, a softly spoken Pashtun, is the spare officer. He meets me with a pick-up and five ANA soldiers, including Javed, a soldier whom I know from HQ Company. On the way out of the FOB we throw boxes of halal rations, unappealing biriyani packed in India, into the back of their pick-up. I've got a small team in one Snatch: a signaller – Lance Corporal Bow – and a top-cover bloke, with Finny driving as usual. We're taking the British platoon to provide the manpower; everyone else is required to guard the perimeter of our compound in case there's another full-frontal attack like the one in March. For the third time in as many days we bump along the pot-holed 611 back into town.

At the District Centre, the British platoon occupy the unfinished building. My team with the ANA occupy a small room opposite the Chief's *hijra*. We park the Snatch wagon close to the building and man the radio. Having done a radio check to the FOB, I'm eager to patrol into town before sunset.

I put Javed at the front and Captain Ahmed just behind me. We're leading two sections – eight-man teams – from the British platoon. The third section of the platoon will stay at the District Centre as a Quick Reaction Force, which I can call on the radio carried by Lance Corporal Bow. The District Centre would be left empty but that's not a worry as it's crawling with the Chief's militia.

As we make our way into the dry riverbed running east towards the 611 and the top of the bazaar, I realise that we're the first foot patrol that Sangin has seen in a very long time. The Canadians came through in their armoured vehicles and the US special forces raced through in their Humvees, but this is the first fully dismounted patrolling that's been done by Coalition forces.

We're without headdress or sunglasses. I've got my para helmet clipped with a karabiner to the rear right-hand side of my webbing vest. My pouches contain five magazines of 30 rounds each (there's one fitted on my rifle), two bandoliers of 5.56 ammunition (300 rounds), two smoke grenades, a red phosphorus grenade and a high-explosive grenade. In addition to this, in my left chest pocket I've two super-absorbent dressings and a morphine injector, marked with a big 'M' on the outside of the pouch. In my right chest pocket I have my GPS and spare batteries for my radio, which is clipped onto my left shoulder with the headset jammed to my left ear, held on by an elastic strap over my forehead. My vest also has flat zipped pockets on the front, holding a map and a second magazine for my 9mm pistol, which hangs down my right leg in a green canvas holster. The black plastic one that I got in Kandahar broke the night before we left Tombstone so Jim, my bunk-bed neighbour, gave me his, angry that dealing with the interpreters' pay and other staff work in Camp Tombstone was not going to give him a reason to wear a combat holster.

All of this, with my three-litre water pouch, body armour, rifle and pistol, weighs easily about twenty kilograms, a hot and uncomfortable but manageable burden. Lance Corporal Bow stoically carries a good deal more than twenty kilos with his HF radio set. We've removed our sunglasses to allow us to look people in the eye and appear less threatening, but it's perhaps a meaningless improvement to a bunch of 'feringhees' (white people) wandering around like sweaty Robocops.

We walk up the dry riverbed in staggered file, with men on alternate sides. Approaching a bridge that takes the 611 over the riverbed we come into a poultry market. Squawking beady-eyed white chickens are stacked up in wire-mesh crates on rickety stalls of wooden poles and plastic sheeting. Ascending to the main road, we move south onto the main bazaar. It's six o'clock and the men of Sangin are doing their evening shopping. Their response to our presence is discreetly curious and sometimes friendly. I greet those whose eyes I meet in Pashtu – '*Staray mashay*' ('May you not be tired') – and a restrained wave, my hand coming to rest over my heart, a demonstration of sincerity.

Halting the patrol via the radio allows us to get chatting in

the middle of the bazaar. In a baker's stall two men are surrounded by rows of fresh naan bread. The younger man is
busy at the oven, while the elder with a white beard is at the
front, selling it.

'Why are you here?' asks the old man.

'To help secure the town so that it can be improved,' I
reply, drawing closer.

'How? What improvements?'

'Well, that's for the people to decide and then the government can make it happen.'

Suddenly I'm aware of how grandiose and pompous I
sound. I can't give concrete examples of 'reconstruction' projects because there aren't any happening – not yet at least. I
want to be able to tell him that there'll be a new school for his
children, electricity, new wells, new roads, but I can't. I now
feel a bit silly. The old man gives a non-committal slow nod
of the head and tugs at his beard. He offers me a naan bread.
I accept and, determined to pay for it, tease out a roll of
Afghanis stuck into the top of my body armour and give him
a fifty note, about a dollar. I fold the crisp bread in half and
stuff it into my map pocket, closing the zip to conceal it. I get
thirty-eight Afghanis back in change, and continue strolling,
with Tamim by my side.

On the other side of the bazaar some of the British soldiers are trying in vain to buy toothbrushes, making up for
the fact that they were 'crashed out' of Camp Bastion with
only their patrolling kit and no personal comforts. With
Tamim's interjection the shopkeeper is very willing to do a
bulk deal: ten brushes for two dollars. The soldiers are
delighted; they can share them out and not have to double

up. Moving to a fruit stall I buy a kilo of mangoes. The young turbaned seller is friendly but uncommunicative. Having paid a couple of ragged Afghani notes, I give the blue plastic bag to Tamim so that I can carry my rifle with both hands.

It's a prosperous place, judging by the array of goods on sale, and cars in a reasonable state of repair pass by frequently. Having come through the main bazaar, we break west and start heading towards the District Centre. As I pass a public call office sign it strikes me as extraordinary that a phone line has reached Sangin. There's also mobile coverage; the Chief is frequently on his cell phone.

Back at the District Centre, I throw my kit into the front of the Snatch and go up onto the roof, just with my rifle and pistol. In the dusk the Chief chatters away with a few of his gang, sitting on plastic garden furniture, having enjoyed the sunset. The slight breeze evaporates the sweat from my shirt and is pleasantly cooling. The Chief looks profoundly calm. His right hand clicks a loop of turquoise prayer beads, his thumb pulling two at a time over the forefinger into his palm. He wears a simple white *shalwar qamiz* and black shoes; they're of a 1970s loafer pattern, black leather with big heels, worn without socks. They're a testament to his status; he can afford not to wear sandals.

Looking north from the roof top I see a series of low bare hills unfolding like a rumpled silk sheet. The Helmand River, broad and fast-flowing, emerges from between them, cradled in broad grey gravel banks, passing the compound not more than a couple of hundred metres distant to the west. Another few hundred metres in the same direction the far side of the Sangin valley rises, barren and abrupt, silhouetted now by a faint bronze glow. To the east, the town sprawls out for a couple of kilometres. Far above the bazaar, a pair of kites engage in a playful staccato dance.

Haji Mirwais, the Chief's second-in-command, offers me his pouch of naswar. Now practised in its use, I accept and place a pinch under my tongue. Reclining in my chair, a tingling relaxation rises, weighing my body down. My thoughts rise in a swirl of ineloquent euphoria. I'm touched by his simple sharing gesture; I feel included.

The Chief stands abruptly and we follow him down the stairs from the roof into his *hijra*. Thin mattresses clad in dark velvet have been placed around the wall. The chief sits opposite the door and I settle on his right as befits my status as his guest. After we begin to chat, however, I place Tamim in between us so he can more easily interpret some of the more difficult and fast-flowing Pashtu. Haji Mirwais is on my right and the rest of the gathering is made up of the Chief's militiamen.

On top of a long orange cloth before us the tea boy places long naan breads, a large metal dish of stew, a plateful of boiled mutton cuts and a plastic basin of whey with a ladle sticking out. I'm the only one given a glass. The Chief fills it and then drinks a long draught directly from the ladle before returning it to the basin, from where it's picked up by another diner. The naan is cold but still fresh and the stew, which turns out to be naan slices drenched in tomato sauce and mutton dripping, is hot and delicious. We use little strips of nan bread as pincer-spoons, deftly arched between the fingers and thumb of the right hand. The chief puts

chunks of the choicest mutton – stringy grey meat and bul-
bous lumps of white fat – onto my piece of bread. Determined to be an ideal guest, I swallow the fat, though it turns
my stomach.

When we've eaten our fill, the dishes are removed. All the
leftover bread is placed in the middle of the cloth and gathered up into a bundle, ready for the next meal. Tea is served
in little glasses and we begin to chat. The Chief is curious
about my faith.

'How frequently, Captain, do you pray?'

'Well . . . We pray whenever we like, probably once or twice
a day.'

'And do you fast?'

'Not really. We can give up something we like for forty
days, like chocolate.'

'So, what do *you* give up?'

'Umm . . . I gave up grapes last year, and this year I didn't
really give up anything.'

The Chief nods and strokes his moustaches, looking
slightly nonplussed. His name, Haji Khan Mohammad,
reflects the fact that he has completed the Haj, the pilgrimage
to Islam's holiest shrine in Mecca, and is clearly devout. My
representation of Christian practice seems flimsy and incon-
sequential, in stark contrast to the faith of the men around
me, whose religious fidelity and sense of complete certainty
for a brief moment I envy.

Thanking the Chief for supper, I leave the *hijra*, walking
out into the warm evening. Our Snatch is parked at the front
of the building, backing onto the dirty veranda behind its
high stone pillars. Relieving Lance Corporal Bow, I settle

down to 'stag on'. He cheerfully extracts his sleeping bag from his kit and leaves for the doss-room opposite the *hijra*. We're sharing it with the ANA, although Captain Ahmed has taken his guys onto the roof to sleep; it's cooler and the wind from the river keeps the mosquitoes away. I sit in the back of the Snatch with the radio set on the vehicle's roof, to get a better signal back to FOB Robinson. Lance Corporal Bow has strung up a tactical radio so we can speak to the British platoon next door. I send a situation report to FOB Robinson telling them that all is well, the platoon house is up and running, and we've had a pretty positive response in the bazaar. In reply I'm told to expect the British Colonel early tomorrow for the Shura.

The night is quiet. I mull over the baker's question from earlier on. It gets me thinking about what the plan for Sangin is exactly. I would like to have given my questioner some better answers about how our presence might improve things. Currently, of the three lines of operation (security, development and governance) much discussed prior to deployment, only the first is present in Sangin. We can provide security by patrolling around the town but we can't start development projects, which are the key to winning hearts and minds. Nor can we get involved in governance and counter-narcotics.

Now that the Army is in Sangin the other agencies should be with us. We've had a friendly response from the population so far and *now* is the time to show them how their livelihoods might be improved by supporting us. This is our window of opportunity. I cast my mind back to the glib jargon I heard from the DfID girl in Colchester before deploying. She needs to be here now with us, making it happen. Initially some 'quick-impact projects' would be ideal – perhaps repaving a road – to generate extra civilian employment and keep the population sweet. A few thousand dollars from their huge budget would be incredibly well spent buying a bit of sympathy from the population until their trust can be won with more enduring projects. Also, the Foreign Office needs to be here providing some public information, telling the population what's going to happen with the poppy, otherwise they'll assume the worst – that we're here simply to put an end to the poppy and destroy their livelihoods.

CHAPTER 8

'As far as I can tell, they're on our side'

May 2006: Sangin, Helmand Province, Afghanistan

Under the mulberry tree the Shura gathers. High green boughs shade white-turbaned elders. The rich mahogany of their faces is amplified by the cleanness of their clothing. Some, with long white beards, are ancient, their bark-like skin deep-lined and wizened. They're unarmed and one old whitebeard has a child cradled on his knee. It's a tender and incongruous sight in a place where a man's hands are normally clutching an AK.

Cross-legged and crammed together on top of a colourful expanse of woven plastic matting, they form an untidy hollow square around Colonel Shirdil, who sits at the base of the tree. Above him a yellow songbird sits in a little cage hanging from a lower bough. The British Colonel and I are on his left.

Shirdil begins: 'In the name of God, the most merciful and beneficent . . . I am from Badakhshan, my father was Tajik but my mother was a Pashtun.'

This means that he understands the Pashtun honour code – the *Pashtunwali* – and wants to help solve their problems. After repeating this sentiment at length he eventually gets around to asking the forty or so elders to voice their concerns. The Chief of Police has been deliberately kept away to allow an honest discussion, and the District Chief has stayed away to keep the whole thing impartial. From the front row of cross-legged figures an old man rises and having, like Shirdil, evoked the name of God with a '*Bismillah ar-rahman ar-rahim*', replies:

'The police have beaten many people in this town. They have also taken money from them. There is nothing we can do to stop them ...'

He continues to give a general description of barbaric police behaviour but does not give any details of specific incidents. Several others do the same. It's clear they're not willing to speak freely, possibly due to the presence of some militia who have slowly gathered at the flanks of the meeting to eavesdrop. This is frustrating; the Shura is supposed to be our chance to get an honest description of the situation in Sangin without local politics interfering. It's impossible to tell who's sent the militia; they may be the District Chief's men or might even have been sent by the Chief of Police. Sensing this, Shirdil gets up and shoos them away. Then he settles back down, and asks the elders to resume their contributions.

An old man stands and, lifting the tail of his *shalwar qamiz*, reveals some violet bruises just below his rib cage. 'I was beaten by the police after an argument. They wanted money from me ... What was I to do? I cannot fight them, I am too old.'

He sits back down. No one else seems very keen to offer up any more details so, after a slight pause, the British Colonel describes the proposed solution: a new auxiliary police force nominated by the elders themselves.

'If you choose twenty-four men whom you can trust, they would be the basis of a new police force that is not corrupt and has the support of the people.'

'But these men will have their own loyalties. Each side will plant their own man to spy on the others,' says one old man.

'It's impossible for it not to be corrupted,' adds another.

A succession of negative voices condemn the idea. The rivalries at play in Sangin are clearly more numerous and complex than it might seem to us on the surface. We've very little understanding of a situation probably involving violent blood feuds between tribes and families, narco-economics and Islamic fundamentalism. What knowledge we've gained in the past few days is superficial to say the least and no foundation for making decisions about what to do here now we're in the middle of town. Shirdil invites the elders to come to FOB Robinson the following day to discuss the idea further in private. There's lukewarm acceptance of the invitation and suddenly the sitting mass rises to a stand, breaking into a noisy cacophony of vigorous chatting. The Shura is over. An old man gives Shirdil a handful of fresh purple figs carried in the knotted corner of his shawl. Above him the songbird flutters with agitation at the sudden movement around its cage then comes to an uneasy rest.

The Taliban have not been mentioned at all during the Shura, but the Colonel, standing listening to an old man, suddenly grabs me.

'This old boy says there's Taliban in the bazaar right now. Let's get in there and show 'em who's boss.'

'OK, sir, we'll be there in five minutes,' I reply, making for the Snatch to get the team together.

Ten minutes later we're patrolling into the bazaar. I'm calm but super-alert. I'm at the front with Captain Ahmed and the ANA, followed by two British sections. I've got Finny and Lance Corporal Bow just behind me.

'Keep fucking switched on guys, it might get noisy,' I advise as we turn into the main bazaar.

'Livin' the dream, sir,' replies Private Finau, with only a little bit of irony.

The bazaar is free of Taliban, or at least no one shoots at us. We receive the same discreet friendliness and occasional curiosity as the day before, although it's quiet as no one does their shopping in the midday sun. On the way back in, the British Colonel zooms past in his wagon and gives a wave, on his way back to the FOB. I stop at the fruit stall and buy two small green melons, a gift for the Chief.

Tramping back to the district centre, the sweat streams down my face and back. We should really have had something better to say to the Shura about what we're doing here. The elders have a great deal of influence over the rest of the population, so we if we had a 'reconstruction' line of operation or a poppy alternative we could have been promoting them, rather than just suggesting the half-baked auxiliary police idea which went down like a lead balloon.

Back at the District Centre, I go into the middle room with Shirdil to meet the Security Chief of Sangin. It seems he's another government representative. How his role relates to the District Chief and Police Chief is unclear. We sit on the floor of the dark, dank room. The Security Chief is a big man in his forties with powerful limbs and swollen feet. Dark rings about his eyes and a bulging white turban enhance a look of controlled ferocity.

He leans forward and speaks quickly. 'I am the youngest of three brothers; the eldest is now in the parliament in Kabul, my other brother was murdered by the Taliban. That is why I want to kill them.'

Colonel Shirdil takes notes; these become a list of suspected Taliban and their locations, mainly villages in the north of the valley. The Security Chief is adamant that the details should be noted correctly and uses his hands a lot, drawing illustrations on the palm of his left with the forefinger of his right. He has lots to say and Shirdil's list grows. Tamim is also taking notes in my pocket book, scribbling quickly with a blue ballpoint; the lilting Persian script is beautiful though hastily formed. The Security Chief does not accuse the District Chief of any Taliban involvement but the fact that he's not in the room with us and we're here without his knowledge suggests to me that, oddly, he is not trusted. Having said his piece, the Security Chief trails into silence. He's assured by Shirdil that the information will be acted upon and sent up to the British and Afghan headquarters. As we shake hands and leave the murky room I reckon that, given our intelligence vacuum in Sangin right now, this information could be priceless.

Now at 1500 the afternoon heat is overwhelming. It pounds down like an invisible suffocating blanket. Lance Corporal Bow is stagging on in the back of the Snatch, picking at a ration pack.

'How's it going, Corporal B?' I ask.

'Yeah, all right, boss,' he replies in his cheerful Essex lilt. 'I was gonna eat but my guts feel a bit weird.'

'Go and sleep, I'll stag on.'

'Nah, you're all right, boss, Finny's taking over in a minute anyway.'

Cheered by his good humour, I go myself to our doss-room. Manipulating my body armour into a reluctant pillow, I stretch out on the stained carpet with my rifle tucked in beside me. Despite the fetid stench of new sweat and ancient dirt I succumb immediately to the afternoon's soporific power.

Two hours later I'm on the roof with the Disctrict Chief's second-in-command, Haji Mirwais. We're due to patrol out shortly so I'm scanning around the town with my binoculars just in case anything of interest is happening.

Haji Mirwais clearly knows about the meeting with the Security Chief. 'Maybe Captain, he gave you names of the Taliban in Sangin?'

'Mmm . . . Maybe. I wasn't really listening.'

'Many people that he says are Taliban are the ones he does not like, the ones he has a feud against,' he says quietly. 'He wants you to help him.'

'It's a very complicated situation, I think,' I say, in complete honesty

'Captain, in your home do you have a girlfriend?' he asks with a smile

'Yes, I do,' I reply, amused by the very abrupt change of subject

'So, you are enjoying lubshub?' he asks with a raised brow

'Lubshub?' Turning to Tamim, I find him chuckling gently.

Happily he interprets: 'Yes, loveshove, you know, when you are together with your girlfriend,' he explains, rubbing his pointed index fingers back and forth, side by side, in demonstration

'Oh, right, *loveshove* – yes, of course! I enjoy it whenever possible.'

Laughing at the sudden appearance of this rhyming slang, which Tamim later explains is a Hindi film import, the thought of gorgeous Lucy in idyllic Oxfordshire seems almost too remote to even believe. Like many others, I have stripped my kit of all pictures and addresses of loved ones. Intended as a security measure, it also prevents distracting memories of whoever you're missing. Her face floods into my mind and then vanishes as I clamber down from the roof to get my patrol kit ready.

Leaving the District Centre on foot, we patrol northwards following a deep, fast-flowing irrigation channel which runs parallel to the river and passes the District Centre at the foot of its compound. To our right, small fields of rich green wheat are tightly interwoven with mud-built farmsteads and great clumps of mulberry trees. Drenched in the orange light of early evening, the wheat stalks are buffeted slightly by the pleasant breeze coming off the river. Leaving the mud track we break east into the farmland, stepping carefully along an intricate network of irrigation streams. Javed is on point about ten metres ahead of me, with Captain Ahmed just behind him looking back every few paces for my directions.

The farmland surrounding us is incredibly fertile, well nurtured and orderly. There appears to be little if any poppy grown in this ultra-fertile zone; wheat is probably the priority near the water as it's a very thirsty crop. Without stopping, I pick sweet white mulberries as I pass under their heavily laden boughs and stuff them into my mouth.

Approaching a farmstead, Tamim, off to my left, raises his hand suddenly. 'Stop! stop! There is a girl washing,' he says, retreating and pointing over his shoulder. A blue shawl briefly flickers behind a row of trees.

'Hey Javed! Ahmed Jaan! Let's go!' I shout, waving them back towards me. We backtrack.

Tamim, at my side, is shaken. 'If we go near their women, they will kill us.'

Giving the dwelling a wide berth, we continue on our route. Keeping a sharp lookout for people, I hope that the blue shawl, the first glimpse I've had of a woman in Sangin, is also my last.

We're in a difficult position in Sangin; we need to 'dominate' the town with patrols to show its inhabitants that we're securing it, but this in itself might cause offence. Just the presence of a bunch of British soldiers – even with a few Afghans mixed in – is potentially deeply antagonistic, especially if the majority of the population aren't aware of our purpose. This is a tribal society that adheres strictly to a code of honour, the *Pashtunwali*, and will not hesitate, as Tamim has pointed out, to respond violently to any offence. We must be careful not to blunder around, otherwise we'll end up becoming a big target for everyone, not just the Taliban.

As the fields are gradually replaced by scruffy concrete compounds we come to the main road, the 611. We're north of the bazaar at this point and, crossing the road, we head past a vast cemetery that dominates the eastern half of the town centre. The dusty, barren expanse is covered with grave mounds, their ends adorned with pairs of fragmented flat stones poking up in opposite diagonals. Some graves are further marked by large green flags, the colour of Islamic obeisance. A stone pillar and a clutch of green and black flags mark a shrine of some sort. Keen to avoid it, we move quickly past it away from the cemetery.

Having crossed the 611 again, we head through more close-knit agricultural dwellings and fields, back towards the District Centre. I'm pleased that we've been literally right around Sangin, unhindered. We have, it seems, complete freedom of movement.

Back at the District Centre I stag on in the back of the Snatch. I give a 'sitrep' – a situation report – to the headquarters in FOB Robinson, telling them what we've been doing, and then set about cleaning my rifle.

Sangin is really quite prosperous, judging by the rich farmland, the well-stocked bazaar and the numerous cars on the main road. The economy seems to be booming, and of course this is on the back of the poppy grown throughout the region. Sangin, I'm guessing, is the centre of the opium trade for the north of Helmand, where opium barons, having collected the harvest from local cash-croppers, sell on the unrefined opium to traffickers who'll take it either north through the Hindu Kush and onwards to Central Asia or south to Pakistan.

There's clearly a thriving, lucrative industry in Sangin which will make it a really tough nut to crack: what we offer as an alternative to the poppy will have to be equally lucrative, or perhaps made more attractive by additional developmental benefits like healthcare and education. I'm now slightly desperate to know what the alternative will be and hoping that the development people and the Foreign Office are going to put in an appearance soon.

Near the back of the wagon a few of the Chief's militia are leaning around a motorcycle that is a faithful replica of a Japanese original, only the name badge is imperfect – it's upside down and reads HODNA.

Intrigued by my presence, one of the militiamen wanders over and leans on the back door. Not much more than a gangly youth, his beard is short and wispy. A thick thatch of black hair emerges in a messy fringe from the arched front of his shiny prayer cap, adorned with plastic gems.

He peers quizzically in. 'What are you doing?'

'Listening,' I reply, pointing to the headset on my left ear.

Nodding, he takes a small comb from the chest pocket of his grimy brown *shalwar qamiz* and runs it through his beard. An AK is slung comfortably under his arm, decorated with tight bindings of pink plastic cable and little reflective stickers of holy Qur'anic calligraphy. A pink nylon flower pokes from its muzzle. He strikes me as rather whimsical, hardly the fearsome Mujahid of Afghan legend. One of his fellow militiamen appears by his side and stares at me. His bloodshot eyes, lined with black kohl, are watery and blinking. I ask for the comb, and it's handed to me. I run it through my beard, pleased that my growth far exceeds theirs. I'm fond of my beard; it's like a calendar of my time with the Afghan Army, a physical testament to being 'out there', immersed in a foreign culture. I draw the comb from my ears down to my chin, enjoying its cleansing, scratchy relief. I then bush out the sides, adding as much volume as possible.

As I hand the comb back, the militiaman refuses it. 'Keep it, it's spoilt now.'

His words sting me. 'Very well,' I reply. 'I'll treat it as a gift.'

But it is not. He has made plain his contempt for me as an unclean infidel. It's disheartening: I regard my beard as a cultural asset, a symbol of maturity and social standing; but it now seems a bit superficial. I put the comb in my pocket as the militiamen wander off.

Having been relieved by Finny, I go up to the roof to sleep. The night's breeze is preferable to the stench and stuffiness of the doss-room, which now reeks of sweaty feet and old food; the tea-boy has left a pot of stew in there to store overnight. The rooftop is scattered with prostrate sleepers. In a corner a pair of militiamen are on sentry behind a barricade of leaking sandbags. They sit on white plastic chairs and survey the river. Unrolling a blanket, I can see the top of the Snatch wagon just below me. Over by the main gate a gaggle of militia sit in a circle under the birdcage, talking quietly and smoking hashish; a peal of helpless laughter occasionally rings out. Lying on top of the blanket I cover myself with my sleeping bag and, enjoying the brilliant stars, drift off.

Back on stag in the small hours I sit uncomfortably in the wagon. Before dawn the militia descend from the roof for prayers. Immediately adjacent to the District Centre a small mud building serves as a mosque, recognisable as such only by a loudspeaker attached to a crooked wooden pole at its front. It has a pretty little pale blue door and window. The men make their ablutions in a fast-flowing irrigation stream next to the mosque. The loudspeaker seems not to work and they make their way silently to prayer.

We're due out on patrol at five, so just beforehand Lance Corporal Bow comes and transfers the radio from the top of the wagon into his backpack.

As dawn breaks we're heading south through small farmsteads. As usual I've got the ANA at the front with me. Moving around a field of wheat along a narrow path, we're overtaken on our flank by the British soldiers from the rear of the patrol moving straight through it, leaving trails of trampled stalks.

Moving back along the path, I ask the Lieutenant commanding them to steer his men onto the path. 'Otherwise the farmer will be a bit gutted to find our tracks.'

The Lieutenant's response is suddenly angry. Perhaps upset at being given advice in front of his men, he flares up. 'Mind your own fuckin' business, my blokes know what they're doing. You're just along for the ride,' he spits out.

'What? If it weren't for the ANA we wouldn't be on this patrol, *they* make it possible, we've got to do everything with them – that's the whole fucking point,' I retort.

An awkward silence settles and I turn away, moving back along the path. By now the tail end of the patrol is moving through the field so I jog along the path to get back to the front. Rather than angered, I'm disappointed by the platoon commander. I know he's tired and under pressure but he should realise it's supposed to be a 'joint' operation with the ANA. Their presence is small but of critical importance, isn't it? Without Javed and Captain Ahmed at the front of the patrol surely we'd appear as a bunch of foreigners doing our own thing. Perhaps we do anyway, despite their presence? Really, the patrol should be all Afghans with a couple of Brits giving advice, but that's not going to happen if our Kandak continues to sit tight in the FOB. As for the wheat, it's not the end of the world but we must try to avoid offending people whenever possible.

Having emerged from the farmland, we move onto the 611 and head north, towards the bazaar. Captain Ahmed stops for a chat with the man running the southern petrol pump. Drawing close, I greet him and accept his offer of a glass of water. He's short and grimy with a straggling grey beard.

Despite his humble appearance he has a keen curiosity. 'Tell me, are you going to prohibit the growing of poppy?' he asks, smiling.

'Well, we will offer an alternative – something else for people to grow . . .'

'What?' he asks, still smiling.

'Well, it's not certain, but there will be other benefits, like improvements in the town . . . That is, development,' I reply, disappointed at the hollowness of my words.

Sensing my unease, he does not question me further, but makes a prediction. 'If you try to stop the poppy in Sangin, there will be much trouble,' he says, his smile now replaced by a look of mild anguish.

'We won't do anything too hasty, I can assure you,' I reply, sensing that his words are very true.

Thanking him for the glass of water, I bid farewell with my hand on my heart. The gesture is returned. Captain Ahmed and I return to the road and the patrol continues.

Passing through the bazaar, we receive the usual discreet

friendliness and passive stares. I quickly purchase a kilo of small yellow mangoes. From the bazaar we move westwards, down into the dry riverbed, and head back towards the District Centre. The riverbed is full of livestock, at least two hundred head. Brown jostling flocks of sheep and goats are attended by men and boys, some catching animals, some conversing at the side. As I approach, their sun-darkened faces become clearer, adorned with long unkempt beards and simple off-white prayer caps. These men are the Koochi, a nomadic Pashtun tribe of herders. Grazing their beasts across all of south and east Afghanistan, they dwell in tents and visit towns to sell their livestock. They're shocked to see us.

Catching the gaze of two men who appear to have stopped their conversation mid-flow, I greet them. 'Salaam alaykum.'

They stare intently at me, without response.

'When do you hold this market?' I ask, undeterred.

Judging that my presence has stunned them into silence and they're unable to understand my artless Pashtu, I move away to look at the herd while Tamim converses with them. The sheep and goats chew their cud hurriedly. They seem healthy and have bloated, wobbling tails of fat which make them look ridiculous. Leaving them behind, we head towards to the District Centre which is nearby, at the end of the riverbed. Tamim tells me that the livestock market happens twice a week, on Mondays and Thursdays.

Having returned to the compound, I join Captain Ahmed and his men for breakfast. We settle down in a small circle on the plastic matting under the mulberry tree. It's an idyllic setting: the morning sun, yet to gain its ferocity, bathes the garden in a soft light, catching pink cherry blossom and small orange flowers among the grass. It's like a bizarre military picnic. Captain Ahmed offers me the ladle from a basin of whey. I drink and return it. Tearing strips of fresh naan bread, we plunge them into plates of thick clotted cream sprinkled with coarse white sugar. It's utterly delicious. Soon finished, it's followed by little greengages and tea. I mull over my argument with the platoon commander. I'm fond of Ahmed and his little band of men. So far they've been reliable and perfectly willing. Though small in number, they do at least give us a bit of an 'Afghan face' and hopefully more credibility among the population. I'm hoping that one of our ANA companies might soon replace the British platoon so that there only have to be a couple of Brits in the District Centre and it's the ANA running the show.

A Pashtun in his early thirties, Captain Ahmed has crooked dirty teeth and a short beard sprouting in scraggly patches. Soft-spoken and very patient, he seems to be well-liked by his soldiers. He's not really a talker and says the odd word to his men but not much else. I tell him that I'm grateful for his help with the patrolling and that he and his team will probably be relieved tonight by a new team from the FOB. He nods happily.

As his soldiers get up and leave he says quietly, 'Captain Leo, remember that everyone here has some connection to the poppy, even the Chief, everyone . . .'

'Surely the Chief is trying to stop it – no?' I ask, with deliberate naivety.

'He'll do whatever is most beneficial for him in all things. If the Taliban are here he'll support the Taliban, when the British are here he supports the British.'

His words trail off as one of the militia walks behind us to the mulberry tree and takes down the songbird's cage.

I'm unsure how seriously to take Captain Ahmed's warning, but to be honest I don't feel unsafe at the moment. I'm not stupid enough to believe that everyone is on our side and I'm well aware of the duplicitous nature of Afghan politics, but so far I trust the Chief, or at least trust him enough to feel he wouldn't endanger our lives while we're on his turf. What would be the point of that? Like everyone else he's keen to hedge his bets.

Even so, after today's patrol I do feel an increasing uneasiness about the clumsy, ill-informed nature of our presence in Sangin. We're running the risk of offending people simply by being here, but we're not using the opportunity to achieve anything. Good intentions and hand-shaking will count for nothing without anything concrete to back them up. We desperately need some proper intelligence people from Helmand Task Force headquarters to help us work out what's going on in Sangin with local politics, opium and the Taliban, and the bureaucrats from DfID and the FCO need to get up here and get busy alongside us.

After thanking Captain Ahmed for breakfast, I go through the garden down to the irrigation channel, following the man with the birdcage. The channel is a dozen feet wide, with deep, fast-flowing blue-green water. On the bank, shaded by dense greenery, the man is squatting on his haunches, washing the cage, splashing handfuls of water across its floor. The songbird rests unsteadily at the top of the cage, surrounded by pink plastic flowers. The man refills a little water vessel attached to the bars of the cage. From a bag in his pocket he pours a small amount of birdseed into a tiny dish, and places it carefully inside. Seeing that he's happily absorbed in his task, I leave him and wander back up towards the District Centre.

On the radio in the back of the wagon, I speak to HQ. We've still not received any orders about how long we're here for and who else might be joining us but I'm hoping to get clarification of this from whoever brings our water and rations resupply. I'm told that it'll come some time today. Tamim and Finny are waiting at the back of the wagon, listening in; they break out into big smiles when they hear about the resupply as they're both due to go on R&R, and they need to get back to the FOB to catch the Chinook when it flies in tomorrow.

As I slump in the back of the wagon, listless with the rising heat, a Toyota Land Cruiser screeches to a halt and disgorges a group of the District Chief's men. From the back they unload what looks like a pair of black footballs swaddled in thick white polythene, and bustle excitedly into the *hijra*.

'What's that?' I ask Haji Mirwais as he follows them in.

'It is opium, it's been confiscated and will be destroyed.' Without stopping he disappears into the *hijra*, firmly closing the door.

Incredulous, my confidence in the Chief and his men is shaken. As Captain Ahmed warned, *everyone* is connected to the poppy in some way. I want to believe that it really will be destroyed but I just can't be sure.

The resupply arrives in the early evening and brings rations and water but no new information about who's coming to join us or the plan as a whole for Sangin. As we unload boxes of MREs and mineral water, one of the sergeants with the resupply looks wide-eyed at a gaggle of militia gathered by the front gate.

'Fucking 'ell, sir, d'you feel safe here?'

'Yeah, we're all right, we've got mangoes and everything,' I reply, keen to jest.

'What about this lot? They look a bit nuts to me,' he says, glancing again at the militia, now sitting in an untidy circle, generating thick plumes of smoke.

'They're OK. As far as I can tell, they're on our side,' I say, half-convincingly.

With the resupply, Captain Ahmed and his guys are replaced with a new team of ANA, four young Tajiks. It seems that no more ANA are available.

As the resupply convoy leaves, I'm fairly gutted that no one has arrived to give our presence here more purpose and nothing seems to have been developed in terms of the plan for Sangin as a whole. I feel like we're sitting here wasting precious time while the Helmand Task Force headquarters appear to be doing nothing about it. I'm not sure that things will be peaceful for much longer; we're a fairly big target and the Taliban, or whoever, are most probably sizing us up before making their move. Unless we show the population some sort of progress they won't support us when the shooting starts and may even turn against us.

'Where the fuck is the DfID bird now?' I ask myself, irate with disappointment.

If they're too risk-averse to come into Sangin then we ought really have a bag of money ourselves to start some high-profile basic projects, to buy some sympathy until the real development can start. 'Whatever the Comprehensive Approach was supposed to be,' I tell myself, 'this is not it!'

Declining supper with the Chief, I bed down in the doss-room with a churning in my guts. Shortly I'm gripped with stomach cramps and, grabbing my head-torch, scurry through the dark garden to the stinking squat toilet and submit to a paroxysm of uncontrollable liquid-shit diarrhoea. Standing up, I move out of the toilet, pausing next to a patch of six-foot sunflowers. My stomach turns as my mouth is filled with a rush of water. Heaving, I vomit great arcs of toxic yellow puke, exploding through my throat and splashing onto the sunflower stalks. With eyes watering I shudder between each round, desperate not to taste the remnants stuck at the back of my mouth.

After the convulsions have subsided I return gingerly to the doss-room. I'm passed by Lance Corporal Bow heading for where I've just been, with the same affliction. It seems that while sleeping in the doss-room, the filth has penetrated our bodies. Curling up on the greasy carpet, clutching my stomach, every fibre of my body screams 'sickness'. I'm exhausted and yet I cannot sleep.

CHAPTER 9

'It seems we've been played'

May 2006: Sangin, Helmand Province, Afghanistan

Wrenched from a half-slumber by a hand on my shoulder, I make my way to the Snatch wagon to stag on. In the grey light of early dawn, I relieve the new driver who replaced Finny yesterday. Light-headed and dry-mouthed, I break open a bottle of mineral water and down it steadily. Up until now I've been drinking the local water from a tank in the doss-room which has chunks of ice floating in it. The militiamen bring in a great block of ice daily, and it sits slowly melting on the floor of the dusty veranda as they hack bits off whenever they feel like it. An ice-cold drink of water here is simply luxurious; however, I reckon I ought to stick to mineral water until I'm better. The quivering in my bowels has subsided a little and although I'm chronically dehydrated from all the puking, that's now passed, probably because I've nothing left to puke up. I reckon if I fast for the day and just drink water I'll be back to normal by tonight.

Lance Corporal Bow, however, has got more puking to do and has visited the toilet three times in the last hour.

'Fucking hell, Corporal B, you may as well just stay down there!' I call out after him as he scurries past again.

'I need the exercise, boss.'

Moments later great strangled heaves sound from the toilet as he retches repeatedly, with impressive vigour.

By the afternoon, Lance Corporal Bow is still puking, and although I'm feeling a bit better, I've still got the shits. I'm now keen for him to see a doctor.

On the radio my request for our team to be rotated with another is agreed in the late afternoon. After rapidly bidding farewell to the Chief, assuring him we'll be replaced and thanking him for his hospitality, we leave the District Centre, waving the militiamen goodbye. Numbed by the illness, I'm ambivalent about leaving. Anyway, I expect I'll be back in a few days.

Back at FOB Robinson we find the mentoring team having a barbecue. They've rigged up half an oil drum, now full of embers, and a griddle of American-issue burgers and spare ribs. They're from ten-man ration packs and come with burger buns sealed in green foil vacuum packs which taste like cream crackers dipped in paraffin. I nibble the corner of a spare rib and decide to continue my fast for a bit longer.

Colonel Shirdil is there, munching a burger, and I can't help thinking he should be getting a grip of his Kandak and getting some troops together to replace the British platoon at the District Centre. Moving to one side of the barbecue, I back-brief the commander of the British team that's about to go down there, telling him what the situation is and where exactly we've been on patrol.

After unloading my kit from the Snatch I tramp through the ankle-deep dust to our corner of the compound. A new construction has emerged: up against the wall next to the camouflage net three plywood walls sprouting four-inch nails are covered by a battered tarpaulin to form a room.

CSM Johnstone appears from a tarpaulin flap at the side. 'Fuckin' hell, sir, I thought you'd gone native. Welcome back.'

'Thanks! I can see you've been busy,' I reply, ducking through the door flap

'Just tryin' tae get us some shelter frae this bastard dust.'

Inside, a waxy yellow light and stifling heat are generated by the afternoon sun. The CSM has set up our mosquito nets on sheets of plywood and arranged old ammunition tins as seats, so it's looking pretty homely. It's just me and him in here; Finny got away on the Chinook for R&R and Stoddy is bunking up with the American medic in the American training team's compound. Apparently we're due to move over there when the Americans leave with the Herati Kandak. Until then we're making do, but the new shelter looks fairly pukka.

Outside I look under my poncho: the wind has brought an inch of dust into my former wardrobe. Toppling it over, I move it into our new home. Laid sideways, it provides an excellent tabletop. Hanging my kit on an array of four-inch nails I feel content with my new bed space. Taking my pistol I move back outside, wandering over to the plunge pool.

When the American Special Forces first constructed the camp, the land was leased from a local farmer on the condition that the Americans enabled him to continue to draw water from a well on the site. Their engineer, clearly a bright spark, created a system of pipes with a pump to channel water through the perimeter and sensibly included a deep plunge pool in the system, made from a plastic water tank cut in half. Happily, the troops inside the perimeter get to wash properly and the farmer's crop, which naturally is poppy, flourishes.

Keeping my combats on I jump into the pool, four feet square, and submerge myself fully in the wonderfully cool, cleansing water. Sitting briefly on the bottom, I blow a flurry of bubbles through the water. Standing, I scrub my beard and head with soap and, taking off my combats, scrub them too. Wearing only my dog-tags, I lather up and submerge, over and over. I feel invigorated and well again. The illness and filth of the District Centre have been washed away. I put my boots and wet combats back on and stroll towards our shack, drying as I walk in the evening sun.

I'm not clean for very long. CSM Johnstone and I weigh down the door flap with ammunition boxes under the strange blue light of a cylume, a chemical light stick which once initiated glows for a couple of hours. The door flap however, part of an old tent, is an imperfect fit and can't stop the dust billowing in defiantly after each gust of wind.

I'm resigned and the CSM is angry. 'I'm fuckin' threaders wi' this. It's the worst place I've ever been.'

But despite his venom I know that he's simultaneously relishing the challenge, the feeling of being 'out there' in this almost comically absurd filthy hole.

By the time I crawl into my mosquito net I'm ingrained with dust. A thick uniform layer has settled on my sleeping bag. I stretch out, masking my face with a cotton sweat rag. I'm woken from a stifled sleep by the battering of the wind on our fragile walls. The cylume has dimmed and though I can't see the dust that penetrates our walls I can feel it accumulating about my head.

In the morning, the wind has gone. I break my fast with pineapples in syrup from an American ration pack and make my way down to the ANA side of the base to find HQ Company. They're located in a watchtower on the west side of the perimeter, overlooking the river and the 611 road.

Ramadan the tea boy is cooking and greets me with a smile. 'Salaam alaykum. How are you, Captain?'

'Alaykum salaam. I'm very well, Ramadan. Where is Captain Hameed?'

'In the river, washing,' he replies, pointing down the dusty slope in front of us towards the green foliage of the river bank. In among the trees a couple of ANA vehicles are parked up and some figures are splashing around in the shallows.

The watchtower, a tall construction of sandbags and timber, is well ordered with clean plastic floor matting. It's homely because they live in it. On the high, narrow windows, facing all directions, rests an array of Kalashnikov weapons including a long sniper rifle. Pir Ahmed arrives and we drink tea sitting outside, facing the river. The company seems to be a bit thin on the ground, and they can't all be in the river.

'Pir Ahmed, where are all your men?'

'On leave, Captain. We have only eighteen men in the company now, so we can only just man our two watchtowers.'

This is sickening. With so few men HQ Company is hamstrung and ineffectual, just like the Kandak as a whole. At this rate the battalion will never be able to find sufficient men to increase the ANA presence at the District Centre in Sangin, especially as Colonel Shirdil isn't keen on the idea anyway. The company's inability to actually do anything due to a lack of manpower has been a persistent theme since the first day of training and I'm now utterly frustrated by it.

Sighing with resignation I move on to a practical issue that we hopefully *can* solve. 'Pir Ahmed, could you by any chance find me a kettle?'

Without speaking he jumps up, has a quick rummage inside the watchtower, and reappears with a shiny tin kettle, its new golden glaze untarnished. 'Take it, Captain, it's yours.'

Having dug a shallow pit next to our shack, I get a little fire going with some timber fragments, leftovers from CSM Johnstone's building frenzy. I rest the kettle over the flames on a trio of stones; its 'Made in China' sticker quickly ignites as the kettle blackens. I'm chuffed at Pir Ahmed's kind gift; not only is it better than an issue mess tin for brewing up in, but we can also heat our MRE packets in it rather than using the fiddly chemical-reaction heaters that come with each pack and never really get them piping hot.

Seeking some more substantial fuel I make for the large pile of firewood outside the baker's hut and notice that the door is ajar and nobody is there. Inside, the deep pit of the oven is cold and a few plastic vessels and rags are all that remain on the dusty floor. Mohammad Qasim has gone, probably back to Gereshk. Deflated, I gather an armful of wood and continue brewing up.

After tea I make my way over to our makeshift headquarters, as I'm the 'watchkeeper' – the officer on duty overnight. On the way I pass the British 105mm gun line, a messy concoction of shelters gathered under a suspended parachute to the rear of the big guns. At the side, a group of young British Artillery soldiers, tattooed, deep brown and dusty, take turns on a pull-up bar. Wearing shorts made from cut-off combat trousers and boots, their shouts of encouragement mingle with cries of mock-derision and laughter.

The operations room is in a watchtower on top of the mud building that houses the American training team. Climbing up the rickety wooden steps onto the flat roof, I remember meeting the Alabama National Guard guys up here and being surprised at their .38 hunting rifle, but it doesn't seem so bizarre now. This is where all operations are supposedly controlled from. Crucially, it's the communications hub of the unit. As the overnight watchkeeper I must be ready to react to any event that might occur involving our troops on the ground and get the more senior officers like the Colonel out of bed if anything really serious occurs. It's basically the same as stagging on except you've got a couple of signallers with you, listening to the radios.

Settling down on a piece of battered garden furniture, I scan the horizon with binoculars. The sun is now a fat glowing orange, falling rapidly towards the horizon. The river reflects its light and is, quite simply, beautiful. I can see the grey mass of the town but no real details. The two signallers with me have a radio each; one's listening to the Helmand Task Force channel, the other to our team at the District Centre. I'm hoping for a quiet night so I can doze in my chair; the best thing about being up here tonight is that I'm away from the evil dust.

At around midnight the team commander at the District Centre comes on the radio and says he's received a warning from the District Chief. Apparently there's a Taliban convoy heading for the District Centre, intending to attack it. This is serious. I inform Helmand Task Force headquarters, and the Colonel's second-in-command, a Major, rushes up to speak to the District Centre on the radio.

The team commander's voice is terse. 'We've got a Taliban convoy approaching from the north . . . probably four vehicles . . . I request aviation to take a look and HE [high explosive] and illum [illumination] on standby...'

'Roger . . . Wait,' replies the Major. Grabbing the other radio, he fires off a series of questions and then resumes his previous conversation. 'We can't get aviation for another forty-five minutes but you can have illum.'

Minutes later there's a series of almighty poundings from the gun line. A white spark ignites in the black sky, at least six kilometres away. Its brilliance increases as it floats slowly downwards and then splutters out, just as the next one has reached its climax – the six rounds are perfectly timed to give a continuous screen of light.

However, the commander is unsure what he's seeing. 'Mmm . . . There are two vehicles in the riverbed due north . . . They've got their four-way flashers on . . . Request more illum on the same location.'

Another six rounds are fired up.

'They're leaving . . . They're driving off.'

It sounds a bit bizarre. I've not heard of the Taliban driving around with their hazard lights on.

The team commander comes back on the radio. 'I think this is just bullshit to test our reactions . . . The Chief keeps asking when the helicopter's coming . . . I think we're being tested.'

It seems we've been played. I know the Chief is a bit of a shady character but I'm reluctant to believe he's set on betraying us to the Taliban. Perhaps he's testing us for his own reasons or perhaps it's just a muddle and the vehicles really were a Taliban convoy and were scared off by the illumination. The only thing that's certain is that the team in the District Centre are not happy. 'We do *not* feel safe here . . . The militia are threatening us,' says the commander, now agitated. 'I request to extract at first light.'

'OK, if you don't feel safe then extract,' replies the second-in-command, deflated.

I'm also disappointed, or rather, confused. We simply don't know who's for us and who's against us, yet without any intelligence sources we're unable to find out. Either way the town's inhabitants must have been entertained by the fireworks: they were probably glad it wasn't high-explosive shells we were chucking into town. By the time I come off stag the team has extracted from the District Centre, so there's no one at all in Sangin. Perhaps it's a good thing, seeing as nothing is happening with the reconstruction side of the operation, and they won't just be sitting there like a big target waiting to be hit.

Plodding back through the fine ankle-deep dust towards our shack, I pass the gun line again. They're taking advantage of the cool of the early morning to clean one of their guns, thrusting a great cleaning rod down the long barrel like a Napoleonic naval gun crew. Chattering away, their banter is boisterous; they're clearly jubilant that, after two weeks of tedium in the filthy dust, they've finally fired their guns.

Back in the shack, I get a brew on with CSM Johnstone. He was put on standby to go out with the Quick Reaction Force.

This group would have gone to support our team at the District Centre if it had 'gone noisy' when the illum went up. Consequently he's been up most of the night.

'I dinnae mind. I'd rather be sat in a wagon waitin' to go than tryin' to sleep in this sandpit.'

Agreeing with his sentiment, I make us instant white tea using the sachets of powder. These only come in British ration packs, so I was delighted to be able to liberate them from a box of 'Menu A' that I found while watchkeeping. Two sachets of tea and one of sugar is the perfect combination. I make the CSM's in his issue black half-pint mug and, having lost my issue mug, use the bottom half of a mineral water bottle, which warps slightly as I pour in the boiling water.

Our peace is interrupted by the beating of a Chinook's twin rotor blades. One circles high above us in protective over-watch as its partner, like a massive squat insect, swoops down towards the landing site outside the FOB, generating a sudden dust storm. I clamber onto the perimeter to watch. Static, with its rotors still turning, the helicopter disgorges a gaggle of troops from its tailgate, who make a crouched run off the landing site. Another gaggle makes the opposite movement and, tailgate up, the Chinook promptly rises directly upwards, banks sharply and quickly fades away. Just beyond our perimeter a group of ANA are left among the scattered remnants of their makeshift watchtower, blasted apart by the Chinook's downdraught. Laughing, they half-heartedly set about collecting the pieces.

The troops who've arrived on the Chinook turn out to be a platoon of Gurkhas, to replace the British platoon that's just left on the same helicopter. Having been called to the operations room by the British second-in-command, I meet their platoon commander, an attentive softly-spoken Nepali CSM. I'm required to go with them to recce a location for a new platoon house in Sangin. The Colonel, who's gone to Camp Bastion, has directed that we must get back into town. We're going to the Security Chief's house this time, and I'm required because I've met him.

In the mid-afternoon we rattle into town with the Gurkhas. The Security Chief's house is at the north end of town, beyond the bazaar. It's a vast concrete pile, surrounded by a high-walled compound. Having parked up we have to wait a few minutes for the Security Chief to appear from an outbuilding, as he wasn't expecting us. He has to send one of his lackeys to find the key to the main house. He gives me a smile of recognition as we enter. Although it's empty at the moment the security Chief is not willing to let us use his compound as a base.

'My wife and children will soon be moving in here, for their security. With my wife present I regret that it would be impossible for your troops to be here.'

Despite this, he says at length that he's very keen to help us fight the Taliban and that his men know how to use a GPS. After speaking he takes off his dark turban and re-winds it over his little white skullcap. His deft strokes are a joy to watch. The left hand feeds the material upwards, the right winds it, using the palm then the back of the hand in an unconscious rhythm.

The unlived-in house has a musty smell. It's grand but horribly tacky; the room we're in has a thick fitted carpet, decorative wooden cladding on the walls and a faux-gold door handle. Getting up to leave, we make a cordial farewell.

It's unfortunate that we can't use the Security Chief's compound; it would afford excellent arcs of view over across the northern half of Sangin. I don't really buy his excuse for not having us there, but it's hardly surprising that he doesn't want his fancy new house turned into a patrol base by a gang of foreign soldiers about whom the population may not be ultimately very sympathetic. Though he supports us – from what I've seen so far – it's probably a bit much to ask to have us in his house. Anyway we may as well just mount patrols from the FOB; it's much more discreet than staying in the town.

Driving back into the FOB, I'm surprised to see some new arrivals spread out in the middle of our compound, sorting through their kit. It turns out to be a few EOD (Explosive Ordnance Disposal) bomb-disposal blokes and a UAV (Unmanned Aerial Vehicle) team. They've got a little hand-launched radio-controlled aircraft from which a camera beams back a bird's-eye view of the ground. This is good news; the next time we get a threat warning we can send the UAV up to take a look before putting troops onto the ground. Unfortunately it doesn't work at night but still, it's a step in the right direction. But there are no military intelligence personnel, nor any development or Foreign Office people among the group of dusty new arrivals. Baffled by their absence, I return to the shack.

Stripping off my webbing vest and body armour, I vent my disgust to CSM Johnstone, who is reassuringly sanguine.

'Dinnae worry aboot that lot, sir, they'll be sittin' on their arses wi' fuckin' air-con in Kandahar.'

The following day the Gurkhas deploy to the police station, to use it as new platoon house. Surprised, I discuss it with the second-in-command, who, with the Colonel away in Camp Bastion, is overworked and fed up.

'The Colonel has directed them to occupy the police station so that's where they're going.'

'But surely the Chief of Police is just as bad as the District Chief or probably worse, isn't he?'

'Well, maybe, but we need to be in town . . . and we're not going to find anywhere better,' he says, exhausted.

'But all the civilians hate the Chief of Police, that much we do know.'

'Well, we haven't got any choice really.'

What makes it even more absurd is that no ANA at all are going along. They're supposedly all occupied guarding watchtowers, down to the last man. That means none of the mentoring team will be there either. The police compound really isn't an ideal platoon house; apart from the fact that the Chief of Police is probably a murderous criminal, the town can't be clearly seen from it and it's vulnerably exposed to the hills on its eastern side.

'Christ! This is a pantomime,' I exclaim to myself.

A grim realisation falls over me: there is no plan at all behind any of this. What I had suspected is now suddenly clear. Its not that we're struggling to implement it, it simply doesn't exist. A series of disjointed ill-considered directives from headquarters is all that exists here. Everything else, all the well-meaning reconstruction stuff, is an illusion. The setting up of the platoon house and the time spent there now seem to have been an egotistical folly.

'This is a cluster-fuck,' I gasp under my breath. 'If it wasn't dangerous it would be laughable.'

At this moment the fact that we're surrounded by the hostile sands of the 'Desert of Death' no longer seems funny.

Despairing, I give the Gurkha commander a patrol trace – a sheet of clear plastic on which I've drawn coloured lines marking our routes in town. When he puts it against his own map he'll know where we've been previously. The colourful squiggles merge as I roll the trace into a translucent tube and hand it over.

Shortly after the Gurkhas depart the Herati Kandak also leave. This allows the British team to move into the American accommodation: two rows of metal shipping containers with a wooden door on the front, fitted with an air-con blower. CSM Johnstone is jubilant to at last be away from the dust as we cram our kit into the tiny room. We've got two other blokes in with us so it's a tight fit.

I've not yet arranged my kit when I'm struck down again with diarrhoea and vomiting. To guard against its spread through our ultra-close living quarters I'm isolated – sent back, with unwelcome irony, to our deserted shack.

The compound is devoid of people. Only the sad remnants of our ramshackle bivi positions remain in the dust. The shack, now empty except for my mosquito net, rifle and some water bottles, is stiflingly hot. Suddenly agitated, I smash the wall with the sole of my boot until one of the sheets of plywood splinters free of its nails and flops outwards. The air remains still. Sitting uneasily on a wooden pallet, I guzzle mineral water mixed with sachets of Gatorade, left by the Americans, to replace the water I'm losing with my twice-hourly bouts of liquid shitting.

The doctor brings over another sickie – Lance Corporal Bow who, like me, is well practised at diarrhoea and vomiting. As I'm no longer puking the doctor gives me more antibiotic pills, and tells me to continue eating to flush the bacteria out of my body.

As the sun sets I put my mossie net outside, hoping for a still night. I'm pleased to have some company. Lance Corporal Bow doesn't have much to say but he is, as ever, cheerful. He's blissfully unaware of the futility of our presence here. The satisfaction from his day's work comes from getting the radios working. He's the essence of unquestioning dependability, quietly tolerant of illness, futility and danger. I respect him deeply.

The UAV team appear and practise their take-off procedure. One of them runs along and throws the little plane in the air while another fiddles with a control box. It rasps away and, a few minutes later, makes a crash landing into the far side of the compound.

Time passes in a vacuum, a cycle of drinking Gatorade and going to the toilet repeatedly. The only anticipation is the consistency of my next shit.

We're distracted from our tedious isolation by the arrival of a resupply convoy from Tombstone. Standing on the perimeter wall we watch the elongated snake of vehicles – British, American and Afghan – approach under a towering dust cloud.

The distant roaring of the vehicles is interrupted by the pounding *crump!* of a muffled explosion.

'Fuck! IED!'

We train our rifle sights onto the convoy. An Afghan vehicle is half-toppled over, listing on its right side, surrounded by a swirl of smoke and frantic, scurrying figures. They're about five hundred metres away and through my sight I can see them pulling at the cab of the pick-up truck. The rest of the convoy is static with their troops dismounting, checking the area around their vehicles for more IEDs (improvised explosive devices).

More ANA arrive on the scene in pick-up trucks packed with soldiers clinging onto the back. They've come out from the FOB presumably to assist the casualties and allow the convoy to get moving again.

To the right of the wagon that's been hit is a small village, a cluster of perhaps two dozen low mud compounds mingled with trees and surrounded by a few patchy green fields of wheat.

The ANA, now dismounted, are making for the village in an extended line of little jogging figures. A flurry of shots crackles. As the ANA disappear among the houses the agitated popping of shots continues. This doesn't look good.

'Jesus, what are they doing, Corporal Bow?

'Dunno, boss. I think they're barking.'

'You're right, whoever planted the IED's not gonna be hanging around in the village.'

The shooting continues for another few minutes. The British Quick Reaction Force arrives in a pair of Snatch wagons and the convoy slowly moves forward. The ANA trickle out of the village and remount their wagons, joining the convoy. The two Snatch wagons remain static, guarding the smashed ANA vehicle, waiting for an American Humvee to come and drag it into the camp.

Once recovered, and returned from my isolation, I go over to see HQ Company. It's still my job to supposedly 'mentor' Captain Hameed, but in reality, because they're such a small group and they're just manning the watchtowers, all I can do is pay social visits and hope to advise him.

As I enter the little office Captain Hameed greets me with a smile. I'm pleased to find Abdul Qadir, the company second-in-command, is also present, newly returned from his leave. He was in the convoy that got IED'd but happily is unscathed. We settle down on the matted floor to drink tea and nibble the sweet Panjshiri raisins he's brought with him from home. Captain Hameed tells me there were three ANA casualties from the IED, and by God's mercy no one died.

'And in the village?' I ask. 'Were there any casualties there?'

'Maybe,' he replies, unconcerned. 'These people are all against us. If they attack us, we must attack them.'

'But surely that makes the problem worse. If you speak to them, they may give you information to help us.'

He remains unconvinced. 'They do not want to help us. They are all criminals.'

I want to shout him down, but it's not a good time to be discussing hearts-and-minds tactics when they're clearly upset. An awkward silence falls on our little circle.

Keen to change the subject, I turn to Abdul Qadir. 'How is the Panjshir valley and how is your baby daughter?'

'Thanks be to God, she is well,' he replies, a warm smile

spreading across his face. 'And the trees at home are full of fruit.'

Ramadan enters with a basin. Onto aluminium plates he doles out big splodges of reddish sticky rice, and passes them round. Though simple, it's delicious. The interior wall facing me holds a slogan, elegantly scrawled in white chalk. Around it, little pink roses hang from the cracks in the rough mud plaster finish. As the others chatter, I ask Suhail, a Pashtun interpreter accompanying me in Tamim's place, what it means.

'It's saying that it was the Shura-e-Nazar who defeated the Soviets, so they can beat anyone. It is a slogan of the Tajik Northern Alliance . . . one of the Mujahideen groups.'

He speaks quietly, unwilling to be drawn into a sectarian discussion.

As we work our way through the stodgy rice with our fingers, a rifle shot cracks outside. Our actions frozen, we look up from our rice, mystified. Captain Hameed jumps up and rushes outside.

'Probably an ND [negligent discharge] – you know, an accident,' I say flatly.

A minute later, Captain Hameed returns, settling back down in the circle. 'A man has been killed, in the mosque, shot in the face. I'm not sure if it was on purpose.'

As he plunges his fingers back into his rice, we silently follow suit and resume our lunch.

Leaving the office, Suhail and I pass the mosque doorway, a few metres away. I look through the door. A squatting group of ANA soldiers stare silently at a green canvas sheet hiding the corpse. A blue-black puddle shrouds one end. It does not move me, perhaps because I can't see him. I want to lift the sheet and see the man's face – I imagine it must be caved in – to make it more real, and test its impact.

As we walk back to the other side of the FOB, we see the vehicle blown up by the IED, dumped at the side of the track. The rear half is shredded: a mangled mess of punctured metal. Shrapnel holes are scattered across the cab; the passengers, though gravely injured, are clearly very lucky to be alive. It's perverse that the soldiers in this pick-up survived and yet one has just been killed accidentally in the mosque.

Back at the accommodation containers I avoid a big group of officers chatting around a home-made picnic bench. A few more Captains arrived with the resupply convoy and there's not really anything for them to do. They've come up from Tombstone only because they're bored – especially Jim, who's had the good grace not to ask for his holster back.

Sitting down to chat with CSM Johnstone, I tell him about my lunch, but he's not interested. He went with the Quick Reaction Force to assist the convoy after the IED and saw Captain Hameed in the village.

'I seen him knock doon an old man. This old boy had a bag o' peas, and Capt'n Hameed ripped it frae his hand and punched him in the face. Knocked him clean over. It was fuckin' shockin'...'

'You're right,' I reply, sighing with resignation.

Inwardly I scoff at the recollection of arguing while on patrol about our troops walking through a field of wheat.

CHAPTER 10

Desert of Death

June 2006: Helmand Province, Afghanistan

Now in Camp Tombstone, I've a whole day to kill before going over to Camp Bastion and getting the Herc to Kabul and then a flight to Brize Norton. R&R! Ten days of 'rest and recuperation' in the UK. 'Fucking bring it on!' is my new whispered mantra. I'm chuffed to bits; I had avoided thinking about it until the moment I was told to be on the next Chinook out of Sangin.

In the dry sterility of Tombstone, I struggle to prevent my imagination making sudden flights of delicious fantasy about seeing Lucy and gorging on champagne. I'm determined not to believe that it's definitely happening until I'm actually on the RAF's Tristar, taking off from Kabul, as the R&R flights are infamous for savage delays.

At supper I revel in the fresh fruit and salads. The crunchy iceberg lettuce is a delectable treat after the monotony of bland MREs and Afghan rice.

Our dormitory is only half occupied now, by a bunch of officers mentoring an ANA logistics battalion. The occupants of the beds around my top bunk are all in Sangin. Their excess kit and personal effects remain in an odd assortment on top of their beds. I'm right in anticipating that on the lower bunk next to mine Jim, still in Sangin, has left his mini DVD-player at the top of one of his plastic trunks. Having arranged the little player on the dusty shelving unit, I stretch out in a camp chair and am completely absorbed by two hours of Napoleonic seafaring heroics.

Rising before the sun, I run rings around the inside of the perimeter. I'm hopelessly craving R&R now that it's suddenly here. Trudging around the little camp I can think only of Lucy. Now remembered, her face dominates my every thought, like a genie free of its bottle.

Having showered, I pull on my combats, a clean spare set.

One of the young officers from the logistics unit comes up and blurts out, 'Jim was killed last night. With two others . . . There was a contact.'

'Fuck . . .' is all I can manage in reply.

My stomach lurches and starts to fall. Sitting down, I put on my boots. Slowly buckling on my holster – *his* holster – I walk over to the operations room.

'The UAV crashed west of the river and the Gurkhas went to recover it. That was late last night,' the watchkeeper tells me in his soft Welsh tone.

'They got contacted and couldn't move so the Quick Reaction Force went out to give them a hand but got ambushed here.' He points to a map on the wall: there's a big red pin near a thin blue line, the Helmand River, just above a rash of black dots marking Sangin town.

'That's when Capt'n Phillipson got shot . . . Shot in the face.'

'Fuck,' I whisper to myself

'They got his body back to the FOB and then went out again to try to reach the Gurkhas, this time up to the north,' he continues, tracing the line of direction with a pencil point on the map. 'But they got ambushed again and the UAV Sergeant Major lost an arm, blown off by an RPG, and a Corporal was shot in the chest but he's all right. At that stage Apache went up and the 105 guns in the FOB fired. The Paras sent out B Company from Camp Bastion to help everyone extract. So they're all back in the FOB now and the Paras are in the town.'

'What about the ANA, did they go out with the QRF?' I ask.

'They went out but when it kicked off they bolted and left their wagons with the lights on and engines running, so the Taliban fuckin' stole 'em,' he replies quietly.

In the dormitory I return the DVD-player to the plastic trunk, carefully replacing a *Wild Geese* disc into the player, leaving it as I found it. The trunk contains a stash of cards from his family. There's one of a silly cartoon dog from his mother. With a falling sensation in my stomach I quickly close the lid and go outside.

Over at the interpreters' hut I seek news of Tamim; he should be back from his leave by now. From a sitting circle of interpreters drinking tea, one of them rises and tells me that his return is unlikely.

'Captain, he will not come back, he has gone home to be married.'

'I didn't think it was happening so soon,' I reply, thinking, surely Tamim would have told me about it?

'Well, take his number and give him a call,' he continues. He scrawls a string of digits into my notebook, copied from his mobile phone. Declining his offer of tea I thank him and leave.

Back in the dormitory I clean my rifle; it'll stay in the armoury while I'm on R&R. A Sergeant Major comes in and asks which is Captain Phillipson's bedspace. I show him. Unfolding a big brown cardboard box he packs the contents of the bedspace into it. By the time I've finished cleaning my rifle, the Sergeant Major has left with the box and the bedspace is empty.

In the afternoon I'm over at Camp Bastion waiting for the flight to Kabul. Walking through the lines of yellow half-cylindrical tents, a 3 Para officer I know from Sandhurst passes and greets me. He's excited about an imminent arrest operation.

'We're out a bit later after some high-value targets. It's bound to go noisy.'

'What planet are you on?' I think, as I wish him good luck. This is not a game, a chance to fulfil personal fighting fantasies. If we want a fight we'll get one here, a thousand times over, but to what end? Violence will surely breed more violence, until the whole thing is beyond our control.

The shock of the morning's news has compressed my frustration into anger. I want very badly to talk about the whole thing, to share it and be told that sense will now prevail, at the tragic price of this death.

The Camp's headquarters is a quadrangle of low canvas tents and elaborate radio antennae encircled by a thick earthen barrier. Passing the gate guard, I enter one of the tents through a door flap into a stuffy interior, yellow under fluorescent tube lights. Keen to find out what we're going to do, now that disaster has struck, I find the liaison officer responsible for our team. He's our link to this headquarters and has been relaying the orders to us from Helmand Task Force HQ in Lashkar Gah.

'What's the form?' I ask, approaching his desk. 'Are we pulling out of Sangin or what?'

'Mmm, no. One of the Para companies is going to stay on at the District Centre. Other than that the plan's not really changed, Leo.'

'What plan?' I retort, flashing with anger. 'There is no plan . . . We fucking well made it up as we went along going into Sangin, you know that.'

'Easy, mucker, it's not my fault this has happened,' he says plaintively.

'This is fucking nonsense. We blundered into that town not even knowing where our objective was, and we've sat there like a bloody great target doing fuck-all.'

'Mate, chill,' he says standing and raising his palms

'Don't tell me to fucking chill!' I want to grab his pasty white face and smash it on the desk between us. 'This is a fucking disgrace! More blokes'll die up there, for no reason, and we're doing fuck-all about it.'

Flushing red, he sits back down and looks intently at his computer screen. Other officers in the tent glance awkwardly at me. I'm making a scene. Breathing heavily I turn about, push past the canvas door flap and leave, angered even more now by my lack of eloquence.

In the large tented cookhouse I make myself tea in a polystyrene cup. The Sky News headlines flash in noisy repetition across a TV screen, watched by a few off-duty blokes wearing PT kit and flip-flops, their weapons lying next to their chairs.

'First British Soldier Killed in Helmand' comes up in bold, above a simple map of the Province with 'Sangin' enlarged on a red pointing arrow, followed by some archive footage from somewhere in northern Afghanistan. The soldier's anonymity means his parents are still uninformed. The camp's internet and phone cabin is still closed with an 'op minimise' sign on the door, in order to prevent those in camp communicating his name to the media before his parents have the news. This unintentionally provides all other parents of those in Helmand, aware that an unnamed soldier has been killed, with ample opportunity to imagine that their child is dead. The suspense of waiting can only end when someone else's son has their photo flashed up on the news, and the collective trauma of anticipation is passed onto a few individuals whose lives are shattered.

Sick of the Sky News intro music, I move outside and join the crowd for the pre-flight roll call. The gathered troops are jubilant to be leaving for R&R and banter boisterously until a voluntary hush falls as a list of ranks and names is called out and each one is claimed by a shouted reply.

As we wait for a brief from the logistics corporal, I chat to an Artillery CSM whom I know from the first operation going into Sangin; he rode in the back of Sergeant Stoddart's dilapidated ANA wagon. He left Sangin on the same Chinook as me and is disappointed.

'Gutted to have missed it, boss,' he says as we talk quietly.

I know he's not being macho, he really means it. We both know that it will have inflicted on most of the participants one of the most intense experiences of their lives so far, and for some the worst experience ever – seeing a friend shot through the face. Because of this and despite this it holds a tragic allure for near-miss non-participants. He's done probably twenty years in the Army and yet as a professional soldier still craves opportunities to risk everything and relish life through avoiding death.

I know he really means it because I feel the same. I'm angry at the death of a friend and know that it marks the arrival of catastrophe for his family, the people of Sangin, and the British and Afghan soldiers in Helmand, and yet I feel guilty for my absence when CSM Johnstone and everyone else was in the thick of it. I've missed out for not having been there, in the fatal contact. My anger is contradictory, and this compounds my anger.

In Kabul the tedious checking-in procedure is repeated for the Tristar flight to Brize Norton. A nurse escorts a man to the check-in desk; he's dressed in trainers, jeans and a colourful shirt, with his left arm now a fat cocoon of immaculate white bandage. He's the CSM from the UAV team, a casualty of the fatal contact. He recognises me and we chat briefly.

His gruff Mancunian voice is very chirpy. 'I reckon I'll get at least two hundred grand in compensation for this,' he says, pointing his chin to the stump. 'I'm fockin' made!'

On the plane, I stare out of the port-side window, struggling to avoid conversing with an over-friendly officer from ISAF headquarters.

'How's it going in Helmand?' he asks

'It's a disaster,' I reply, staggered that he doesn't already know this.

'A catastrophe,' I continue, as he widens his eyes in surprise. 'We've blundered into Sangin and other places and achieved fuck-all . . . The whole reconstruction bit is just nonsense, it's non-existent on the ground, it's just not there. Going into the north is a blunder, a full-on military blunder and all the blokes can do now is fight to survive.'

He's taken aback by my response and the conversation dies. Disconsolate, I resume my window-staring in silence. After so much uncertainty over the previous months, certain truths are now starkly clear. I know that this is the start of terrible violence and that we've lost this campaign before it's even started. I know that soldiers dying in Helmand is pointless. I know that our artillery shells and Apache helicopters will, in a tragic replay of Soviet clumsiness, kill countless Afghan civilians while pursuing a nebulous enemy. I feel foolish for believing so wholeheartedly that in coming to Afghanistan I would be part of something intelligent, meaningful and constructive. I know now that our entry into Helmand has been ignorant, clumsy and destructive – a vainglorious folly.

My faith in the establishment to which I have devoted my life for more than five years has proved to be ill-founded. I feel angry at this betrayal, and angry at my own foolishness. A feeling – not a decision, but a slowly rising knowledge – comes to me that I will leave the Army and voice my anger.

The Hindu Kush spreads below us, an unending carpet of miniature brown peaks. Casting my mind back to Rich Holmes's funeral, I swear at the thought of more funerals to come.

*

With the death of Captain Jim Phillipson, Sangin exploded into violence. The District Centre, occupied by the Parachute Regiment, became the scene of the fiercest fighting experienced by the British Army since the Korean war.

In late June Captain David Patten and Sergeant Paul Bartlett were killed near FOB Robinson.

In early July Corporal Peter Thorpe and Lance Corporal Jabron Hashmi were killed on the roof of the Sangin District Centre and Private Damian Jackson was killed in the town.

In August Corporal Bryan Budd was killed in the town during an action for which he was posthumously awarded the Victoria Cross.

In September Lance Corporal Luke McCulloch was killed in the town.

*

London, October 2006. The Major General's door is unmoving. In a sweaty state of trepidation I replay back and forth the events of the last few weeks.

After returning from Afghanistan I headed off alone to travel across Asia, using the three months' 'terminal' leave due to me at the end of my service. Just before departing, however, I spoke to a journalist about Afghanistan. I was forthright; I told her exactly what I thought of the situation, and about my personal decision to leave the Army.

Ten days later I was buying horses in Kazakhstan, cutting a deal with a toothless farmer for a pair of stocky ponies that I intended to ride the length of the country into neighbouring Uzbekistan.

'I'll be back tomorrow to collect,' I told the chuckling farmer, as I handed over grubby wads of the local currency.

Dossing down that night in the house of an American Peace Corps worker whom I'd met in the local town, I checked my e-mail – the last opportunity to do so for probably a couple of months. Stacked with messages, my in-box told a frantic chronology of events. The write-up of my interview with the journalist had made the front page of last weekend's *Sunday Times*, with my picture splashed across the front page of its *News Review* section. On the following days the story had become front-page news in the rest of the national press and had also been seized upon by American and international networks. I was amazed by the magnitude of interest generated by a member of the Army publicly criticising the campaign in Afghanistan. Perhaps Kazakhstan wasn't remote enough for me to get away with breaking Army rules that forbid speaking to the media.

A dozen e-mails from the likes of ITN News and *The Today Programme* requested interviews and another dozen, mostly from fellow officers serving in Afghanistan and Iraq, offered support. There were also a couple from the furious Scots Guards Adjutant. 'Where are you? You must return to London immediately' was followed by: 'Telephone the Commanding Officer now ... The longer you ignore this message, the more serious the consequences.'

Twenty-four hours later I was on an Air Astana flight bound for Amsterdam, having resold the ponies to the toothless farmer to his utter delight and considerable gain, and spent the cash on the airfare. I'd weighed up the odds and decided against doing a runner; I didn't want to be declared 'absent without leave' and face arrest on my eventual return to the UK, as hinted at by the Scots Guards Commanding Officer when I spoke to him on a crackling Peace Corps satellite phone:

'This has made waves at a ministerial level . . . The Chief of the Defence Staff has personally demanded your retrieval . . .'

Landing at London Gatwick, bearded and filthy in my riding breeches, I returned immediately to Wellington Barracks to be charged with misconduct. I'd broken the rules by expressing my opinion on the British strategy in Afghanistan, to the possible detriment of that campaign, went the official line.

For the next month I endured the tedious machinations of the Army's disciplinary system. I explained myself repeatedly, an investigation was made, and professional reports and character references were gathered from various sources. Finally my case file was ready to go before the Major General for his judgement.

The Aide-de-Camp answers the phone again. This time it's from next door.

'The General will see you now,' says the ADC, gesturing with a forced smile towards the tall oak door.

Moving into the huge and richly furnished office, I close the door softly behind me. Slamming my heels left-right onto the floor, I stand to attention in a formal halt before the Major General's desk.

'Leo, how nice to see you,' says the Major General, without irony. A rangy giant of a man, his charm and good humour are legendary throughout the Foot Guards. For a moment I'm also really pleased to see him, before assuming a face of contrition.

He opens my case file: an inch-thick stack of papers in a

lever-arch folder. Pulling it free of its binding, he arranges the different annexes before him, his long artistic fingers nudging them into a well-ordered line across the desk top. Full-length portraits of William and Mary stare down at us from behind the Major General. I glance at the red handkerchief billowing from the breast pocket of his dark suit; I'm glad I'm equally well dressed.

'Of course you understand the magnitude of this,' he says, looking up and pulling off his glasses. 'Just how, exactly, did it happen?'

I explain, with frankness, well practised now after a month of repetition.

The Major General nods. 'So your views are, would you say, correctly represented in this article?' he asks, his fingers coming to rest on the *Sunday Times News Review*. I can see my bearded face upside down on its cover.

'Yes, sir, verbatim.' I like him but I feel no regret at all. Perhaps he even *agrees* with me?

'I have little choice but to give you a Letter of Censure . . . The impact of which would of course be much greater were you not leaving the service.'

'Yes, sir,' I reply solemnly. Inwardly I'm not bothered; it means I couldn't command the Scots Guards were I to stay in the Army and I'm barred from joining the Foreign Office, but I'd sooner drive a bus.

'It would be very unfortunate if this were to appear in the media,' the Major General continues softly.

'Yes, sir,' I reply.

'Given that you've waited a month for this interview you may, I think, resume your leave.'

'Thank you very much, sir,' I reply, allowing the hint of a smile to appear. I'm *sure* he agrees with the article.

'You will return to Asia?'

'Yes, sir.'

Emerging into the autumn sun on Horse Guards Parade, I loosen my tie and breath deeply. I know that I'll head east again, as soon as possible, but only after I've set down a few things in writing.

Postcript. CSM Tommy Johnstone, of the Army Air Corps, was Mentioned in Despatches for his bravery while serving in Helmand Province.

Epilogue

Since the first British soldier was killed in action in Sangin in June 2006, the violence sweeping Helmand Province has killed dozens of British soldiers and hundreds of their Afghan National Army colleagues. Countless Afghan civilians have died in the crossfire, Afghan homes lie ruined by British artillery shells and opium production is at an all-time high. The British intervention in Helmand Province has been not only a blundering catastrophe, but a violent tragedy. It is still unfolding as I write.

The soldiers of the Helmand Task Force are suffering a ferocious enemy onslaught in the northern towns of Sangin, Naw Zad, Musa Qala and Kajaki and in the southern town of Garmsir. More than fifty servicemen have been killed and eighty-five wounded in action. Currently, small groups of soldiers are still fighting and dying in these locations.

These troops, under great pressure, have been unswervingly professional and brave. Sadly they are the unfortunate victims of strategic confusion generated by a command hierarchy that is unworthy of their trust.

When, in late 2005, the UK agreed to intervene in Helmand Province as part of NATO's increased engagement with Afghanistan, the challenge could not have been greater. For the previous four years, since the fall of the Taliban, Helmand (like most other provinces lying beyond the reach of the fledgling government in Kabul) had been left untouched by any form of central governance. Opium barons and lawlessness held sway.

The plan at the outset of the British deployment into Helmand in April 2006 was based around a 'comprehensive approach'. Well-documented in British military doctrine, the essence of this approach is that the military must act in concert with other players to achieve results. Another doctrinal inspiration was the 'inkspot' strategy, relating to a successful counter-insurgency conducted by the British in Malaya in the 1950s.

The plan was simple: within an inkspot haven of security the comprehensive approach would be established to nurture civil development and governance. Three lines of operation – security, development and governance – were to run concurrently, all interdependent and of equal importance. The Army secures the inkspot, allowing the Department for International Development (DfID) to initiate development. The Foreign and Commonwealth Office (FCO) would help the Afghans govern themselves and, crucially, drive the counter-narcotics campaign. The overall effect would be the reconstruction of civil society.

Reconstruction is desperately needed as civil society has been all but destroyed by incessant violence in Afghanistan during the last thirty years. A decade of all-out war against the invading Soviet army was followed by inter-factional fighting among the victorious Mujahideen groups, the rise of the Taliban, and their removal by a US-led Coalition, allied to the Northern Alliance. This violence has left the population deeply traumatised, exploited by opium barons, and denied access to healthcare, education, justice and other fundamental provisions of a developed, civilised society.

The Helmand inkspot was to be a limited triangular area of operations based around the provincial capital Lashkar Gah, the nearby town of Gereshk, and the newly created hub of British operations, the dust-ridden and far-flung Camp Bastion.

While the three lines of operation are interdependent and must occur simultaneously, they must also, as a matter of course, be preceded by a rigorous intelligence assessment of the target area and possibly by some form of information campaign. The key to success is winning the hearts and minds of the civil population through tangible developmental improvements such as basic healthcare and education. As success is consolidated the inkspot slowly grows, on a timescale marked in years rather than months.

The insurgent will of course fight this process, but deprived of civilian sympathy and denied freedom of movement he will only manage occasional acts of terrorism within the inkspot. Overwhelming targeted violence is the just response to such a threat, because the safety of the civilian population and their trust in the security forces is quite simply the be-all and end-all of the entire strategy. High-intensity war-fighting on a broad front, with civilians dying as collateral damage, is therefore a nightmare scenario of failure. Tragically this has come to pass in Helmand.

In the early stages of the deployment a spectacular digression from the comprehensive approach was made: the British command deployed small teams of British and Afghan troops to occupy remote northern towns of the Province.

These teams were deployed despite the fact that DfID and the FCO had absolutely no effective practical measures in place in northern Helmand. Two of the three lines of operation were missing. The troops, deployed in isolation, had no real means of winning hearts and minds; they could offer no practical developmental improvements and were unable to even state the British policy on opium production. Their presence soon became antagonistic; like honeypot targets, they attracted anyone fancying a crack at the invading infidel, seemingly no better than the Russians before them.

Once attacked, these teams were quickly sucked into lethal high-intensity war-fighting, which is still raging. Over-exposed and often outgunned on the ground, British troops have had to rely on close air support (British Apache attack helicopters and American A10 'Tank-busters') and artillery (105mm guns). This escalation of violence is their primary means of survival. But these weapons are not the surgical tools best used by the counter-insurgent: they are blunt-edged, indiscriminate and have killed numerous civilians.

The decision to scatter small groups of soldiers across the north of Helmand, in isolation, in an intelligence vacuum and with complete disregard for the most basic tenets of counter-insurgency was, quite simply, a gross military blunder. Its exact provenance is uncertain, but it was probably the result of political pressure from London and Kabul, requests from the Provincial Governor keen to extend his authority, and an impatient overconfidence within the British command.

It would be absurd to suggest that war-fighting on a broad front, supposedly 'drawing out' the Taliban, is a necessary prelude to the reconstructive phases of the comprehensive approach. Violence begets violence, as thousands of new local recruits, previously uninterested in radical Islam, are drawn to the Taliban cause, hungry for revenge after civilian deaths in their communities.

Because of the failure to properly establish security anywhere in Helmand, developmental reconstruction work is occurring nowhere. Without guaranteed personal safety, DfID and FCO personnel remain in their compounds, if indeed they are present at all. As the Governor of Helmand pointed out to the BBC in October 2006: 'Promises to get projects up and running have not been kept and there hasn't even been a DfID representative in Helmand for two months ...'

Security cannot exist without development and development cannot begin without security. The Helmand Task Force is achieving neither.

Afghanistan produces 92 per cent of the world's opium. According to the United Nations' *Afghan Opium Survey 2006*, Helmand Province has a phenomenal 42 per cent share of that production. Poppy-growing *is* the economy and the livelihood of the vast majority of the rural population. Exploited by middlemen, these poor cash-croppers have no other choice. The opium industry is closely linked to funding the Taliban. It is therefore incredible that the FCO failed to carry out any kind of *practical* counter-narcotics strategy at the start of the Helmand campaign. Despite counter-narcotics being a British responsibility for Afghanistan as a whole (under the Bonn agreement of 2001) there was, at the start of the campaign, no functional plan at the provincial level. Unless poppy-growers are informed about viable alternatives and what their future might hold, they will only assume that their livelihoods are under threat and react with hostility. Months into the campaign, senior planning officers in the Helmand Task Force headquarters were unable to articulate the British counter-narcotics plan. Meanwhile, the narco-economy is booming: by British Foreign Minister Kim Howells's own admission Helmand's poppy production hit a record high in 2006, with a staggering 162 per cent increase from the previous year.

The British face a broad spectrum of opposition in Helmand. The enemy cannot simply be described as 'Taliban'. A Helmand poppy-farmer can hang up his hoe over lunchtime, pick up his Kalashnikov, shoot at the British and be back in the fields for the rest of the afternoon. The farmer has nothing ideologically in common with the Taliban but they may share a common aim, for example the absence of foreign troops, for different motives. If the real enemy is hard to identify and looks very similar to local civilians, intelligence-gathering must compensate for this. Unfortunately, in the early stages of the deployment, in places like Sangin British troops suffered from a worrying lack of sound intelligence. This was due probably to the fact that the mechanisms in place for its gathering and analysis were run by desk-bound staff officers lacking field experience of

Afghanistan and devoid of reliable sources. The result was a dangerous ignorance of local tribal, political and social structures, and the intricate manner in which these interweave with Islamic radicalism and opium production.

Looking forward, I firmly believe that a smaller British military presence would be much less offensive and potentially more effective than a large conventional force. Small numbers of determined Afghan-experts, having spent years in the country and gained a profound knowledge of local culture, language and politics, might discreetly be able to guide the Afghans in solving their problems largely themselves. This approach has started in a very minor way; the bearded members of the operational mentoring teams seek to enhance the capability of the Afghan National Army. Their effectiveness is limited by the high turnover of personnel (in accordance with the British six-month tour cycle), but the improvement of the ANA is a sensible platform on which to base an eventual but very distant military exit strategy.

This 'discrete effect' approach should apply equally to the military's partners in the comprehensive approach. Counternarcotics and development must be driven forward in the field by risk-taking practical operators, disinclined to stay at their desks in Lashkar Gah or Kandahar.

Discrete effort inside Afghanistan will, however, be futile without action at the strategic, international level. Diplomacy beyond the porous and lawless border with Pakistan should aim to inhibit the opium market, and stem the flow of well-equipped young 'jihadis' desperate for martyrdom against NATO soldiers. Resolving these issues is a fundamental precursor to future success in Helmand Province.

The British forces in Helmand, unsupported by the other arms of government and plunged hastily into isolated peril, have lost the battle for hearts and minds before they had a proper chance to win. In 2006 more than 4,000 civilians were killed 'collaterally' in Afghanistan, many in Helmand. This lost ground will take a generation to regain.

We cannot fight our way to a solution. A peaceful, developed Helmand cannot be won by the sword, and the longer we try, the greater the tragedy.

Leo Docherty

March 2007

LOVE LESSONS

www.**kidsatrandomhouse**.co.uk

Love Lessons

Illustrated by Nick Sharratt

DOUBLEDAY
London·New York·Toronto·Sydney·Auckland

LOVE LESSONS
A DOUBLEDAY BOOK 0 385 60836 5

Published in Great Britain by Doubleday,
an imprint of Random House Children's Books

This edition published 2005

1 3 5 7 9 10 8 6 4 2

Text copyright © Jacqueline Wilson, 2005
Illustrations copyright © Nick Sharratt, 2005

The right of Jacqueline Wilson to be identified as the author of this
work has been asserted in accordance with the Copyright, Designs
and Patents Act 1988.

Papers used by Random House Children's Books are natural,
recyclable products made from wood grown in sustainable forests.
The manufacturing processes conform to the environmental
regulations of the country of origin.

Typeset in Century Schoolbook by
Palimpsest Book Production Limited, Polmont, Stirlingshire

RANDOM HOUSE CHILDREN'S BOOKS
61–63 Uxbridge Road, London W5 5SA
A division of The Random House Group Ltd

RANDOM HOUSE AUSTRALIA (PTY) LTD
20 Alfred Street, Milsons Point, Sydney,
New South Wales 2061, Australia

RANDOM HOUSE NEW ZEALAND LTD
18 Poland Road, Glenfield, Auckland 10, New Zealand

RANDOM HOUSE (PTY) LTD
Endulini, 5A Jubilee Road, Parktown 2193, South Africa

THE RANDOM HOUSE GROUP Limited Reg. No. 954009
www.**kids**at**randomhouse**.co.uk

A CIP catalogue record for this book is available
from the British Library.

Printed and bound in Great Britain
by Mackays of Chatham plc, Chatham, Kent

For Mary, Rachel and Rebecca

I hate my dad.

I know lots of teenage girls say that but they don't really mean it. Well, I don't *think* they do. I don't really know any other teenage girls. That's one of the reasons why I hate Dad. He keeps me a virtual prisoner.

I'm interrogated if I slip down the road to Krisha's Korner Shop. I'm not allowed to go into town by myself. I can't go to see any films. I can't eat in McDonald's.

Dad even fussed about me making a simple bus ride by myself to go to Miss Roberts for maths tuition. He took my sister Grace and me out of school ages ago, when I'd just gone into the Juniors and she was still at the finger-painting stage. Dad said *he* was going to educate us.

1

We were left to get on with it for ages, but this summer we had a home visit from a Mr Miles, who was from some kind of education authority. He wanted to know what provision Dad was making for my GCSE coursework. Dad said he didn't believe in examinations. Mr Miles smiled through Dad's tirade, obviously having heard it all before. He looked at Grace and me when Dad ran out of steam.

'What do you want to do when you're older, Prudence and Grace?' he asked.

Grace mumbled something about working with animals. Dad won't let us have any proper pets because he says he's allergic to them. Grace has a lot of secret, unsatisfactory pets, like the blackbird in the garden and the toads in the compost heap and for a while she kept a wormery hidden under her bed. Grace's pets are not exactly cuddly.

'You'll certainly need to pass lots of exams if you want to be a vet,' said Mr Miles.

Dad snorted. 'You'll find our Grace has got no more brains than a donkey,' he said unkindly. 'She'll get a job in a shop somewhere and be happy enough.'

'In your bookshop?'

'She can help sell the books, but I doubt she's up to the business side of things,' said Dad. 'But Prudence can do all the cataloguing and buying and book fairs.'

'Is that what you want to do, Prudence – run your father's business?' said Mr Miles.

I swallowed. 'I – I'd like to go to art college,' I said.

Dad glared at me. 'For goodness' sake, I've told you to forget that nonsense. You don't need to go away to college to learn drawing and painting; you can do that already.'

'But I *want* to go, Dad.'

Dad was furious with me for arguing in front of Mr Miles, but decided not to pursue it. 'All right, all right, go to art college, waste three years, see for yourself,' he said. He nodded triumphantly at Mr Miles. 'I guarantee she can pass her art GCSE standing on her head.'

'I dare say,' said Mr Miles. 'But I think you'll find art colleges require quite a few GCSEs, plus three good A-levels. You're going to have to make more provision for your daughters' education, Mr King, especially now Prudence is fourteen. Otherwise we might have to pursue the matter through the courts.'

'The courts!' said Mum, panicking.

'You've got no power to do any such thing,' said Dad, hands on his hips, his chin jutting. 'You can't stop parents home-educating their children.'

'Not if they've been home-educated right from the start. But your girls have attended school in the past, so I think you'll find we have every power. However, let's hope we can avoid any unpleasant action. We all want what's best for Prudence and Grace.'

Dad seemed sure Mr Miles was bluffing, but

nevertheless he fixed up for me to go to this Miss Roberts for maths tuition on Wednesday afternoons.

I only went once. It was unbearable.

Miss Roberts used to teach maths at a girls' school way back in the sixties. She seemed preserved in that time, still teasing her limp grey hair into a bouffant style. Her pink scalp showed through alarmingly. I kept staring at it as she bent over me, trying to explain some supposedly simple point about algebra.

I couldn't understand any of it. I wrote down random letters of the alphabet but I couldn't tease any meaning from them. I expect letters to arrange themselves into words. If I'm doing sums I need numbers – though I'm actually useless with numbers too. I can't always add up accurately. The shop takings rarely balance on a Saturday when I help out.

Miss Roberts tried hard to be patient with me. She explained it over and over again, raising her voice and speaking very s-l-o-w-l-y. Then she switched to geometry in despair. I could draw wobbly circles with her old compass and construct reasonable squares and rectangles with my own ruler but I didn't know what any of them *meant*.

I paid her the twenty pounds for the tuition and she gave me a cup of tea (the milk was so old it floated in little flecks on the tan surface) and a stale custard cream.

'Don't look so woebegone, Prudence,' she said.

'Your father says you're a very bright girl. I'm sure you'll catch on in no time.'

I made an extreme effort to swallow the sour milk-biscuity paste in my mouth and thanked her politely.

I didn't go back. For the last three Wednesdays I've walked into town and spent my tuition fee. Sixty whole pounds.

I've never had so much money in my life before. Dad gives Grace and me one pound every Saturday. He behaves as if he's bestowing solid gold upon us, and even has the nerve to lecture us, telling us not to waste it on rubbish. I've always saved mine up to buy sketchpads and soft pencils and coloured crayons, bought one by one.

Grace spends hers all at once on sweets – a bar of chocolate or two, and a handful of gummy snakes. She gollops the chocolate in one go but she keeps the snakes, lining them up on the arm of the sofa, red and yellow and green like a slithery traffic light. She plays with them, giving them names and personalities, but she can't help licking them affectionately so that they all get very sticky. She tries to save them till Sunday, though she sometimes can't stop herself biting off a head or two on Saturday night.

Grace isn't three or four, as you might expect. She is eleven years old and very weird.

I know I am very weird too. I can't seem to help it. I don't know how to be a proper teenager. I bought a couple of teenage magazines out of my stolen tuition money. They were astonishing, especially the problem pages. I knew I didn't look anything like girls my own age, but I didn't realize my experiences were so different.

I've had *no* experiences; *they've* had plenty. The girls writing to the problem pages spoke a different language and behaved as if they were from a totally different planet. They wore astonishing clothes and got up to astonishing things with their boyfriends. I read these letters feeling hot, my heart beating.

The only letters I could identify with in any way were the ones where the girls moaned about their mums and dads. They said they couldn't stick their parents. Their mums wouldn't let them have a nose stud or platform heels; their dads nagged about bad marks at school and got mad if they didn't come home till midnight.

'They should try having *my* mum and dad,' I muttered, as I flicked through them by torchlight under the bedcovers.

'What?' Grace said blearily, propping herself up on one elbow. 'Are you still awake? What are you doing?'

'Just reading my book. Go back to sleep,' I said.

But Grace has bat ears. She heard the rustle of the pages. 'That's not a book, it's a magazine! Let me see!' She leaned over from her bed. She leaned far too eagerly and fell out with a yell.

'Shut *up*, Grace!'

'Ouch! I've banged my elbow – and my knee!' Grace whimpered.

'Ssh!'

'It hurts,' she whispered. She came scrabbling into my bed. 'Please let me see, Prue.'

'You won't tell Mum?' I hissed.

Grace sometimes has terrible attacks of conscience when she worries and frets about some tiny little thing she's done wrong and then suddenly blurts it all out to Mum when they're having a cuddle. Grace is far too big for cuddles now but she still wants them. She's like a large lollopy dog, desperate to be patted all the time.

I didn't waste my breath warning her not to tell Dad. Even Grace isn't that mad.

'I swear,' she said. Then she whispered all the worst words she knew, swearing like a trooper. We might live like princesses locked in a tower but you can't go down the street without hearing boys blinding away and drivers yelling. Also, very strangely, Dad sometimes swears when he's in one of his tempers, foul words frothing out of his mouth. If Mum or Grace or I ever said just one of those words he would murder us.

I showed Grace the magazines. She handled them reverently, as if they were the finest first folios, easing over the pages and smoothing them out. She looked at all the photos of teenage girls and stroked their clothes longingly. She started reading the problem page and then snorted with shocked laughter.

'Ssh!'

'What's this girl going *on* about? What does she *mean*?'

7

'Oh, for heaven's sake, Grace, you know the facts of life,' I said, although I wasn't clear what a lot of it meant either.

I had secretly looked at several volumes of Victorian erotica which Dad bought in a book auction, presumably by mistake. I found them right at the bottom of the box, under a Norton set of the Brontë sisters. They featured a bizarre vicar, Reverend Knightly, with a large congregation of ever so lusty ladies. There were extraordinary colour plates showing the vicar cavorting in his dog collar and very little else. I found them comical but not particularly disturbing. They were adults, figments of someone's imagination, and one hundred and fifty years old. The girls in these magazines were real.

'Oh I *wish* I had a boyfriend,' said Grace. 'Do you think Dad will ever let us go out with boys, Prue?'

'I don't *want* to go out with boys,' I said, not entirely truthfully.

For years and years I'd had a private pretend friend, an interesting and imaginative girl my own age called Jane. She started when I read the first few chapters of *Jane Eyre*. She stepped straight out of the pages and into my head. She no longer led her own Victorian life with her horrible aunt and cousins. She shared *my* life with my demented father.

Jane was better than a real sister. She wasn't babyish and boring like Grace. We discussed books and pored over pictures and painted watercolours together, and we talked endlessly about everything. Sometimes we didn't talk silently enough. I knew my lips moved and occasionally I started muttering without realizing. Grace knew I made up imaginary games inside my head and resented it.

'You're doing it!' she'd say when I muttered, giving me a nudge. 'Tell *me*, Prue, go on. Make it up for me.'

'Make up your own games,' I said, which was unfair, because she wasn't much good at it.

I'd started up a new and even more private pretend game recently, after Dad had taken Grace and me on an educational trip to the National Gallery in London. Dad had an old guidebook to the gallery and was all set to inform us relentlessly, but the gallery had long since rearranged all its rooms. Dad couldn't match up the text in his guidebook with any of the paintings and became more and more frustrated and irritable.

Grace barely looked at each painting, trudging with bent head, her feet dragging on the floor. She murmured obediently whenever Dad seemed to demand a response, but that was all.

I didn't say much either. I was flying through this new magical world of religious Renaissance painting, so pink and blue and glittery gold. It was as if I'd sprouted my own beautiful set of angels' wings. I'd always painted wings plain white, but now I saw they could be shaded from the palest pearl through deep rose and purple to the darkest midnight-blue tips. Some of the angels' wings were carefully co-ordinated with their gowns like matching accessories. Others had unusual, eccentric colour combinations like red and gold and black, with a white gown. One particular fashionista angel was strolling along the sandy path with a golden-haired boy about my age, holding a fish.

When we were little Dad used to read aloud to us every day from a large and unwieldy Victorian Bible. Dad had been very religious until he had a row with our vicar. He'd gently suggested to Dad that home-schooling was all very well, but Grace and I needed more of a social life so we could make some friends. Dad blew his top and had no time for the vicar, his church, or the entire Christian faith after that.

He put the Bible back on the shelves as stock. I was sorry when it sold, because I loved looking at the wonderful Doré illustrations. I remembered a lot of the Bible stories, so I knew that the boy with the fish and the angel friend was Tobias. He was dressed in colourful medieval garb, with dashing bright-red tights. I tried to imagine a modern teenage boy prancing about in scarlet stockings. Still, some boys wore their jeans skin-tight. The Tobias in the painting obligingly put on blue jeans and a white T-shirt and smiled at me.

He came home with me that day as my new imaginary friend. Poor Jane got elbowed into the background. Tobias and I read together, painted together, walked together, whispered together. He spoke softly right into my ear, his cheek very nearly brushing mine.

Now I imagined him kissing me, touching me, like the girls and their boyfriends in the magazines. But then I imagined real boys, with their foul mouths and grabbing hands, and I shuddered.

'I don't like boys,' I said.

'Boys like *you*, Prue,' said Grace. She sighed. 'It's not fair. I wish I was pretty like you so boys would turn round and stare at me.'

'I bet they only stare because I look such a freak,' I said.

Mum made most of our clothes from remnants from the Monday market stall. I'm fourteen years old and yet I have to wear demure little-girly dresses with short sleeves and swirly skirts. I have a red-and-white check, a baby blue with a little white flower motif, and a canary yellow piped with white. They are all embarrassingly awful.

Mum used to make appalling matching knickers when we were little, threaded with very unreliable elastic. Our baggy shop-bought white pants are only one degree better. Still, I have *proper* underwear now. I used my maths tuition money to buy a wonderful black bra with pink lace and a little pink rose, and two matching knickers, wispy little things a tenth of the size of my plain girls' pants.

I locked the bathroom and tried them on, standing precariously on the edge of the bath so I could peek at myself in the bathroom cabinet mirror. I loved the way they looked, the way they make *me* look.

I hadn't dared wear them yet under my awful dresses because Grace could so easily blab. I'd have to wash them out secretly myself rather than risk putting them in the laundry basket.

'Do we look like freaks?' Grace asked worriedly.

'Of course we do. Look at our clothes!'

Grace considered. 'I *like* my dresses, especially my pink one with the little panda pattern – it's so cute,' she said. 'Would you have liked that material for your dress, Prue?'

'No! I can't stick little pandas or teddies or bunny rabbits. For God's sake, I'm *fourteen*.'

'Do you think *I'm* too old to wear my panda dress?' Grace asked anxiously.

There was only one answer but I didn't want to upset her. 'I suppose your pink panda dress does still look quite sweet on you,' I lied valiantly.

'It's getting a bit small for me now anyway,' Grace sighed. '*All* my dresses are tight on me. I wish I wasn't getting so large and lumpy.'

'It's just a stage you go through. Puppy fat.'

'*You* didn't,' she sighed again. 'Dad keeps going on about me getting fat. He says I shouldn't eat so much. He says I'm greedy. Do you think I should go on a diet, Prue?'

'No! Take no notice of him. He just likes to nag, you know that. Anyway, you can't diet *just* yet. I've got you a surprise.'

I'd felt so mean spending all my tuition money on myself, though I knew Grace would never manage to keep any present I bought her properly hidden. The only way I could buy her a treat was to get her something edible, to be quickly consumed.

'A surprise!' said Grace, clapping her hands.

'Ssh! I was keeping it a secret, to cheer you up next time Dad goes off on one of his rants, but you might as well have it now.'

I climbed out of bed and went to scrabble in my knicker drawer. My hands found the flimsy satin and lace of my new underwear. I secretly stroked them in the dark, and then searched again until my fingers slid over the crackly cellophane of Grace's surprise.

'OK! Here we are!' I slipped back into bed and thrust my present into her hands.

'What *is* it?' she said, unable to see properly in the dark.

I flicked the torch on to show her.

'Oh *wow!*'

'Shut *up!* Do you want Dad to hear?' I said, nudging her.

'Sorry. But, oh Prue, it's so *sweet!*'

There's a special chocolate boutique in the shopping centre. It's Grace's all-time favourite shop even though she's never even set foot inside it. Mum buys chocolate off a market stall. It's always a funny make and past its sell-by date, but it's cheap, and that's all Mum cares about.

I was going to buy Grace a pound of posh

chocolates in a fancy box, but then I saw this big white chocolate bunny in the window, clutching an orange marzipan carrot. I knew she'd love it.

'What shall I call him? Peter Rabbit? Benjamin Bunny?'

'Can't you ever make up your *own* names, Grace?'

'You know I can't. *You* think up a lovely name for him.'

'There's not much point. You'll be chomping away at him in two seconds. Knowing you, there won't even be a little chocolate paw left by midnight.'

'I'm not going to eat him. He's far too wonderful. I'm going to keep him for ever,' said Grace, but her fat little fingers had already undone his ribbon and peeled off his cellophane. She sniffed his creamy ears ecstatically. 'Oh, he smells heavenly!'

'So eat him, silly. That's what he's for.'

'I *can't*! Well, perhaps I could eat his carrot? I don't want to spoil him. Still, maybe I could just lick one of his ears, to see what he tastes like?'

'Go for it, girl!'

Grace stuck out her tongue and licked. And licked again and again and again. And then all by themselves her teeth started chomping and the chocolate bunny was left disturbingly hard of hearing.

'Oooh!' Grace murmured blissfully. Then she shone the torch on him. She saw what she'd done. '*Oooh!*' she wailed, her tone changing.

'It's OK, just eat his head up quickly. It's what he's *for*.'

'But it's *spoiling* him. Why am I such a greedy guts? Look, he's got a horrible gap in his head now.'

'He's fine.'

'No he's not. I want him to be whole again,' Grace said, looking as if she might burst into tears.

'Well, his ears are in your tummy. If you gobble up the rest of him quickly then his body can join up with them, and they can squidge themselves together like plasticine. Then he'll be whole in your tummy and it will be his own private burrow.'

Grace giggled uncertainly, but started chomping on his chocolate head. She offered me one arm because she felt he could manage on three paws. I'd imagined him so vividly I felt a little worried myself. It was like feasting on a real pet rabbit.

'You eat your rabbit all up yourself, Gracie,' I said.

'It's the loveliest treat ever,' she said indistinctly, mouth crammed with chocolate. 'But when did you buy it?' She paused. The obvious hit her. '*Where did you get the money?*'

'Keep your voice down!'

'I'm *whispering*.'

Then we heard the bedroom door open along the landing. We held our breath. I snapped the torch off and Grace leaped into her own bed. We

15

heard footsteps: the pad and slap of old slippers.

'It's OK, it's only Mum,' I whispered.

We heard her padding right along the landing, past our bedroom, down the stairs to the first floor, above the shop. Each stair creaked as she stepped. Our mother is a heavy woman.

We heard her in the kitchen, opening the fridge door.

'She's having a midnight feast too,' I muttered.

'Not a patch on mine,' Grace whispered, daring to take another bite.

Mum came trudging up the stairs again, slower now, breathing heavily.

'Should I save a little piece of rabbit for Mum?' Grace asked.

'No!'

'But she loves chocolate.'

'Ssh!'

'Not now. In the morning,' Grace persisted.

'Shut up or she'll hear us.'

It was too late. The footsteps stopped outside our door.

'Girls? Are you awake?' Mum whispered.

'No!' Grace said, idiotically.

Mum opened our door and came shuffling into the room. 'You should have gone to sleep ages ago,' she said. She came over to Grace's bed and bent over her. 'Are you all right, lovie?'

'Yes, Mum,' said Grace.

'What about you, Prudence?'

'I'm fine,' I mumbled, giving a little yawn to make her think I was on the brink of sleep.

'Are you hungry, Mum?' Grace asked. 'We heard you go down to the kitchen.'

'I was just getting a glass of milk for your dad. He's not feeling too clever. He keeps getting these funny turns.' Mum sounded very anxious.

'He should go to the doctor,' I said.

'You know what your dad's like,' said Mum. 'Prudence, why don't you try talking to him? When he's in a good mood? He might just listen to you.'

I pulled a face in the dark. I hated being Dad's favourite. It didn't really mean much anyway. I couldn't get him to do anything he didn't want to do. No one could.

'I'll try mentioning the doctor,' I said. 'But I don't think it will work.'

'You're a good girl,' said Mum. 'Well, night-night, then.'

She kissed Grace, patted my shoulder awkwardly and then waddled out of our bedroom, her hand held stiffly in front of her so she wouldn't spill the milk.

'You are a moron, Grace,' I hissed.

'Sorry!' she said. She took another big bite of chocolate bunny. 'Oh yum yum, happy tum!' She fell asleep in mid-munch, and started snoring softly.

I lay awake for a while, talking to Tobias.

I woke early and had another quick read of the teenage magazines before smoothing them out and hiding them under my mattress. I rescued the crackly cellophane from the bed and hid that too. It would be stupid to risk chucking it in the bin. In his maddest moments Dad would rootle right through the rubbish, mostly to berate Mum for buying the wrong things.

I went and got washed and then dressed in the red-and-white-check girly number. I plaited a strand of hair with scarlet thread and fastened it with three red beads. I wished I had red lipstick, but Dad wouldn't let us use make-up. It was a chilly morning so I stuck on my red cardigan too, an odd hand-knitted garment with a pixie hood.

Grace was still sound asleep, her lips crusted

with white chocolate. I hoped she'd have a good wash before she came downstairs for breakfast.

I heard snoring from Mum and Dad's bedroom so I thought I'd have the kitchen to myself. I made myself a cup of tea and then settled down at the kitchen table with my sketchpad and new watercolours, trying to reproduce the Tobias and the Angel painting from memory.

The back door suddenly opened, making me jump violently. My paintbrush blotched red paint, so that poor Tobias grew a massive muscly thigh.

'Good morning, Little Red Riding Hood,' said Dad, tweaking the limp woolly hood on my back.

I struggled into Winsome Daughter mode.

'Hi, Dad,' I said brightly, mopping at my painting with a hunched-up Kleenex. I was terrified that Dad would see my paintbox was new, bought with my stolen maths tuition money.

'Made a mistake?' said Dad, putting the kettle on to boil again.

'Well, you startled me a bit. I thought you were still asleep.' I closed the paintbox quickly, so that he wouldn't notice the paint palettes were pristine.

'I was just having a breath of fresh air in the garden.' Dad breathed in and out ostentatiously. 'Clearing the cobwebs.'

He swung his arms and beat his chest to indicate fitness. In actual fact he looked awful, very pale and drawn, his face so tense I could see the muscles jumping in his eyelid and temple.

He was wearing his old sleeveless padded jerkin. It had once been green but now it was a strange sludge colour. His shirtsleeves were rolled up very neatly in his usual painstaking way. His exposed arms were so thin that his long ropy veins looked about to burst through the skin.

'Are you all right, Dad?' I asked.

'Of course I am!' He glared at me indignantly. 'I'm in the pink.'

There was nothing remotely pink about his grey skin.

'What about these funny turns?' I said, chancing it.

It was a mistake.

'What's your mother been saying? There's nothing whatsoever wrong with me. Just because I had one little dizzy spell. She makes such a fuss.' Dad's eyes narrowed suspiciously. 'I suppose she's recruited you in her get-me-to-the-doctor campaign?'

'What?' I said, feigning ignorance. I tried hard to change the subject. 'What do you want for breakfast, Dad? Toast? A poached egg?'

'Not if *you're* poaching it, Prudence. It'll either be raw and runny or hard as a bullet,' said Dad, putting the poaching saucepan on the stove himself. 'You want to take some lessons from your mother.'

Dad had been a confirmed bachelor until Mum won him over with her Yorkshire puddings and treacle tarts. I knew she was an excellent cook but I didn't like that kind of old-fashioned

British food, all the pies and pastries and sauces and custards constructed from scratch. I hankered after convenience food and takeaways.

Grace and I knew every meal choice on the menu of the Kam Tong Chinese restaurant and the Ruby Curry House on our parade of shops but we'd never been allowed to eat there. We'd never even been able to order from Pete's Pizza takeaway round the corner, although Grace and I had spent ages choosing the perfect combination of toppings from the leaflet that came through the door. The only takeaway food we ever had was fish and chips once a month, and we'd even missed out on that recently because Dad had a bilious attack and blamed it on 'that greasy muck'.

I watched Dad fussing around with the poacher. He held an egg in either hand. 'You'll have one too, Prue?'

'No thanks, Dad.'

He tutted. 'You could do with the protein. You don't eat enough – unlike your tubby little sister.'

'Don't tell Grace she's tubby, Dad, she hates it,' I said.

'Don't *you* tell me how to talk to my own daughter, Miss Saucebox,' said Dad, poking me in the back. Then he patted my shoulder to show he was only joking. He leaned over, peering at my picture. 'That's not bad, girl,' he said.

'Not bad' is high praise from Dad. I couldn't help glowing.

'Our little trip to the National Gallery obviously inspired you,' Dad said proudly.

'It was wonderful. So, do you really think I'm good at art, Dad?'

'You know you are,' he said. 'In fact we *might* just collaborate when you're a wee bit older. You could design the dust wrapper for my Magnum Opus.'

Dad has been writing this so-called book ever since I was born. There are odd pages and half chapters all round the flat, typed on Dad's ancient Remington portable and scribbled over again and again with his cramped copperplate corrections. I've read pieces here and there and can't make sense of any of it. It's supposed to be a history of the world, but Dad seems mostly concerned with Kingtown, where we live, and how it's changed for the worse over the last thirty years.

Mum always arranges the discarded pages reverently, as if they're Ten Commandment tablets straight from God. She calls it Dad's Magnum Opus too, without a hint of irony. When Grace was a bit younger she thought Dad was writing about ice creams and showed a passing interest until I explained that Magnum Opus is Latin for 'great work'. Now we have a private running joke that Dad is writing an encyclopaedia of ice creams and we invent new extracts covering exotic flavours.

I decided I'd tell her Dad's idea and design a private dust wrapper for her amusement. Dad would be sitting in our bookshop with a Magnum in one hand, a Cornetto in the other, with Grace and me on either side of him carrying trays of ice-cream tubs for him to sample.

Dad saw me smiling and misunderstood. 'I'm not joking, Prudence. I really think you'd be good enough one day.'

I took a deep breath. Golden opportunity time!

'Maybe I'd need a little training, Dad,' I said casually, as if I didn't really care.

Dad raised his eyebrows and sighed. 'I'm not sending you to blooming art school,' he said. 'How many times do I have to get it into your thick head? Now don't go all droopy-drawers on me. You can paint as much as you like in your spare time. Anyway, they don't *paint* at art school now, they just faff around with blocks of concrete and dead animals and pretend all that crap is *creative*.'

I didn't bother replying. I stared at my painting of Tobias and the Angel. They smiled at me sympathetically with their rose-madder lips.

'If you've set your heart on further education, then you might as well go to a proper university,' said Dad. 'We'll show that interfering berk from the education authority. You'll pass all his exams with flying colours. How are you getting on with your maths tuition?'

I blinked. 'Fine, Dad,' I said quickly.

'I thought you said you couldn't understand a word she said?' Dad said suspiciously.

'And *you* said I just needed to apply myself – and I have,' I said. 'Dad, I'm sure your poached egg's ready. I'll make a pot of tea.'

I clattered around, and felt very relieved when Mum came thudding downstairs in her old pink mohair dressing gown. She's been wearing it ever since I can remember. It was a mistake right from the start. She looks like giant walking candyfloss.

'You two are early birds,' she said brightly. 'Oh, are you making breakfast, Prue? You're a good girl. Poached eggs – mm, lovely.'

'No, she's not making the poxy poached eggs; *I* am. And mine's ready now, but I suppose you want to nab it, so I'll just have to start all over again for mine,' said Dad.

'Oh no, dear, you have it. I'll make my own,' Mum twittered.

They started a totally pointless argument about eggs, while I packed up my painting and made tea and toast for four, thankful that I'd somehow managed to skirt round the maths tuition inquisition.

I relaxed too soon. We were still sitting at the breakfast table fifteen minutes later, Mum fussing, Dad irritated, Grace in her teddy pyjamas sleepily scoffing half a packet of cornflakes, when we heard the post come through the shop letter box.

'More blooming bills,' said Dad. 'Run and fetch them, Prudence.'

I ran. I fetched. I didn't even think to sort

through the little wad of envelopes. I saw there was one white handwritten envelope but I didn't wonder who it could be from.

I'd written a very good showy essay for Dad on the significance of letters in Victorian fiction – and yet I was thick enough to hand it straight to him. Dad shuffled the envelopes, opening them with his eggy knife, chucking several bills straight into the bin.

'We can't just ignore them, Bernard,' Mum said anxiously.

'Yes we can,' said Dad.

'But we're going to have to pay *some*time.'

'I don't know what with,' said Dad, flapping another sheet of paper at her. 'This is from the bank. "Overdraft . . . not acceptable . . . blah-di-blah." Jumped up little penpusher. I don't need *him* to point out my financial circumstances, thanks very much.'

That letter went in the bin too. Mum twitched, peering over at it, ready to whisk it out the minute Dad left the room.

He binned the next letter too, barely reading it.

'What was that about, dear?' Mum asked anxiously.

'That interfering creep Miles from the education authority. He's still banging on about Prudence's GCSE coaching. Demanding details, tutors' names, timetables! God almighty!'

'Well, that's OK, dear. We've got Prue started at Miss Roberts's. Then maybe we can manage

25

some science tuition later on. But you'd better write and let him know. Just in case he might turn nasty.'

'Let him try! Now, what's this?' said Dad. He slit open the white envelope, took out the sheet of paper and read the letter. He sat very still.

'Prudence?' he said quietly.

My heart started thudding under my red-and-white checks. 'Yes?'

'This is a letter from Miss Roberts,' Dad said ominously.

I swallowed. Grace nudged up close to me.

'Oh dear,' said Mum. 'Doesn't she think Prue's been making any progress?'

'Well. You could say that,' said Dad, spinning it out. His whole body was tensed, ready to spring.

'Now don't go getting cross with her, Bernard. It's not her fault she finds maths a puzzle. I'm sure she's doing her best,' said Mum.

'Yes, she's doing her best, all right,' said Dad, his voice rising. His pale face flushed purple. 'Doing her best to make a monkey out of me!'

He shouted it, spit spraying into the air. Then he wavered, wobbling sideways so that he had to clutch the table.

'Don't get so het up, please,' Mum begged. 'Are you having another funny turn?'

'Yes, I am – and it's no blooming wonder!' Dad said, through clenched teeth. He leaned over the table at me. 'How *dare* you!' he yelled, thumping the old scratched pine so hard that all the plates and knives and spoons rattled.

26

Grace reached out and held my hand under the table.

'What has she *done*, Bernard?' Mum asked. 'Has this Miss Roberts complained about her? Maybe she's simply too strict for our Prue.'

'Miss Roberts hasn't complained, as such. She's simply a little perturbed. She hasn't seen hide nor hair of Prudence for the last three weeks.'

'What?' said Mum. 'But – but why? Did you get lost, Prue? Why didn't you go?'

'Well?' Dad shouted, leaning so far over the table his face was nearly touching mine.

'I went once and I couldn't understand a thing. I just didn't see the point,' I muttered.

'I can't believe I'm hearing this!' Dad bellowed. 'Why didn't you come and tell me, after your one obviously disastrous visit?'

'I didn't want to,' I said, right into his face.

'You didn't want to. Even though you knew Mr Miles is all set to leap into action and slam your mother and me behind bars for not giving you a proper education?'

'He won't put us in prison! Will he?' Mum said weakly.

'Of course you won't go to prison, Mum.'

'Oh, Miss Know-It-All! Only you know damn all, even though you think you're so smart. You need to get to grips with maths, even if you're just going to waste your time at art college. Remember that, missy. You thought you could swan off and do your own thing, tell bare-faced

27

lies to your own father, waste everyone's time
and money—'

He stopped short, his mouth still working
silently though he'd run out of words.

'Bernard? Do calm down – you're getting
yourself in such a state. You're making yourself
ill!' said Mum, catching hold of his arm.

He brushed her away as if she was some
irritating insect. He focused on me. His face was
still purple. Even his eyes were bloodshot with
his rage. 'What about my money?' he screamed.
'What have you done with my eighty pounds?'

'Sixty. I paid the first time.'

'Don't you dare quibble with me! Sixty, eighty,
whatever. Hand it over immediately, do you hear
me?'

'I can't.'

Dad struggled to draw breath. He looked as
if his head was about to explode, shooting eyes,
teeth, tongue all over the table. 'I said *hand it
over immediately!*'

'I can't, Dad. I've spent it,' I said.

Dad reeled. 'You've spent eighty pounds of my
money?' he gasped.

'Sixty pounds, Dad. Yes. I'm sorry,' I said
weakly.

'Whatever did you spend it on, Prudence?' Mum
whispered.

I swallowed, unable to say.

'She spent it on me. On chocolate. Lots and
lots and lots of chocolate,' Grace gabbled
desperately.

'I might have known. You greedy little fool!' said Dad in disgust. 'So you stuffed your great gut with *my* hard-earned money.'

I was suddenly so angry I wasn't frightened of Dad any more.

'Don't talk to Grace like that, Dad. It's horrible, and it's so unfair. I *didn't* spend the money on chocolate. Grace is just saying that to protect me. I spent it on other stuff.'

'*What* stuff?' said Mum, who'd never spent sixty pounds in one go in her life.

'I went to McDonald's, I bought magazines, I got a special box of watercolours from the art shop—'

'That wouldn't use up eighty whole pounds! Give me what's left!'

'Sixty, Dad, *sixty*! I spent all of it. I bought some underwear too.'

'Underwear?' Dad gasped. 'What sort of an idiot do you take me for, Prudence? What did you really buy?'

'Oh my lord, you're not on drugs, are you?' said Mum.

I'd never had the chance to smoke so much as a Silk Cut, never swallowed anything more sinister than an aspirin. The idea that I'd somehow been hobnobbing with drug dealers was so ludicrous I couldn't help smiling.

Dad's hand shot out. I felt such a whack on my cheek that I nearly toppled sideways.

'Take that smirk off your face! Now tell me what you spent eighty pounds on, you little liar.'

Grace started crying, but I was too angry for tears.

'It was *sixty* pounds, Dad — don't you ever listen? And I *told* you, I bought my watercolour paints, some food in McDonald's, some magazines . . . and some underwear.'

'Show me!' said Dad.

'Don't, Bernard! Of course she can't show you,' Mum said. She looked at me worriedly, putting her hand on my scarlet cheek. She rubbed at it, as if she could wipe the slap away.

'I'll show him,' I said. 'I'll go and get it.'

'No — don't, Prue!' Grace wept. 'She really did buy me chocolate, Dad, a great big bunny, I swear she did.'

'Ssh, Grace. Dad won't believe you. He thinks we're both liars. Well, we'll show him.'

I strode to the bedroom, pulled open my drawer, found my beautiful new bra and knickers, took hold of them in each hand, ran back and threw them down on the table in front of Dad.

He recoiled as if they were hissing vipers. We all stared at the pink satin bra, the padded cups standing out proudly, edged with black lace. The wispy matching knickers curled in an S shape, barely wider than a ribbon.

Behind the table the family's damp underwear hung limply on the airer, grey-white, baggy, slackly elasticated, almost interchangeable.

'You sleazy disgusting little trollop!' Dad shouted. 'You're no daughter of mine.'

'I don't *want* to be your daughter. You're the worst father in the whole world!' I shouted back.

He clutched his chest as if I'd punched him. Then he fell forward, his head going smack against our old table. I thought he was literally banging his head with rage. I waited for him to sit up again.

Dad stayed where he was.

'Oh Bernard!' Mum whispered.

'Dad?' said Grace.

The kitchen was suddenly appallingly silent. I stared across the table.

I had killed my own father.

We stayed sitting still for a second, staring at Dad. It was Grace who suddenly sprang into action, surprising all of us.

'We should bang his chest and give him the kiss of life!' she said, running round the table towards Dad.

She took hold of him fearfully, pulling him backwards into an upright position. Very bravely, she tilted his head, took a deep breath and blew into his mouth in a ghastly parody of a kiss.

We had never kissed Dad on his mouth in our lives.

Seeing my poor sister behaving so valiantly jerked me into action too.

'An ambulance! I'll dial nine nine nine,' I said.

'No, no, your dad won't go to hospital,' Mum wept, though Dad was clearly past arguing.

I dialled anyway. Someone at the end of the line asked me which service I wanted. I asked for an ambulance and gave our address.

'I should have asked for the police too,' I said. 'So they could come and arrest me.'

'Don't be so silly,' said Mum, rushing round, starting to clear the table. Her hand hovered over my pink and black lace underwear. 'Take these, Prue, quick!'

I stuffed them in the pocket of my frock and went and stood beside Grace. I watched her labouring over Dad.

'You're doing it too quickly. And shouldn't you pinch his nostrils?'

'*You* do it, Prue,' said Mum.

I had a go, although it was awful shoving my head so close to Dad, feeling his coarse moustache scratching my lips, his false teeth clunking against mine. I scooped them out, feeling I was violating my own father.

Mum tried too, though she seemed as reluctant as me. She kept stopping and peering at him fearfully, as if he was about to strike her for being so impertinent.

My cheek still throbbed from his slap. I started pacing up and down, peering out of the window for the ambulance, as if I could summon it up instantly by willpower.

'Get . . . Dad's . . . pyjamas,' Mum gasped, in between breaths.

'I'll pack a case for him, Mum,' Grace said quickly.

33

It seemed bizarre, finding nightclothes and a toothbrush and a flannel for someone who might already be dead. He still wasn't moving at all, and his eyes were semi-shut. Mum hovered above him, bent over awkwardly, her head on his chest. I thought she might be hugging him, but she was listening for a heartbeat.

'I think I can hear it. You listen, Prue. It *is* his heart, isn't it?'

I couldn't tell if the drumming in my ear was my own blood or his. I hated breathing in Dad's stale old-book, old-sweat, old-jersey smell. His mouth was lopsided now, as if he was silently groaning. He looked like an old, old man.

'Oh Dad,' I said, and I started crying. 'I didn't mean to make you so angry. I'm sorry. Can you hear me? I'm so so sorry.'

There was a knock on the shop door downstairs. The ambulance people were here. They gently prised me off Dad and examined him carefully.

'Is he dead?' I sobbed.

'No, no! He's unconscious, dear, but he's not dead. We'll get him to hospital as soon as possible.'

'He hates hospitals,' said Mum.

'Can't help that, love. We can't leave him here in this state. Are you coming with him?'

'Yes, of course, he's my husband.'

'What about the girls? They'd best stay here.'

Mum looked at us, biting her lip.

'Do you want me to come, Mum?' I said.

34

Mum drew in her breath, hugging her huge chest, her hands hanging onto her elbows. 'No, dear, you stay and look after Grace. I'll ring you from the hospital. You be good girls and – and try not to worry.'

The ambulance people strapped Dad onto a stretcher and manoeuvred him out of the kitchen and down the stairs, Mum treading heavily behind with the carrier of his things. Grace and I followed them downstairs and through the shop, as if we were in some strange procession. We watched from the shop doorway as they slotted Dad's stretcher into the ambulance and helped Mum clamber inside too.

The Chinese people stood on their restaurant doorstep, watching. They nodded at us sympathetically. 'Your dad?' they said, and the woman pointed to her heart.

When the ambulance drove off she asked us if we'd like to come and sit with them.

'No, no, it's very kind, but we're fine,' I said firmly.

Grace pushed me when we were back inside our own shop. 'I wanted to see what their place is like. And they might have given us some chow mein and chop suey – I *so* want to know what it tastes like.' Then she clapped her hands over her mouth. 'I didn't mean that. Dad's right, I *am* a greedy guts. Oh Prue, this is all so awful. I can't believe it, can you?'

'Remember when we were little and Dad sent

us to bed in disgrace and then we'd curl up and pretend to be different people?'

'Yeah, I liked it best when I was Kylie Little Bum and you were Janet Air and I sang and you painted and we lived in our own penthouse flat,' said Grace, sighing. 'You're always so good at making everything up.'

'Maybe it isn't good. It takes over from your real life and you start to believe it. Like when I bought the knickers and bra. I was pretending to be like the girls in the magazines and then when I argued with Dad I was kidding myself I was like little Jane Eyre standing up to Mr Brocklehurst – and yet look what I've done.'

'He'll get better, Prue. The ambulance people said he was just unconscious. So maybe he just fainted because he was so mad at you?'

'Don't be daft, Grace. He wasn't just *fainting*,' I said.

'Well. Whatever. But it wasn't *your* fault. You didn't make him ill.'

'I did, I did. I don't know how I could have yelled back at him like that.'

'I thought you were brave. I'd never dare. But I get on Dad's nerves more than you do. It's because I'm so fat and so stupid. No wonder he likes you best,' Grace said, with no hint of resentment.

'I think Dad's the stupid one. You're much much much nicer than me. You'd definitely be *my* favourite, Gracie,' I said, and I put my arms round her.

We had a long hug and then broke away, looking at each other anxiously. The kitchen seemed spookily quiet in spite of the loud hum of our old fridge and the tick of the clock. We both watched the second hand edging its way round each numeral.

We'd rarely been in the house by ourselves. We'd frequently fantasized about days of freedom together but now we were too frightened and guilty to do anything but stand and stare.

'When do you think Mum will come back?' said Grace. She swallowed. 'I mean, I know you don't know either, but do you think she'll be back by lunch time? And what should we do about the shop? Will we open it up?'

'There's not much point. How many customers do we get?' I said.

I went to the waste bin and fished out all the bills. 'Look, final demand, final demand. And – oh God, look at this one – they're threatening to take Dad to court, Grace. I think he's going to have to close the shop anyway, even if he gets better.'

'But what will he do? Do you think he'll publish his Magnum Whatsit?'

'Oh, come on, Grace, he's never going to finish it.'

I thought of Dad only an hour ago, admiring my Tobias and the Angel painting and telling me I could illustrate his precious book. I started howling.

'Oh don't, Prue! Dad will be all right, I'm sure he will be,' Grace said, clutching me.

'I was so *mean* to him. I let him down so. And if we're really in all this debt it's so awful that I spent all his tuition money. No wonder he was so cross. How must he have felt when I thrust my bra and knickers right in his face?' I pulled them out of my pocket and tugged hard at them, but they wouldn't rip. I rummaged in the kitchen cupboard for the scissors.

'No! Don't! *I'll* have them if you don't want them,' Grace said quickly.

I stared at her.

'I know they wouldn't fit me, but I could just keep them like – like secret ornaments,' she said. 'They are *so* beautiful. Where did you get them from?'

'Mallard and Turners. Their underwear department.'

'You went there by yourself? You lucky thing!'

We looked at each other. We had the perfect opportunity to slip out now and go round all the forbidden shops, but of course we couldn't.

'We can't go on a jaunt, not while Dad's so ill or—'

'I know,' said Grace, sighing. 'So what *shall* we do?'

'Perhaps we ought to get on with our work, same as any other day. That's kind of pleasing Dad, isn't it?'

So we cleared the kitchen table and got out our books and notebooks and pens. Grace tried to do a passage of English comprehension. I tried to read a chapter of a French children's book.

We sighed and stared into space a lot, unable to concentrate. I made myself a cup of black coffee to see if that would jerk me into attentiveness. Grace got the cereal packet and the sugar bowl and dipped and nibbled between sentences.

I threw my French book across the room after an hour and got out my paints and my Tobias and the Angel picture, deciding to finish it. I tried talking to Tobias in my head but Grace kept interrupting.

'Can I use your paints too?' she begged. 'I want to make Dad a Get Well Soon card.'

I was scared it was a bit late in the day for a Get Well Soon card but I didn't dare say it. I hated Grace using my paints because she always put too much water on her brush and turned the neat little palettes into muddy pools, but I decided I'd better be kind to her.

She laboured long and hard over her card. She used the back of the cornflake packet so that it would stand up stiffly. She drew our bookshop, dutifully painting each individual book red or green or brown or blue, although they merged into each other as one long book blob. Then she drew Dad, a little skinny man with a frowny face. She drew Mum, a big blobby woman with black dots for eyes and similar dots all over her dress. All the dots ran so that it looked as if Mum and her dress were weeping copiously. She drew me in a corner, reading a book, my hair very thick and bushy so my face seemed hidden by a black cloud. She drew herself wearing her favourite pink panda dress, like a big raspberry meringue.

'Have you finished? That's so good,' I said.

'It's not. I'm rubbish at painting. I could see the way I wanted it to be in my head but it won't come out right on the paper,' Grace sighed. She looked at it worriedly. 'I've made Dad too small.'

'He *is* small. Smaller than Mum.'

'He looks like a stick, like he'll snap any minute,' Grace wailed. 'Help me make him look bigger, Prue.'

'He's fine,' I said, but I stopped applying delicate touches of gold ink to the Angel's halo and helped her lengthen Dad's arms and legs.

'He still doesn't look right. He's like one of those insect thingies with long legs,' said Grace.

'Daddy-longlegs,' I said.

We laughed though it wasn't a bit funny. Grace looked as if she might cry again any minute.

'I wish Mum would come back,' she said. 'Is it lunch time yet?'

It was only just gone eleven but I made her French toast to cheer her up. We had another round each at half past twelve, and finished all the flapjacks in the tin, and ate an overripe banana mid-afternoon.

Mum didn't get back till five. Her eyes were red, and she was clutching a sodden handkerchief.

'He's dead!' I whispered.

I started sobbing. So did Grace.

'No, no, he's not dead. There, girls. I'm so sorry – you must have been very worried. I was in such a state I forgot to check I had any change for the phone call. I had no idea they would take so long. It's a nightmare, a total nightmare. Your dad's going to be so angry with me when he realizes he's in hospital. Well, maybe he *does* know. It's hard to tell.' Mum started crying too.

'Is he still unconscious then, Mum?'

'Well, his eyes are open and maybe he understands. But he can't speak, you see.'

'What do you mean? Has he done something to his throat?'

'No, no. Your father's suffered a stroke, girls. It's affected his speech and he can't use his arm and his leg.'

'But he'll get better, won't he, Mum?' said Grace.

'They don't know, darling. It's too early to tell at this stage.'

I went running out of the room. I threw myself on my bed. I couldn't bear it. I knew it was all my fault.

A stroke is such a strangely inappropriate term to describe what's happened to Dad. The word 'stroke' implies something soft and subtle. Dad looks as if he's been bashed repeatedly down one side. His head lolls, his mouth droops, and his right arm and leg sag as if they're broken.

Mum had warned us but it was still terrifying walking along the ward of the stroke unit and going into Dad's room. The man slumped in the bed was a Guy Fawkes caricature of our father.

We stood on the threshold of his room, all three of us. Dad's eyes were closed, but he mumbled something.

'Hello, Dad,' I whispered, forcing myself to walk over to his bed.

His eyes snapped open, making me jump. He frowned at me. There was a little dribble down his chin. He tried to wipe it away, looking agonized.

'Shall I wipe it, Dad?' I asked.

He made vehement mumbles, making it plain he didn't want to be helped at all. He carried on struggling after his chin was dry. He kept flinging his unaffected leg out from under the bedclothes, hoping that the rest of his body would follow.

'Lie still, dear. Try to relax,' said Mum.

Dad's contorted face was anything but relaxed. He tried again and again.

'He's trying to get out of bed to go home,' I said.

Dad glared at me, groaning. He resented me talking about him rather than to him.

I went closer, though I really wanted to run away, out of the room, down the ward, right out of the hospital.

'Dad, you can't go home just yet, you're not well enough,' I said.

Dad wouldn't see reason. He became more and more agitated, and when Mum tried to tuck him back under the sheets he punched her arm. It was the weakest, feeblest punch in the world, but it made her cry.

'Now, now, there's no need for tears,' said a nurse, bustling in and putting her arm round Mum. She was nearly as large as Mum, but in an exuberant, voluptuous way. She had glossy brown skin and magnificent plaited hair. 'Mr King's doing splendidly, my dear. Aren't you, lovie?'

43

She nodded at Dad and then stuck a thermometer in his mouth before he could groan at her. He spat it straight out defiantly.

'You're a naughty boy,' she said, laughing. 'You want to have a little game with me? Watch out, though, laddie – I might well stick it somewhere else if you turn awkward on me.'

Dad decided to subject himself to a thermometer in his mouth after all.

'There now. That's the ticket.' The nurse winked at Mum. 'We'll soon get him trained, eh?'

Mum simpered uneasily. 'He hates hospitals so,' she said.

'Well, we're none of us here by choice,' said the nurse. 'I'd much sooner be at home with my feet up watching *Corrie* on the telly.'

Dad groaned again, gargling slightly with the thermometer.

'Hey, hey, watch out or you'll swallow it,' said the nurse. 'OK, let's see how you're doing.'

'How's his temperature?' Mum asked anxiously.

'It's fine, dear, just fine. You're doing well, Mr King,' the nurse said. 'Let's just tidy you up a bit in honour of your visitors.' She smoothed his pyjama collar and combed his sparse hair with her long brown fingers. He did his best to bat her away, groaning something that sounded very much like a bad swearword.

The nurse seemed to think it was too. 'Ooh! In front of your wife and daughters! I'll wash your mouth out with soap if you're not careful,' she said cheerily. She raised her eyebrows at Mum, and then shook her head. Mum shook her head back, though she glanced anxiously at Dad.

The nurse smiled at me. 'So what's your name, dear? I'm Nurse Ray. Little ray of sunshine, that's me.'

'I'm Prudence,' I said, wincing, because I hate my name so much.

'And what about you, sweetheart?' said Nurse Ray, going over to Grace. She'd been skulking fearfully in a corner the whole time.

'I'm Grace,' she whispered.

Dad groaned as if the very sound of her name irritated him.

'Don't look so worried, sweetheart,' said Nurse Ray, chucking Grace under the chin. 'Daddy's only grumpy because he's had his stroke. He'll be his usual self in no time, I'm sure.'

Grace stared at her. Dad was very much his usual self, even incapacitated by his stroke. He didn't *have* any other self. He was permanently grumpy.

'Go and say hello to your dad. It'll cheer him up,' said Nurse Ray.

She encouraged Grace forwards until she was in Dad's line of sight. He saw her approaching. He groaned again.

'Hello, Dad. I've made you a Get Well Soon card,' Grace said bravely.

Dad made little attempt to look at it.

'Hold it up above Daddy's head so he can see it properly,' said Nurse Ray.

Grace waved her card around in the air above Dad. He moaned, his eyes swivelling, as if a vulture was circling above him. He made another attempt to get his leg out of bed. He heaved himself halfway up with his good arm, beads of sweat standing out on his forehead.

'Oh Bernard, don't, dear, you'll hurt yourself,' Mum flapped, patting at him.

'I'm sorry, Mr King, you're stuck with us for a while,' said Nurse Ray, expertly flipping him down on his back and tucking him in firmly. 'It's not going to be for too long. Believe me, we need the beds. We just need you to be a bit stronger and start getting more vocal and mobile. That makes sense, doesn't it?'

Dad groaned feebly, but lay still and shut his eyes.

'That's it. You have a little nap.'

We said goodnight to him and backed out of the room. Nurse Ray came with us, smiling encouragement.

'How long will my husband have to stay in hospital?' Mum asked.

'It's up to the doctors, dear. It'll depend on what sort of progress your husband makes.'

'Will he get better?' I asked. 'Properly better?'

Nurse Ray hesitated. 'He'll get a lot better, I'm sure.'

'Will he be able to talk again? And walk?'

'I dare say. Some people make complete recoveries.'

'But some don't?'

'Your daddy's a fighter, cussed as they come. His type generally do the best.' She seemed keen to change the subject, concentrating on my hideous red-checked dress. 'Is that your school uniform?' she said sympathetically.

'I don't go to school,' I said, blushing.

'They're home-educated,' said Mum. 'My husband teaches them.' She stopped short and put her hand to her mouth. She didn't say any more.

I wondered what on earth was going to happen now.

Mum made us beans on toast when we got home, which was quick and comforting. We listened to the radio while we ate, and then started sewing our quilt. I'd designed the overall pattern and cut out all the little hexagons, Grace tacked as best she could, and Mum sewed. It was so peaceful listening to quiz shows on Radio Four without Dad's incessant interruptions: *'Don't you know that, you fool?' 'Come on, come on, speak up!' 'Fatuous idiot, who does he think he is?'* He addressed the radio speaker, as if all the performers were actually inside, little tiny men, listening.

We knew we had to talk about Dad and what was going to happen, but none of us could bear to spoil the peace. Grace and I went up to bed at our usual time. I was in the middle of reading a biography of Queen Elizabeth I for my Tudor project but I didn't feel like history.

I knelt down by my bookcase and fingered my

way through all my favourite old books. I found my big battered nursery rhyme book wedged right at the back, with weirdly worrying pictures of jumping cows and blind mice and girls with giant spiders. I flicked through this surreal world where pigs went marketing and children lived in shoes and the moon was made of green cheese.

I remembered Dad's pedantic voice enunciating, 'Ring-a-ring-a-roses' and 'Hey diddle diddle'. I'd never been invited to sit on Dad's lap when he read to me, but I'd sit cross-legged at his feet.

'Do you remember Dad reading us nursery rhymes?' I asked Grace.

'I didn't like them because they were scary. He poked me hard and told me not to be so soft,' said Grace.

I hesitated. 'Grace, do you love Dad?'

'Of course I do!' Grace said.

'But sometimes don't you hate him too?'

'Never,' said Grace, sounding shocked.

'Not even when he's being particularly horrid? He's much meaner to you than he is to me.'

'Yes, but that's because I'm thick.'

'No you're *not*! Listen, *I* hate him.'

'You can't say that, Prue, not now he's ill.'

'But it doesn't make him any nicer, does it? Weren't you embarrassed, him going on like that in front of that nurse?'

'She was so lovely,' said Grace. 'That's what I'd like to be now, a nurse. I could look after people and make them better and have them think me special. If I can't pass exams to get to be a proper nurse maybe I could go in one of those big homes and look after old folk.'

'Are you going to help nurse Dad then?'

'Oh! No, I couldn't! I mean, he wouldn't let me.'

'So who *is* going to nurse him?' I said.

I felt terrified. What if it had to be *me*?

I stayed awake hours after Grace nodded off. I heard Mum go to bed, but when I got up to go to the loo her light was still on. I put my head round the door. She was still wearing her pink dressing gown, sitting on the end of the bed, staring into space.

'Mum?'

'Oh Prue!' She had tears trickling down her face.

'Don't cry, Mum.' I went to sit beside her, reaching up and putting my arm right round her large shoulders. 'Maybe Dad will make a complete recovery, like that nurse said.'

'Maybe,' said Mum, but we neither of us believed it. 'I'm just trying to figure out what to do. I don't know what's the matter with me. I don't know if it's living with your dad all these years. He's always told me what to do, and now it's as if my mind won't work. Not that it ever did very much. I was never a thinker, not like you and your dad. I was always in awe of your dad whenever he came in to buy his pie and his sausage roll from the baker's where I worked – you know, where the Chinese folk are now. He knew so much, and he had all his books. He lived in a different world.'

'Well, he obviously fancied the pretty young girl in the baker's or he would never have asked you out,' I said, patting her.

'I wasn't ever pretty, dear. And it wasn't your dad made the first move, it was me. I got up the courage to ask if he'd like me to do any dusting or tidying in the shop. Then I cooked him a meal. That's how it all started.'

'And you've been dusting and tidying and cooking ever since,' I said. 'It's going to be all right, Mum. We'll sort things out together.'

'I don't know where to start. I don't know how I'm going to cope when your dad comes out of hospital.'

'I'll help, Mum.' I took a deep breath. 'I suppose I can take a turn if Dad needs any nursing.' My chest was so tight I could hardly get the words out. Mum shook her head.

'No,' she said firmly. 'That's one thing I do know. You're still only a child, even though you're so clever. I'm not having you take on such a burden. Anyway, you won't be around during the day. You'll be at school.'

I stared at her.

'You'll have to start school, Prue – you and Grace. Your dad won't be in a fit state to teach you, and I certainly can't. There's so much you need to know for these exams. We can't send you for tuition in all the different subjects, we simply can't afford it.'

'I'm so sorry about taking Miss Roberts's money, Mum.'

'Oh well. It's not as if you've made a habit of it. I've felt badly for years that you girls have so little spending money – though I wish you'd spent it on something *sensible*, rather than those lacy little bits of nothing.'

'I know. It's just . . . I so wanted them.'

'Yes, of course you did. Don't you think *I* ever want things?' Mum saw me staring and burst out laughing. '*Not* fancy underwear. Those knicks of yours wouldn't even go round my knee as a garter. No, there's all sorts of things I'd love. Not clothes, I'm not worth dressing.' Mum slapped at her thighs contemptuously, as if they were two great stupid beasts beyond her control. 'But I'd love stuff for the house, all the labour-saving gadgets, and oh goodness, how I'd love a television just like anyone else. I've tried to get your dad to see it's educational but he won't hear of it. He's just books books books. Still, even he can see you can't learn *everything* from books. You need to go to school so you can start studying for your GCSEs. Grace can start too – she needs the extra pushing.'

I'd been begging Dad to send me to school for years and years. I'd read every school book avidly. I'd skied through all the Chalet School books, I'd sniggered at Angela Brazil's *Bosom Friends*, I'd attended St Clare's with the twins, I'd been to Hogwarts with Harry. But these were old-fashioned schools, figments of the imagination.

I thought about Wentworth High School, the grim concrete building three roads away, on the

51

edge of the Wentworth Estate. I'd no idea what it was like inside. You couldn't even peer into the playground, because there was a high creosoted fence, with barbed wire scalloping the top in sinister fashion. I didn't know if it was to stop intruders or imprison the pupils.

I imagined myself walking into that bleak building.

'It won't be Wentworth High, will it?' I said.

Boys from Wentworth sometimes came banging and shouting into the shop, throwing books around, asking if Dad stocked crazy rude titles. He'd order them out of the shop and threaten to call the police. He tried phoning the school to complain, but he said the teachers sounded as uncouth as the pupils.

'Your dad would die if you went to Wentworth,' said Mum. Then she clapped her hand over her mouth. 'No, no,' she said indistinctly. 'We'll send you to Kingtown High. Your dad went there, when it was a grammar school. He'd like to think you were following in his footsteps. Though maybe he'd feel happier if it was an all girls' school. That's it, we'll find you a nice decent girls' school.'

She said it as if she could conjure up a demure convent directly down the road. I saw myself in a straw boater and blazer, arm in arm with my best friend Jane. We'd giggle together and share secrets. It wouldn't matter if we were the odd ones out, because we'd have each other.

I pictured Grace tagging along behind us on

our way to school. I felt sorry for her, so I gave her a best friend too, a roly-poly red-cheeked little girl who loved Grace dearly and stuck up for her whenever she was teased. I even imagined Mum making friends with some of the other mums while Dad nodded benignly in the background, a gentle, frail invalid . . .

We had to go to Wentworth. All the other schools were full up, with long waiting lists.

'We can't go to Wentworth, Mum!' I said. 'We won't go. You need me to help out in the shop now, anyway.'

'We can't risk it. If that education inspector chappie comes back and catches you working then we'll really be prosecuted,' said Mum. 'No, Prue, you're starting at Wentworth next Monday, it's all fixed.'

'But Mum, I don't *want* to go to Wentworth. Look, you *said*—'

'I know what I said. But I can't help it. I don't know what else I can do. For God's sake, can't you try to make this easier for me? Don't you see I'm at the end of my tether?'

I wasn't sure what a tether was. I imagined

a long fraying rope with Mum tied on the end, fat legs dangling.

'OK, OK. Don't you worry, Mum, we'll go,' I said.

'But it'll be *awful*,' Grace wept in our bedroom that night. 'When I go to the sweet shop these girls from Wentworth are always making faces at me and whispering and giggling. I know they're talking about me. And they steal stuff, I've seen them. And the boys are worse, you know they are.'

'Don't go *on* about it, Grace,' I said, because I wanted to drift off with Tobias into our own private world.

'It's all right for you. You're pretty and skinny and clever. You'll make heaps of friends. But what about me? They'll all pick on me and tease me because I'm fat.'

'No they won't. Well, if they do, I'll bash them up,' I said fiercely, though I wasn't sure I could bash so much as a boiled egg.

Grace looked a bit doubtful too.

'Look, if it's really really awful we simply won't go,' I said. 'We'll pretend we're going, but we'll just hang out round the town, go for walks, whatever, just like I did when I was supposed to be seeing that awful Miss Roberts.'

'Really?' said Grace. She sat up in bed and blew her nose. 'Oh Prue, don't let's go at all. Let's just bunk off right from the start. It will be fun!'

'Well, you'll have to keep it absolutely quiet. No blurting it out to Mum!'

'I'll keep my lips totally sealed, I promise,' Grace said.

Mum started fussing on Sunday night about what we were to wear.

'I phoned up on Friday and explained it might be a problem getting both of you kitted out for uniform. I hoped I'd find something in BHS but no one does that green, and even so, the prices are ludicrous. They told me there's a second-hand school uniform shop open every Friday. It's meant to be very reasonable, so you'll be able to get yourselves sorted out. Meanwhile you'll just have to wear your dresses and cardies and explain if anyone asks.'

'Yes, Mum,' we said meekly.

'You've to be at school at quarter to nine tomorrow, to see the headteacher. I expect she's going to give you a little pep talk. There's no need to be nervous. Don't worry, I'll come too.'

We blinked at her.

Mum smoothed down her skirt and then looked at it properly. It wasn't really a proper skirt at all; it was a length of chintz curtain material Mum had hastily stitched together in a depressing dirndl shape. She'd put on even more weight meanwhile. She stared at the big red roses stretched to the limit around her vast thighs.

'Oh dear,' she said. 'I wonder if my good suit still fits.'

'You don't have to come to Wentworth with us, Mum,' I said quickly.

56

'Of course I do,' said Mum. 'Your dad can't go, obviously, so it's down to me.'

'*No*, Mum. We'll look stupid, going with you,' I said.

Mum looked at me, her face flushing as red as her roses.

'Look, I didn't mean because you're *you*,' I said hurriedly. 'We just don't want to walk in with our *mum*. The other kids will laugh at us.'

'Then they'll have to laugh,' said Mum, her chin up. 'I'm coming, Prudence. I need to be there. I've got to make sure you *go* there for a start.' She looked me straight in the eye. It was my turn to blush.

'Oh Mum, we don't want to go,' Grace wailed, and started howling.

Mum sat down on the sofa and pulled Grace onto her lap. 'There now, baby,' she said, rocking her.

'Everything's so horrible and scary and different,' Grace wept.

'I know, I know,' said Mum, rubbing her cheek across the top of Grace's mousy hair. 'I don't want you to go to school, poppet. Heaven knows, I hated it myself. But now your dad's not able to teach you we'll just have to give it a go. And maybe . . . maybe it's time you two learned to fit in more. I just want you both to be happy.'

We looked the picture of misery the next morning, walking to Wentworth in our ridiculous home-made clothes. Mum's suit wouldn't fit her so she was squeezed back into the red rose number, with a red knitted jumper rammed down over her big bosom. Grace was wearing her pink pandas. I told her it maybe *did* look babyish, which hurt her feelings, but she insisted on wearing it because it was her favourite frock.

I cordially hated *all* my frocks, but chose the red and white check as the least offensive. I wore my new black and pink lace underwear underneath, for courage. I hoped it might make me feel like one of the Wentworth girls, confident and sexy and streetwise.

As soon as we set foot inside the great gates everyone stared at us. We trekked across the playground. It seemed as large as the Sahara Desert. I realized that two little strips of hidden lace weren't going to make the slightest difference. Some of the kids had big grins on their faces. It was as if a circus had stopped at their school. We were the clowns.

The girls stood in little groups, giggling. The boys started jostling each other and shouting. Mum looked at Grace and me anxiously and then reached out to hold our hands. She was trying to reassure us but this was a *big* mistake. I snatched my hand away immediately but Grace clung to Mum. That made their jeers increase.

'Let go!' I hissed.

They took no notice, clutching each other. I sighed and marched ahead. I kept my head up and didn't look round, no matter what they shouted. Now I'd jettisoned Mum and Grace I imagined Jane on one side of me, Tobias the other. We didn't care what they called. We were a threesome, cool, aloof, artistic . . .

'God, what do they *look* like? Mum's a walking sofa, the little blobby one's a duvet and the skinny stuck-up cow's a tablecloth!' someone yelled.

I couldn't stay cool. I felt tears pricking my eyes. I turned round and stuck my finger up at them. They all shrieked delightedly. Mum looked shocked.

'Prudence! Don't do that.'

'What did she do, Mum? Prue, what does it mean, doing that with your finger?' said Grace.

'I don't know,' I lied. I'd seen the boys from the estate gesture to each other and worked out exactly what it meant. Grace didn't seem to have any idea at all. She was looking younger than ever, and very frightened.

'I want to go *home*,' she said, hanging back from the school door.

Mum looked as if she might relent. 'I don't see you two learning much in this sort of environment,' she whispered. 'Your dad's going to kill me when he finds out.'

'Let's just leg it back across the playground,' I said.

We looked at Mum pleadingly. She bit her lip, swaying from one Scholl sandal to the other, plucking helplessly at the roses on her hips. 'I don't know what to do for the best,' she said.

Then a man with black hair and a little beard

came up to us. He was wearing a denim jacket and black jeans, and he had a diamond earring in one lobe. We looked at him uncertainly. He seemed very young but the beard surely meant he couldn't be one of the pupils.

'Can I help?' he said.

'My girls are starting at the school. Well, I *think* they are,' said Mum.

He smiled at Grace and me. I usually couldn't stick men with beards but his was small and trimmed and looked cool, especially with the earring.

'I hope you'll be very happy here. Don't look so worried. It's always a bit weird starting at a new school.'

'They've not been to any school, not for years and years,' said Mum, starting to launch into a long and unnecessary resumé of our lives.

He listened politely while Grace and I rolled our eyes at each other, agonized.

'Well, I'm sure everything will be fine,' he interrupted eventually. He nodded at Grace and me. 'I'll maybe see you in the art room sometime. I'm Mr Raxberry. I'm one of the art teachers here.'

'I'm rubbish at art but Prue is brilliant,' said Grace.

'I'm not,' I said, blushing.

'Yes, you are,' said Grace.

I had to shut up or we would have got stuck in a ludicrous pantomime routine.

Mr Raxberry glanced at me. He had a very

intent way of looking, as if he was actually drawing me, noting everything about me. I wished I didn't look such a total idiot in my tablecloth dress. His dark eyes seemed very warm and sympathetic, as if he understood exactly what I was thinking.

He showed us to the office and introduced us to one of the school secretaries. 'Gina will look after you. Good luck! I hope you enjoy your first day,' he said, and then went hurrying off down the corridor.

Gina stared after him wistfully. She would obviously have preferred to look after *him*. She gave us forms to fill in and then told us to wait on chairs outside the headteacher's study.

We crouched there, all three of us, totally unnerved, while great gangs of students careered up and down the corridors, laughing, calling, shouting.

'Why don't the teachers tell them off?' Mum whispered. 'Still, the teachers seem a pretty rum lot. Imagine, that Mr Raxberry had an *earring*. You wouldn't think they'd allow it.'

'He teaches *art*, Mum,' I said.

'I don't know what your dad would say.'

There was a little pause. We were all horribly aware that Dad couldn't manage to say two words together at the moment.

I hunched up on my hard chair, guilt stabbing me in the stomach. Grace reached out sympathetically, and smudged the ink where she'd written her name on her form.

'Oh rats,' she said, sighing.

'Grace! Don't make it all messy,' said Mum. 'Do your name again, and try to keep your writing neat. Look, it's all over the place. Make it smaller, to fit on the line.'

'It won't *go* smaller,' said Grace, gripping her pen so tightly her knuckles went white. She stuck her tongue out as she wrote, concentrating fiercely. Then she peered at my form. 'Oh no! I've done my address wrong. I've mixed up the postcode letters,' she wailed. 'Shall I copy it out?'

'No, it'll look even more of a mess. Just leave it. As if it matters!' I said, though I'd written mine in my neatest printing, using my fine-line black drawing pen.

A smart blonde woman in a black trouser suit and high-heeled boots walked past us into the headteacher's office without even knocking.

'What a nerve! We were here first,' said Mum. 'Do you think she's his secretary?'

She wasn't the secretary. She put her head back round the door in two minutes and beckoned us in. She was the headteacher, Miss Wilmott.

'We didn't think you'd be a woman,' Mum said stupidly.

'Well, I promise you I'm not a man in drag, Mrs King,' she said.

Mum looked dreadfully embarrassed. Grace and I sniggered uncomfortably.

'Welcome to Wentworth,' said Miss Wilmott. 'We're all new girls together. I've only been here since the beginning of term.'

She indicated three chairs in front of her desk. She sat behind it, resting on her elbows, her hands crossed in front of her. They were very pretty hands with beautifully shaped nails, pink with bright white tips, as perfect as a porcelain doll.

Mum hid her own bunch-of-bananas hands in her floral lap. Grace sat on her own bitten fingernails. I made myself sit with my hands by my sides, pretending to be relaxed. I looked past Miss Wilmott at the paintings on her wall. They were mostly creation myths, but I recognized one Nativity scene, with a host of angels flying round above the stable, playing a heavenly version of 'Ring-a-ring-a-roses'. The painting had been in the same room as Tobias and his angel.

Miss Wilmott saw me staring. 'Do you like my painting? It's Italian, by Bellini.'

'No, it isn't!' I said, astonished. 'It's a Botticelli. He paints very differently, in a very poetic and ethereal way. I just adore his work.'

'I'm so pleased,' said Miss Wilmott, though she didn't sound pleased at all.

'She's very into art, our Prudence,' said Mum. 'My husband takes both girls to all the galleries, fills them in on all the details. He's taken such pains with them.'

'Excellent,' said Miss Wilmott briskly. 'Well, I'm determined there's going to be a big emphasis on the arts in Wentworth. I'm sure your daughters will appreciate their art lessons.'

'Oh, not me!' said Grace. 'I don't want to do art, thanks, because I'm useless at it. I'll just do English and history and geography and some nature stuff, but not anything hard.'

'You'll be given a timetable, Grace,' said Miss Wilmott. 'You'll find you'll be doing all sorts of subjects. But first of all, I'd like both of you to do a little test for me so we can sort out which year group to put you in.'

'I can't do tests,' said Grace anxiously, seemingly determined to convince Miss Wilmott she was totally bonkers.

'She panics,' Mum said. 'She's not really that clever – she takes after me, poor girl.' She laughed a false little ha-ha-ha. 'Prudence is the bright one,' Mum continued. 'She'll be top of her class, no problem.'

Miss Wilmott's smile was getting strained. 'We'll have the girls do their assessment tests and then we'll see,' she said. 'Meanwhile, Mrs King, I'd like to remind you that we do have a very strict uniform policy. Can you make sure the girls are kitted out in the regulation green uniform, please?'

'Oh yes, I've got that all in hand. They're going to buy their uniform at the special shop,' Mum said.

'I see,' said Miss Wilmott. She paused delicately. 'Are you on benefits, Mrs King? We do have an excellent free school lunch if that's the case.'

'Oh no, they'll take a packed lunch,' said Mum.

'We're not on any benefits at all, thank you.' Her cheeks were burning.

Miss Wilmott had no idea how she'd insulted her. She'd never heard one of Dad's rants about the Great Unwashed living off the State. Maybe Miss Wilmott thought *we* were the Great Unwashed, and possibly barking mad to boot. Her perfectly manicured nails were starting to fidget impatiently.

'Right then. We'll get Prudence and Grace settled in. School finishes at three thirty.' She gave Mum one more tight smile of dismissal.

Mum sat still, smiling back, not understanding. Grace sat gawping too.

'I won't have to do running or jumping or any games, will I?' Grace said.

'You'll have a games lesson twice a week. I think you'll find it fun,' said Miss Wilmott, getting up.

'But I can't, I've got a bad heart,' said Grace, putting her hand on her chest in a theatrical gesture.

I stared at her. She didn't have anything wrong with her heart. She could obviously lie as fluently as me when she was desperate enough.

Mum blinked at Grace, wondering what she was on about. Miss Wilmott didn't look convinced.

'If you want exemption from games you'll have to bring a letter from your doctor,' she said. 'But I'm sure a little gentle exercise won't do you any harm at all. Now, I really have to go to assembly. I'll settle you down with your tests, girls. Goodbye, Mrs King.'

Even Mum couldn't fail to get the message that it was time to go. She heaved herself upwards and gazed at Grace and me. Her eyes brimmed with tears but she did her best to smile. 'Have a nice day then, girls,' she said. 'I'll be waiting for you in the playground after school.'

'*No*, Mum, we'll walk home ourselves,' I said.

'Well, take great care, dear. Make sure you mind the roads and don't talk to strangers.'

She was treating us as if we were six. It was a relief when she waddled off down the corridor. She turned to wave at us again and again, as if she thought this was the last time she'd see us.

Grace and I sat at adjacent desks in a small room in a special unit called the Success Maker. Another girl sat at the back with some sort of helper. She was stumbling through an early reader book, spelling out the simplest words, often getting them wrong. Two foreign boys were with another teacher. He was making slow, deliberate conversation with them. 'Hello. My name is Mr Evans. I am thirty years old,' he said, expecting them to reciprocate. The boys mumbled and fidgeted, looking round the room, baffled.

I squeezed Grace's hand reassuringly under cover of the desks. She could speak English, she could read fluently. She didn't need to look so worried.

Gina gave us both booklets of questions and

a pen each. 'There we go. You've got an hour and a half.'

Grace flicked through the pages, looking horrified. 'To answer all *this*?'

'Just answer as many questions as you can. Don't panic.' Gina made for the door. She turned and saw Grace edging nearer to me. 'And don't copy either!'

We opened our booklets.

'Oh help help help!' Grace muttered. 'Half of it's *puzzles*. And mixed-up words. Oh, there's that spring cleaning bit from *The Wind in the Willows* – goodie, we can answer questions on *that*.'

I stared at my own booklet, looking for acrostics and anagrams and Moley in his burrow. I couldn't find them. My booklet was full of meaningless mathematical diagrams and sinister scientific formulae. My heart started thumping.

We had different booklets. Grace had one for eleven-year-olds just entering the school. Mine was for fourteen-year-olds starting Year Ten. I didn't know any of the answers. I was as hesitant as the girl reader, as baffled as the two boys. I stared at the paper long after Grace started scribbling away, her exuberant handwriting sloping wildly up and down the page.

I was so unnerved by the maths and the science that I was unsettled by the general intelligence questions too. I could see most of the missing sequences, fill in all the bracketed words, work out every code – but perhaps they were all trick questions? I dithered and crossed out and agonized, then decided to leave them and go back to them afterwards.

There was a passage of Shakespeare, unacknowledged, but it was the balcony scene from *Romeo and Juliet* so it was pretty obvious. I couldn't believe the question. *Do you think this scene was written recently? Give reasons for your answer.* Maybe this was a trick too? I decided to write a proper essay for Miss Wilmott to show her I wasn't a total moron.

I wrote three pages about Shakespeare and his times and the feud between the Montagues and the Capulets. I commented on the difference between courtship in Elizabethan times and nowadays, though I knew little about girl/boy relationships in my own time. It had been love at first sight for Romeo and Juliet. She was only fourteen, my age. I tried to imagine falling so headily, instantly in love that I would risk everything and kill myself if I couldn't be with my beloved.

I conjured up Tobias and wondered what it would be like if he stayed with me until sunrise. I wondered what he'd say, what he'd do . . .

I started violently when a very loud alarm bell rang and rang. I jumped up and grabbed Grace, looking round wildly for flames and smoke. But it wasn't a fire alarm, it was simply the school bell.

'It's break time now,' said Gina, bustling back. 'Time's up, girls. Pass your booklets to me.'

'But I haven't finished! I haven't done any of the stuff on the last two pages,' Grace wailed.

'Never mind. It's not like a real exam. It's just so we can assess you properly,' said Gina, snatching the booklet away from Grace.

I hugged mine tightly to my chest, feeling sick. I'd done far worse than Grace. I'd answered only a quarter of the questions. I just had to hope my essay would be taken into account.

I felt I'd let Dad down. I saw his face screw up with rage and frustration as he tried to berate me.

'There's no need to look so tragic,' Gina said to me. 'I'm sure you've done very well, dear. You've written heaps.'

I'd written heaps of rubbish. I was put in a remedial class.

They didn't *call* it that. It was simply Form 10 EL. I pondered the significance of EL. Extreme Losers? Educationally Lacking? Evidently Loopy? I discovered they were merely the initials of our form teacher, Eve Lambert. But it was obvious that we were the sad guys in the school, the hopeless cases. Some could barely speak English and were traumatized, looking round fearfully as if they expected a bomb to go off any minute. Others were loud and disruptive, standing up and swearing. One boy couldn't sit still at all and fidgeted constantly, biting his fingernails and flipping his ruler and folding the pages in his notebook. He hummed all the time like a demonic bee. Most of my fellow pupils seemed scarily surly. The only girl who gave me a big smile had obvious learning difficulties.

I was the girl supposedly intellectually gifted. This was the class considered appropriate for my abilities. It was totally humiliating to find I could barely keep up. It was like being back with Miss Roberts, only worse. I still couldn't get to grips with maths, though the teacher spoke very s-l-o-w-l-y and CLEARLY, as if superior enunciation would enlighten everybody.

Science was only a fraction easier. I thought I would do well in history and geography but I was used to reading a book and then imagining what an era or a country would be like. I hated this school approach where everything was divided up into topics and you needed to memorize little gobbets of information.

I found French hard too, though I knew enough of it to guess my way through simple books. I discovered I mispronounced all the words. When I was asked to recite the numbers between one and twenty the class started sniggering as I said each number. By the time I said *dix-huit* as 'dicks-hewitt' they were in tears of laughter.

I hoped English would be my saving grace, but I didn't like the teacher, Mrs Godfrey, at all. She looked stylish, tall and thin, almost like a fashion model, and she wore black, with big black glasses framing her dark eyes. She was alarmingly strict, making sarcastic comments about all of us, even the clearly unfortunate.

She told us to write about a poem, 'Adlestrop'. I knew it by heart already so I cheered up. I knew I could write *pages*. I didn't have anything to write *in*, so I went up to Mrs Godfrey's desk at the front of the classroom.

'Feel free to wander at will around my classroom,' she said.

I gathered I *shouldn't* feel free. I didn't know what to do. She didn't look up from her marking. I shifted from one foot to another, not sure how to address her. She made dismissive waving gestures at me while I was making up my mind.

'I haven't got an English exercise book,' I blurted out.

She sighed. 'I haven't got an English exercise book, *Mrs Godfrey*,' she repeated. 'So what have you done with your English exercise book? Have you torn it into strips and scattered it down the lavatory? Have you hurled it frisbee-fashion over the nearest hedge? Have you fed it to a goat for breakfast?'

The class were sniggering again. I waited, crimson-cheeked, for her to complete her comedy routine. She looked up at last.

'What is your name?'

'Prudence King.'

'Prudence King, *Mrs Godfrey*!'

I repeated the ridiculous phrase.

'And you've mislaid your English exercise book?'

'I've never *owned* an English exercise book,' I said. '*Mrs Godfrey*,' I added, emphasizing her name.

This didn't please her. Her eyes glittered behind her glasses. 'Are you being intentionally insolent?' she asked.

I wasn't, but *she* certainly was. I wanted to slap her. She gave me a wretched exercise book and dismissed me back to my desk with another imperious wave of her long white fingers.

I couldn't understand why she was being so deliberately unkind. I decided I'd show *her*. I started writing reams on 'Adlestrop' – and lots of other Edward Thomas poems, bringing in some of the First World War poets too, and mentioning Helen Thomas's lovely book *As It Was*, which I'd found in a dusty corner of the biography section in the shop this summer. I'd read the bit where Helen and Edward go to bed in a lavender-smelling four-poster in a country inn again and again. I had just enough sense to leave this bit out of my essay, but I put everything else in, my hand hurtling down the page.

I thought we'd have to hand our books in to be marked but after twenty minutes or so Mrs Godfrey clapped her hands and went to sit on top of her desk, her long legs dangling, her feet elegant in black high heels.

'Right, class, who shall beguile us first?' she said. 'Daisy, perhaps you'd like to read out your essay?'

Daisy was a very large girl with wild tufty hair. 'Ooh not me, miss, I can't, miss, don't want to,' she said, giggling bashfully.

I could understand why she didn't want to when she read her piece out loud.

'"This is a poem about this place called Adlestrop. It sounds like a nice place. It's a short poem. It's got some funny words like unwontedly."'

That was *it*. I expected Mrs Godfrey to stamp all over her with her high heels, but she was relatively kind.

'Short, but sweet, Daisy,' she said. 'There's no harm in being concise.' She peered over at my scribbled pages and raised her eyebrows. 'All right, Prudence King, perhaps you'd like to share your words of wisdom with us?'

My hands were shaking but I read in a loud clear voice to show her she didn't really scare me. The class started sniggering again. I didn't understand why. This wasn't French. I knew how to pronounce all the words. I only realized why after I'd heard the others mumble through their pieces. It clearly wasn't the done thing to project your voice and read with expression. It was as embarrassing as my tablecloth frock. Even Mrs Godfrey had a smirk on her face.

'That's enough,' she said, long before I'd reached my conclusion. 'It's very kind of you to share your erudition with us lowly mortals, Prudence King, but I think we've had a tad more information than we can absorb.'

So that was it. I couldn't win. I was humiliated in maths and science by my ignorance, ridiculed in French for my mispronunciation, and mocked in English for my enthusiasm.

All right then, I thought. I wouldn't say a word more. I sat silently throughout the rest of the English lesson, refusing to join in a general discussion of 'Adlestrop'. I tried to hold my head high to show I couldn't care less, but it made my neck ache. I was so miserable I was on the verge of tears.

The last two lessons were devoted to PE. I relaxed a little. I was small and strong and whippy. I could run like the wind and catch any ball. I didn't know how to play any sporty games like netball and hockey but I was sure I could learn soon enough.

I followed the others to the gym and found the girls' changing room. Then the obvious dawned on me. I didn't have any PE kit.

The PE teacher, Miss Peters, came bounding up in her pale grey tracksuit, her whistle bouncing on her chest. I steeled myself for another sarcastic charade, but Miss Peters smiled at me with genuine warmth.

'Hello! What's your name then? Prudence? Ah, I love those old-fashioned names. I'm Miss Peters. Is this your first day at Wentworth? Bit of a culture shock, I expect. Right, Prudence, get yourself changed, lickety spit, there's a good girl.'

'I can't,' I said. 'I haven't got anything to change into.'

'You haven't got any old shorts and a T-shirt?' said Miss Peters. 'Oh well, never mind, I've got heaps of spares in my lost property basket, so nil desperandum. There, you learn Latin as a bonus in my PE lessons.'

She handed me someone else's off-white shirt and crumpled green shorts. I clutched them unwillingly, looking round the benches and pegs in the changing room. I couldn't see any cubicles.

'Where do you get changed, please?' I asked.

'Here!' said Miss Peters, waving her arm to indicate the room.

Sure enough the girls were starting to take off their school blouses and skirts as casually as if they were in their own private bedroom. I stared at them, astonished. I didn't even undress like that in front of Grace.

I started undoing my tablecloth frock down the front. It had a zip at the side so it clung too tightly to wriggle out of decorously. I always had to pull it up and over my head. My heart started thudding underneath the red and white checks.

I looked round wildly and saw a toilet sign. I grabbed my things and started shuffling towards it.

'Where are you off to, Prudence?' Miss Peters asked.

'The loo,' I said.

She was way ahead of me. 'Sorry, Prudence, we let Shanaz and Gurpreet change in the toilets, but I'm afraid the rest of you aren't allowed to be modest. Don't worry, we're all girls together – and nobody's looking at you anyway.'

Correction! They were *all* looking at me. I didn't know what to do. I just stood there foolishly, very very slowly unbuttoning and unzipping.

'Prudence, do get a move on,' Miss Peters called. She paused, arms akimbo, waiting.

I couldn't delay any more. She might come and rip my frock off herself if I didn't watch out.

I picked up my hem and tugged. I tried to whip my dress off immediately but my long hair got tangled in the zip. I was stuck with my head swathed in red-checked cotton, my underwear on display to everyone.

'My God, look what the new girl's wearing!'

'It's a *thong*!'

'She's wearing slag's knickers to school!'

'Bright pink lace – oh my God!'

I pulled my hair hard and tore my dress off.

'She's got the bra to match though she's hardly got any boobs to fit into it!'

'Where did you buy your underwear, Prudence? Ann Summers?'

'Who'd have thought it! She looks such a nerdy snob in that mad dress too. Wait till we tell the boys!'

I pulled on my borrowed top and shorts in a panic. Miss Peters shook her head at me as I sidled past her.

'You're at *school*, Prudence. It's plain bra and big knickers in future, OK?'

My face was as pink as my lace pants. I felt they were glowing luridly through my shorts and shirt. Everyone was looking at me, whispering and giggling.

I felt so bewildered. I thought this was the sort of underwear all these streetwise scary girls had been wearing since they were ten years old.

I was so flustered I couldn't concentrate when Miss Peters told me the basic rules of netball. I caught the ball, no bother, but kept running with it. I couldn't understand why people shouted at me when I rushed up to the net and scored a goal. Apparently it didn't count because I wasn't a shooter.

I didn't try after that. I shuffled aimlessly after all the others, not knowing what I was doing, not caring. I tried to imagine Jane running along beside me, but she backed away in horror and went to read her book in the corner. Tobias looked embarrassed for me in my hideous shorts and ambled off on his own. I was left lurching my way through the lesson, friendless.

It was torture getting changed back into my dress when the bell went. Everyone was all set to have another laugh at my underwear. I waited until I was the last girl in the changing room and then whipped my dress on quick.

I was worried about Grace. She'd be waiting for me at the school gate, wondering where I'd got to. I was supposed to go back to the classroom to collect my new books from my desk. I'd been set several pieces of homework. I wasn't sure how to find my way back down all the corridors. I decided I couldn't be bothered. I was determined never to come back to this terrible school so there was no point attempting any of the homework.

I rushed out of the door and peered across the playground. I saw a patch of pink way over at the school gate, but it was sandwiched between two regulation green blobs. I hurried towards them, wondering if Grace was being picked on. She saw me coming and waved – an idiotic exaggerated gesture, waggling both hands. The girl either side of her waved double-handed too. I approached them warily. They grinned at me like three monkeys.

'Hi, Prue! These are my friends, Iggy and Figgy,' Grace gabbled.

'I'm Jean Igloo,' said Iggy, baring her braces. She gave a mock shiver and mimed a dome in case I hadn't quite caught on.

'I'm Fiona Harrison,' said Figgy, flicking her long limp hair away from her long limp face. 'I've been Figgy ever since I made friends with Iggy. Plus I love figgy pudding, yum.'

'I'm Piggy,' Grace announced proudly.

She didn't need to explain. She did anyway, puffing out her cheeks and patting her fat stomach. I wanted to die for her but she seemed thrilled to bits with her new name.

I wondered if Iggy and Figgy had simply made up this nickname rubbish on the spot and were all set to make a terrible fool of Grace, but they seemed such sad loser girls themselves it didn't seem likely. But then maybe I was an even sadder totally lost girl myself. I hadn't made any friends, not even two such pathetic girls as these.

They seemed genuinely fond of Grace, telling her she mustn't panic if she couldn't do her homework, because she could always copy off them. They both gave her their mobile phone numbers, and Grace gave them our home land phone number.

'Grace!' I said. 'What about Dad?' He would go demented if an Iggy or Figgy rang asking to speak to her. Then I remembered Dad was stuck in the stroke unit and currently unable to speak to anyone.

Grace looked at me and tapped her forehead, indicating I was mad. 'Dad isn't there,' she said.

'Yes, but we'll be out visiting him this evening.'

'Yeah, but, like, that's not going to take, like, all night,' said Grace, grinning at Iggy and Figgy.

She was talking like them already, raising her eyebrows and sighing as if *I* was the sad sister.

'Come on,' I said fiercely, grabbing hold of her by the wrist.

She wriggled away and did the maddening wave again. Iggy and Figgy did it too.

'What's with all this waving? You look a total idiot,' I hissed at her.

'It's our secret club wave,' Grace said.

'Oh yes, very secret, you're all so subtle when practising it,' I said. 'Correction. You look like *prats*.'

'Why are you being so horrible?' said Grace. 'I'm just trying to fit in and make friends. Isn't that what you're supposed to do when you go to school?'

'You could be a bit *selective* about your friends,' I said, miming the handwave, while bucking my teeth and flipping my hair.

'Don't,' said Grace, going red. 'I *like* Iggy and Figgy.'

'Yes, well, they obviously *don't* like you, calling you Piggy. That's a hateful nickname.'

'It was my idea, not theirs. It's not hateful, it's funny. I think you're just jealous because I've made two friends and you haven't,' said Grace.

She saw me wince. 'Yeah, it looks like you've been *too* selective,' she said.

'I wouldn't want to be friends with anyone at this stupid school. I hate everyone in it. I don't intend to come back here ever,' I said.

I started running. I dashed into the road, not thinking where I was going, acting like a crazy person. There was a squeal of brakes and a loud honking of a car horn. I stopped still, disorientated, feeling a total fool. Grace was screaming in shock behind me and some guy was winding down his car window, ready to shout at me.

He didn't shout. He shook his head at me and said softly, 'You must be in a hurry to get home.'

It was Mr Raxberry, the art teacher.

'I'm sorry, I just wasn't looking,' I stammered.

I turned round to Grace. 'Stop that screaming!'

'I though you were going to be killed!' Grace whimpered.

'I did too!' said Mr Raxberry. 'But I try not to make a habit of exterminating my pupils, especially on their first day at Wentworth. Get back on the pavement before another car comes along and really knocks you flying.'

I shuffled back to the kerb, still feeling incredibly stupid, but pleased he was being so sweet about it. I thought he'd drive off but he parked the car beside us.

I squeezed Grace's hand to calm her down, and show her I was really sorry for being so mean. She squeezed back and stayed clinging to me.

Mr Raxberry smiled at us both. 'How did it go then, girls?' he asked.

'It was OK!' said Grace. 'I've got these two friends, Iggy and Figgy and—'

'Grace,' I interrupted, scared she was going to go through the whole Iggy-Figgy-Piggy saga all over again.

'We're friends,' Grace persisted. 'They're going to help me because I don't know heaps of stuff. Still, the teachers say I'll soon catch up as I'm still just in the first term.'

'That's great,' said Mr Raxberry. Then he looked at me. 'What about you, Prue?'

He remembered my name!

I didn't know what to say, so I simply shrugged.

'Oh dear,' he said. 'Yep. That was *my* reaction

my first day here. In fact I often feel that way now. But it'll get easier, you'll see. And I think your class is due an art lesson tomorrow. We can check each other out then. Bye now.'

He drove off, waving. I stared after him until his car had gone right down the road and round the corner.

Mum was waiting for us at the bookshop door, rushing out to hug us extravagantly as if we'd just escaped from a bear pit. It *felt* as if I had been bitten by sharp ursine teeth and clawed by big paws. Still, it was so comforting to know that Mr Raxberry understood. Did he really get anxious too? He looked so cool and laid-back with his casual jeans and his earring. It seemed almost impossible. And he was a *teacher*, for goodness' sake. No one could pick on him, tell him off or tease him. Mum wanted to hear all about our day, minute by minute. I couldn't face telling her any of it so I pretended I had to go and get on with homework straight away. I left Grace Iggying and Figgying, munching strawberry jam sponge cake, her mouth red and glistening as if she was wearing lipstick.

I sat cross-legged on my bed, my sketchpad on my lap. I *did* have heaps of homework but as I'd left it all at school I decided to forget about it. I started drawing instead, scribbling any old thing with my felt tips, just seeing what I could jot down. I drew me wearing a real square tablecloth, running like crazy, my hair flying out behind me, my mouth wide and screaming. I was pursued by a pack of bottle-green bears. I drew a car creeping along at the edge of the page, ready to run them all over. I shaded the windscreen, but you could see dark hair, a little beard and the tiny glint of an earring.

I was left in peace until half past five, when Mum closed the shop. She hadn't had a single customer all afternoon, but she still waited until it was five thirty on the dot, carefully consulting her watch.

'Come on then, girls, off to see your father,' she said.

We stared at her pleadingly.

'Mum, do we have to go every day?' I said.

'Of course we do!' Mum said. 'Think of your poor father lying there, waiting and waiting for us. How on earth would he feel if we couldn't be bothered to come? Besides, I've got his clean pyjamas, and a big slice of sponge cake to perk him up.'

'But Mum, Iggy and Figgy are going to be phoning me to see how I'm getting on with my homework – which I'm *not*; it's, like, *way* too difficult,' said Grace, raising her eyebrows and trying out a weird shrugging gesture.

'Stop twitching like that, Grace. And talk *properly*. Don't start talking like that in front of your father, you know it will infuriate him.'

'Everything I do infuriates him,' said Grace. 'It will probably make him worse seeing me. He won't mind a bit if you and Prue go and I stay at home. He'd definitely *prefer* it.'

I glared at her. I didn't want to get lumbered going with Mum while Grace escaped. 'I annoy him too. It was me that made him have the stroke in the first place,' I said.

'Don't, Prue,' said Mum. 'That's nonsense, I'm sure you had nothing to do with it. Come on, get ready, both of you. And don't breathe a word to your dad about going to school – that really will set him off.'

So we walked into town and caught the bus to the hospital. When we got there Dad was fast asleep, snoring, his mouth open, his false teeth slipping sideways over his lip so he looked like Dracula. We drew up chairs beside him and waited for him to wake up.

'Shall I give him a shake?' I said.

'Well, it seems a shame when he's so peaceful,' said Mum. She seemed content to watch him, as if he was a television. Grace and I wriggled on our orange plastic chairs. Dad didn't seem at all peaceful to me. He mumbled and groaned in his sleep, his good left arm and leg twitching. I wondered if he was walking and talking in his dream, unaffected by the stroke.

It must be so awful for him to wake up imprisoned in his half-dead body, unable to say the simplest thing. I felt so sorry for him that I leaned forward and took hold of his bad hand. I touched the limp fingers, as if I could somehow squeeze the life back into them.

Dad's eyes shot open. I dropped his hand quickly. I tried desperately to think of something to say to him.

'Hello. It's me, Dad. Prue. Well, obviously. How are you? Sorry, that's a stupid thing to say.' I was speaking as if I was the one with speech difficulties.

Dad tried to reply, his face screwed up with the effort, a vein standing out on his forehead like a big blue worm crawling under his skin. 'I want . . .' he said, in a new strange thick voice. 'I want . . .'

He couldn't manage to say what he wanted. Mum kept trying to interpret.

'Yes, Bernard? What do you want? A drink of water? A cup of tea? Do you need the toilet, dear?'

Dad groaned and thumped his good left hand on the mattress in frustration. One of the very few words he had left was a very rude term of abuse. He repeated it explosively, saliva glistening on his lips, as if he was spewing bile with his awful insult.

'Ooh, you naughty boy, Mr King,' Nurse Ray said, flitting past.

Dad said it louder, while Mum flushed, blood flooding right down her neck and across her chest.

'He doesn't know what he's saying, poor lamb,' she said quickly.

Dad obviously knew exactly what he was saying. He said it louder still.

It was so sad we wanted to cry, but it was embarrassingly funny too. Grace and I suddenly started spluttering with laughter. We put our hands over our mouths and bit our cheeks, but couldn't control it. Mum was furious with us.

'How dare you mock your father when he's so poorly!' she hissed.

We apologized meekly, but we couldn't catch each other's eye without collapsing. Mum glared at us and produced the slice of sponge cake, making 'yum-yum' noises and licking gestures. She tucked it into Dad's left hand but he tossed it indifferently onto the bedcovers.

'Can't you eat it, dear? Shall I break it up into mouthfuls, would that be easier? Come on, Bernard, you like my special sponge cake.'

'Can I have some, Mum?' Grace asked.

'Of course not! It's for your dad,' said Mum.

'But he's not hungry,' said Grace. She nodded across at his supper tray, still barely touched, though the sandwiches were starting to curl and the sliced banana on his bowl of yoghurt was going brown. 'Can I finish his sandwiches then?'

'No! It's a disgrace – that nurse should have seen to him. He obviously can't manage by himself.'

Mum complained bitterly behind the nurses' backs, but couldn't steel herself to say anything at all to their faces. When Nurse Ray popped her head round the door I dared mumble that perhaps my dad needed to be fed at meal times.

She roared with laughter. 'We've tried that lark, dearie. He spat gravy and mash all over my apron front. He'll eat if he wants to. His left hand's fine, and if he'd only co-operate with our physiotherapist his right hand could get back into some sort of working order.'

Dad said his rude word again when she said the word physiotherapist. Nurse Ray laughed, shaking her head at him.

'Yes, you've fallen out with her, haven't you, Mr King!' She turned to us. 'He won't let us dress him in his shorts, and yet the physio needs to see his legs properly to check the right muscles are working.'

'My husband's never been keen on shorts,' Mum apologized.

'Maybe you'd like to try to get him to practise his exercises? Little and often! These first three months are vital. He needs pretty intensive speech therapy too. His vocabulary is pretty limited at the moment.'

Dad said his swearword again.

'Mr King! Don't say that naughty word in front of your wife and daughters!' Nurse Ray said, pretending to be shocked.

'You could help your dad, Prue,' said Mum. 'You could teach him to say new words.'

'*Respectable* words!' said Nurse Ray, giggling.

'I – I don't know how to,' I said lamely.

'Just chatter to him same as always, darling, and then try to get him to say stuff back,' she said.

I'd never chattered to Dad in my life. He'd always interrupted us. 'Is there any *point* to this story?' he'd say. 'Or are you just in love with the sound of your own voice?'

Dad was the one who always commandeered the conversation. My mouth dried as I tried to think of something to say.

'I've got two new friends, Dad,' Grace said unexpectedly. 'Iggy and Figgy.'

'Shut *up*, Grace!' Mum said sharply.

'It's OK, I'm not going to mention you-know-what. I'm just going to tell him about my friends. Can you say Iggy, Dad? Can you say Figgy? They're easy words.'

Dad didn't try.

'Maybe you'd like to try ultra difficult words,' I said suddenly. 'Like . . . antidisestablishment-arianism?'

Dad had told us that this was the longest word in the English language. He stared at me. His face wobbled and a weird howling sound came out of his sideways mouth. He was laughing!

'An-ti,' he said. 'An-ti.'

'Yeah, ant et cetera, et cetera, et cetera,' I said. 'Or maybe you'd like foreign words? I know. Tell me the name of an Italian Renaissance painter.'

Dad struggled. 'Bot,' he said. 'Bot – bot-bot.'

'Botticelli,' I said. 'Yay! You're not only talk-ing, Dad, you're talking Italian.' Dad thought hard, his brow wrinkled. 'Spag,' he said.

'Spaghetti!' I said.

Dad nodded, but he wasn't finished. Saliva dribbled down his chin. 'Spag *bol*,' he said.

'Spaghetti bolognese, what else?' I said. 'I bet you'd nosh on a plateful of spag bol if they'd serve it up to you!'

Dad frowned. 'No – *nosh*,' he said, prodding at me with his good hand.

He'd always hated any slang. For once I didn't mind him nagging about it. It was such a relief to know that Dad was exactly the same inside – even though I'd longed all my life for him to change.

I gave him a kiss on the cheek when we said goodbye. He batted me away furiously, but he didn't call me the bad word.

'You've always been able to handle your dad,' Mum sighed, as we trailed home from the bus stop.

She was wearing her comfiest shoes, awful boy's lace-ups she found at a jumble sale, but she still lagged behind Grace and me. She was breathing heavily, shuffling Dad's dirty laundry bag from hand to hand.

'Here, Mum, let me carry it,' I said, ashamed.

'That's nice of you, dear,' Mum panted. 'Let me take your arm. You come the other side, Grace. There, isn't that cosy?'

It was anything but. I hated lumbering down the street linked to my mum and sister. I felt a total fool.

'I'll run on home and get the kettle on for a cup of tea for you, Mum,' I said, breaking free.

The telephone was ringing as I got the door open. It always unnerved me. It hardly ever rang. Had Dad had a sudden relapse?

I snatched up the phone and said hello anxiously.

'Hi, Piggy!' two voices squealed in unison.

'Oh for heaven's *sake*. OK, hang on a minute, she's coming down the road,' I said.

I hollered out the door to Grace. She came thudding down the street, cheeks bright pink, her pale eyelashes fluttering, looking alarmingly aptly nicknamed.

She was still on the phone long after Mum had had two cups of tea.

'Do say goodbye now, dear, it'll be costing Iggy's or Figgy's folk a fortune,' she said. She looked pleased, even so. 'Isn't it lovely Grace has made two friends already?' she said.

I barely responded.

'You'll make friends soon too, Prudence, just you wait and see,' said Mum.

'I don't *want* to make friends,' I said.

I knew I sounded pathetic. I stole up to my bedroom, stared at my bear pit drawing and suddenly crumpled it up because it looked so weird and stupid.

I lay on the bed, my face buried in my pillow. Jane came and lay beside me, nestling up close. She understood without my having to say a word. She'd attended Lowood School. She knew how awful it could be. But even Jane had found a friend, Helen Burns. I had no one.

Grace came bouncing up to bed, going on and on about Iggy and Figgy. I pulled the covers over my head.

'Prue?'

I wouldn't answer. I hoped she'd think I'd gone to sleep, even though I was still fully dressed in my terrible tablecloth frock.

'Oh Prue, you're not crying, are you?' said Grace, thumping down on the bed beside me. Her hand squirmed under the duvet. She patted me like a puppy. 'I know, it's so batty, me being the one to like school and make friends and stuff, but it's easier for me. I'm in Year Seven so we're *all* new. And I'm all silly and smiley so people can see I *want* to be friends.'

I couldn't bear Grace being so kind and understanding. Her sympathy somehow made things worse. I still wouldn't talk to her.

I lay awake for hours, hating myself for being such a mean sister. No wonder no one liked me.

'I like you,' Tobias whispered.

Jane had long since stolen away in her shabby button boots, but Tobias was there in the dark, holding my hand. He told me that he liked me precisely because I was strange and passionate and peculiar. He said all the girls in my form were banal and ordinary by comparison.

'I wish there was a boy in my form just like you, Tobias,' I whispered.

8

I felt sick when I woke up the next morning. I decided to stick to my original plan and not go back to school at all. What did I care about Mr Raxberry and his art lesson? He might be sweet to me but everyone else was so awful. Why should I put myself through such horrors?

I could walk to school with Grace and then keep on walking right into town. I didn't have any money to spend but I could window shop or go and browse in the library or walk in the park.

I packed my shoulder bag with sketchbook, crayons and my well-thumbed copy of *Jane Eyre* to keep me going all day long.

'Are you reading *Jane Eyre* in your class?' Grace asked. 'How lovely for you, as it's your favourite book! I bet you'll be top in English, and art, and everything else. I think I'm nearly at the bottom but at least Dad won't know and get mad at me. And Iggy and Figgy aren't, like, total brain boxes. Figgy kept getting the wrong answer in maths yesterday, but she didn't care a bit, she just got the giggles.' Grace giggled too just thinking about it.

I let her ramble on, deciding to keep quiet about my plans. I knew she'd worry and fuss. I didn't want her unwittingly giving me away to Mum.

But as we were walking down Wentworth Road there was a little toot of a car horn. I looked up and Mr Raxberry gave me a little wave.

'Is that the art teacher?' said Grace, as if she really wasn't sure.

'Yes!'

'He's quite nice,' said Grace vaguely. She was looking all around. Then she suddenly grinned maniacally, did her two-handed fool's wave, and scurried forwards on her fat little legs. There were Iggy and Figgy at the gate, grinning and waving back.

I told myself to walk on smartly past the school. Grace was so keen to see her silly new friends she'd barely notice. But somehow my feet in their old red strap shoes were marching me in through the gate.

I had to go. Mr Raxberry would be looking out for me. I didn't think he'd tell on me if I didn't turn up, but he'd maybe worry and wonder where I was. I didn't want to let him down when he'd been so kind to me. He was the closest I'd got to a friend at Wentworth, even though he was one of the teachers.

I didn't know where to go meanwhile. I didn't want to hang around Grace on the periphery of the Iggy-Figgy-Piggy club. I wandered off across the playground, dazed by the shouting, the swearing, the pushing and shoving. I decided to find my way to my classroom and lose myself in *Jane Eyre* for ten minutes. I blundered up and down endless corridors, hopelessly lost. By the time I found it, the classroom was crowded, and there was no chance of slinking to my desk and burying myself in my book.

The girls all gathered round me. I couldn't get them sorted out as individuals, apart from big Daisy with the tufty hair, and smiley Sarah, the girl with learning difficulties. But they all knew who I was, of course.

'It's Posh Prue, in her red-checked tablecloth *again!*'

'Yuck!' said another, holding her nose. 'I couldn't *stick* wearing yesterday's dirty clothes.'

'She's too posh to wash,' someone giggled.

I hadn't realized that most people wore a clean outfit every day. Mum made Grace and me wear the same dress all week, unless we spilled something down it. Our ancient washing machine hadn't worked for months, so Mum had to lug great plastic bags down to the launderette or wash everything out by hand.

I decided to ignore their hostile remarks. I settled at my desk, got out my book and tried to read. The words wiggled up and down the page, refusing to convey any meaning. My eyes blurred. I prayed I wasn't going to burst into tears.

'Hey you, Posh Prue, we're talking to you!'

One girl jabbed at me with her long pointed nail. Another snatched at my skirt, trying to lift it.

'Stop it!' I said.

'Just wanted to see if you've got your slag's underwear on again, that's all.'

'Get off! Leave me alone!' I cried.

I hadn't thought to change my dress but I'd had the wit to leave my beautiful doomed lace underwear at home. However, I knew my substitute grey-white baggy knickers would be equally ridiculed. I was determined to keep them hidden, though four or five of the girls were now scrabbling at my hem, exposing my thighs.

'There are boys in the room, for God's sake!' I shrieked.

They all fell about laughing, making silly 'Ooooh!' cooing noises, like demented doves. One of the bigger boys was lounging on the teacher's desk, legs dangling. He looked over at us.

'Leave her alone, girlies,' he said.

They backed off immediately, giggling and grinning. I stared, surprised. He was the only boy in the class who was remotely good looking. He was tall and slim, with longish fair hair. He'd customized his school uniform, his shirt hanging loose, his sleeves rolled up, and he was

97

wearing cool pointy boots instead of scuffed trainers like the other lads. It was obvious all the girls tormenting me fancied him like mad.

'So why have we got to back off?' said one of the girls. She was the fiercest, and probably the prettiest, with carefully curled dark hair and heavy black eye make-up like Cleopatra. She narrowed her outlined eyes at the boy. 'Are you waiting to have a shufty at the slag's underwear yourself, Toby?'

'Give it a rest, Rita,' he said, laughing at her.

He was called Toby! He did look just a little like my Tobias, though this was a real rough lad, not an ethereal boy with an angel for his best buddy.

I gave him a shy little nod. He winked at me and then carried on chatting to his mates. I knew he'd just taken pity on me. I was new and weird and hideous in my home clothes. He'd put me in the same category as smiley Sarah. He'd protected me automatically without even thinking about it.

It didn't look as if Rita saw it that way. She glared at me.

'Stupid little tart,' she hissed in my face. 'Don't you dare go making eyes at my Toby.'

'Don't worry about it,' I said, picking up *Jane Eyre* again.

My hands were shaking. I hoped they wouldn't notice. I dropped my book and hunted for my new timetable instead. I looked to see when I had an art lesson. It wasn't until the afternoon. It seemed as far away as Christmas. I had God knows how many terrible lessons to get through first, plus a session in the Success Maker.

It was the Portakabin we'd taken our tests in. It was clearly for pupils who were currently utterly *un*successful. Most of them were refugees, with an obvious excuse for their lack of ability in a completely foreign language. Even so, they mastered basic maths and science quicker than I did.

I was the worst student in the entire unit at IT. I couldn't even initially tell the difference between a television and a computer. Mr Widnes the tutor thought I was being deliberately insolent when I sat down in front of the unit television and struggled to switch it on.

'All right, Miss Clever Clogs, stop taking the mickey,' he said, sighing. Then he saw my expression. 'OK, you're obviously not into computers. But surely you've got a *television* at home.'

'We haven't, actually,' I said miserably.

It wasn't for want of trying. Grace and I had begged Dad year after year to let us have a set. Mum had stressed that it would be highly educational, and we'd just watch the arts and nature programmes.

'Educational, my bottom,' said Dad, though he'd put it more crudely. 'They'd just gawp at cartoons and sleazy rubbish – and you'd all get hooked on those wretched soaps.'

So we'd gone without, and consequently felt

more out of touch than ever with the modern world. Mr Widnes clearly thought I came from a bizarrely impoverished background and treated me very gently from then on. I was so stupid trying to do the most basic things and I couldn't even move the mouse around properly. His patience must have been severely tested.

It was a relief to escape the Success Maker at lunch time, but then I had to steel myself for English with Mrs Godfrey.

'Where's your English comprehension homework, Prudence King?'

'I haven't done it yet, Mrs Godfrey. I forgot to take my books home last night.'

I remembered to say her stupid name. I spoke politely. I still infuriated her.

'You don't "forget" to take your books home, Prudence King. Homework isn't a choice, it's compulsory at this school. You will do *two* comprehensions tonight, the one on page thirty-one *and* the one on page thirty-three, do you understand? Come and find me first thing tomorrow morning and hand in both completed exercises or you will find yourself in very serious trouble.'

I wondered what her very serious trouble could be. I thought of Jane Eyre, forced to stand on a table with a placard round her neck in front of all the other pupils at Lowood. I'd rather enjoy standing there like a martyr, gazing over their heads. I tried out an eyeballs-rolled martyr's gaze.

'Are you being deliberately insolent again, Prudence?' Mrs Godfrey said, flushing.

'No, Mrs Godfrey,' I said, lowering my eyes, though of course I *was*. She knew it, I knew it, the whole class knew it. Some of the tougher kids looked at me with a little more respect.

Mrs Godfrey noticed this, and went into serious rant mode. She asked me who on earth I thought I was, said she was sick of my attitude, stated that this was certainly not the way to start at a new school, etc. etc. It wasn't a full Dad-style rant, just an irritating bleat. I wondered why I annoyed her so much. I decided I was glad. How awful to be liked by someone so petty and arrogant and unfair.

I tried the trick I used whenever Dad flew into a terrible temper. I pretended I was in a suit of armour, with a helmet locked protectively over my face. I felt invincible inside my rigid silver suit. No one could get at me or hurt me or harm me.

I kept my armour on all through English and clanked along behind the other pupils when the bell went. It was time for the art lesson at last.

The art block was detached from the main building, in a special shack at the very end of the playing field. It took me a long while to get there. I trudged more and more slowly, as if I was truly clad in armour.

I looked longingly at the school gate. No one would notice if I slipped out now. It was so strange. The only reason I'd suffered this second

101

day of schooling was to attend Mr Raxberry's art class, and yet now I didn't want to go. I felt shy and stupid.

I didn't understand. I was *good* at art. Mr Raxberry wouldn't ridicule me like the repellent Mrs Godfrey. Mr Raxberry was kind. He was so different from all the other teachers. He didn't *act* like a teacher. He wasn't sarcastic or pompous or patronizing. He was gentle and funny and truthful and self-deprecating and sensitive. I could add any number of adjectives, even though I'd spoken to him so briefly. I could write an entire essay on him. I could write pages on a physical description of Mr Raxberry. I could paint his portrait, showing the way he tilted his head slightly, the wrinkles at the edge of his eyes, the softness of his white cheeks contrasted with the dark springiness of his small beard, the diamond earring in the centre of his neat earlobe . . .

I could conjure his exact image in front of my eyes, but I was scared of confronting the real Mr Raxberry. I ran my fingers through my long tangled hair, trying to comb it into submission. I plucked at my hideous dress. I put my hand against my cheeks and felt them burning. I hoped my nose wasn't shiny. I wished I could wear make-up like the other girls.

I wondered whether to trek back into school to find the girls' cloakrooms and check on myself in the mirror there. I was five minutes late for the lesson already.

I stood dithering, wondering why I was in such a ridiculous state. I took several deep breaths, trying to calm down. 'Go *on!*' I urged myself.

I imagined giant hands on my shoulders, pushing me forwards, frog-marching me to the art block. I stumbled along and got there at last, but I still couldn't force myself in the door.

I hung around outside, minute after minute ticking by. I could hear the sound of Mr Raxberry's voice, but not what he was saying. Every now and then the class murmured. Once they all burst out laughing. I longed to be in there, part of things, but I simply couldn't move. I didn't know what was the matter with me. I kept screwing myself up, teeth gritted, fists clenched, but my legs wouldn't move.

Then the art room door suddenly flew open and Daisy rushed out. She barged straight into me. 'What are you doing, hiding there?' she said, shaking her head at me.

I tried to relax my face, but not quickly enough.

'Have you got a pain?' Daisy asked.

I mumbled something vague.

'Is it your period?' Daisy said, sympathetic now.

I felt myself blushing. I knew it was silly, but we didn't even say the word at home. Mum had whispered some stuff about monthlies and bleeding and towels and then left me to get on with it. It was treated like a shameful secret. If Mum saw me rubbing my tummy or getting an aspirin she might whisper, 'Have you got your . . . ?' but she always let her voice tail away before uttering the taboo word. It was odd hearing Daisy discuss it so matter-of-factly.

'Shall I tell Rax you're not well?'

'*No!*' I said, dying at the thought of Daisy discussing my fictitious painful period with Mr Raxberry.

'Well, you'd better go and get cracking then. We're all doing a still life. I'm going to look for daisies for mine – like my name, get it? Rax says I won't be able to find any of them little white daisies but says there are these purply Michaelmas daisies, big ones, growing in the garden. He says no one will mind if I pick just one.'

Daisy hurried past me. I still stood there, motionless.

'Go *in* then, Prudence,' she said, turning. 'Don't look so scared. Rax won't get mad because you're late. He's dead cool, he never gets narked with anyone.'

I gave a little nod, took the deepest breath ever, and then went inside the art room. It seemed happily chaotic, students bobbing about in billowing smocks, setting up all sorts of still life arrangements, chatting to each other and calling to Mr Raxberry.

They were all calling him Rax to his face, but he didn't seem to mind. He strolled around, giving advice, juggling pots and books and ornaments into attractive still life arrangements, laughing as he listened to Rita going on about something.

He didn't have a clue I wasn't there. He couldn't care less.

I decided to slip straight out again while I had the chance. But as I turned he called my name.

'Prudence?'

I stopped, my heart thudding.

'Hi!' He came over to me. It was so strange seeing the real Mr Raxberry close up when I'd been imagining him so vividly. He was smiling at me, his eyes friendly, his head tilted slightly to one side, exactly the way I remembered.

'Did you get lost?'

'No. Well. Sort of,' I stammered idiotically.

'Don't worry. It took me weeks to find my way around. Tell you what, I'll draw you a little map.'

I thought he was joking and smiled.

'Now. We're setting up still life compositions, ones that hopefully reflect our personality, lifestyle, hobbies, whatever.' He looked at me. 'A still life is a fancy name for a lot of assorted objects. Look, here's some postcard reproductions.'

I shuffled them politely. I recognized most of them but held my tongue. I'd learned that some teachers thought you were showing off if you told them you knew all about something.

'Let's find you a little quiet spot in the midst of this bedlam.' He glanced round and saw an empty desk near Rita.

I couldn't bear the thought. 'How about over there?' I said quickly, nodding at the opposite corner where Sarah was happily splodging paint, her tongue sticking out with concentration.

'Great. Yes, keep Sarah company – but I think you'll need some kind of overall. Sarah gets a bit over-enthusiastic sometimes.'

'I haven't got one.' I looked down at my awful dress. 'I don't care if I get covered in paint, it won't matter in the slightest.'

Mr Raxberry raised his eyebrows but didn't argue. He found me paper, a couple of paintbrushes and six new pots of paint.

'OK, now it's down to you,' he said.

It was simple. I set up the paint pots, one paintbrush, the handful of postcards, and took *Jane Eyre* out of my school bag. I smoothed out my paper and started blocking in the shapes.

'You're doing that wrong,' said Daisy, bustling back with a handful of purple flowers. 'You paint *with* the paint pots, they're not supposed to go in the picture.'

'I *want* them to be part of my still life,' I said.

'But that's daft,' said Daisy.

'She's not daft, she's clever,' said Sarah. She smiled at me. 'We can do what we want. I'm painting red, lots and lots of red. I love red. I love your dress.'

'You're the only person in the whole world who loves this dress, but I'm glad you do,' I said. 'OK, I'll paint some red too. I'll paint the red paint pot first.'

'Nutters,' said Daisy, and barged past.

Sarah and I painted companionably. Sarah hummed tunelessly as she painted, but it was quite a soothing sound. I concentrated hard, so so so wanting to impress Mr Raxberry. He was wandering round the classroom, talking, rearranging, suggesting, trying to get everyone to settle down.

He came over to Sarah, holding a Red Delicious apple, a chilli pepper and a crimson china teacup.

'Hey, more red things for you to paint. Let's mix up your palate and get lots of lovely different shades of red. A bit of yellow here – go on, splodge it around with your paintbrush, that's right. There, that's a perfect pepper colour.'

Sarah laughed delightedly. I loved the way he talked to her. Some of the teachers treated her like a baby, some of them simply ignored her, and some treated her warily, obviously uncomfortable. Mr Raxberry treated Sarah with gentle respect and she clearly adored him for it.

'I love you, Rax,' she said, when he let her take a bite of the red apple.

'You're a very sweet girl, Sarah,' he said. 'Don't take a bite of the pepper now, it'll be much too hot and you'll be in serious trouble with your teeth if you bite my china teacup.'

Sarah giggled at the joke. Then Mr Raxberry came over to me.

He stood silently, looking.

I sat silently, waiting.

My mouth dried. I could feel my heart thumping. It had been so horrible when hateful Mrs Godfrey had been scathing about my English essay, but I could bear that. I needed

Mr Raxberry to like my artwork. I needed it badly. I didn't dare look up to see the expression on his face.

Daisy was watching. 'She's done it wrong, hasn't she, Rax? You're not meant to paint the pots and brushes, you're meant to do your own still life, aren't you? Like me with my purple daisies.'

'No, she's got it absolutely spot on *right*,' said Mr Raxberry.

I breathed out.

'You and your Michaelmas daisies are right for you, Daisy. Prudence feels that art materials and books are right for her.'

'Boring,' said Daisy, pulling a face.

I swallowed. 'So it's OK?' I whispered, still not looking up.

'You know it is,' said Mr Raxberry. He paused. Then he said softly, 'You're going to be the girl that makes my teaching worthwhile.'

I started to get into this new strange routine. I went to school, I stumbled through the fog of lessons, I went to Mr Raxberry's art class and the sun shone, dazzling me, and then I went to the stroke unit every evening and endured thunderstorms with Dad.

It was so unfair. I had to do all the talking to him. Mum contented herself sorting Dad's laundry and trying to feed him sloppy snacks — yoghurt and ice cream and cold rice pudding — though his false teeth were now firmly back in place and all too snappy.

Grace pressed herself right against the wall of his room, as if trying to burrow right through it into the toilet next door. She said nothing at all unless directly questioned. Sometimes her hands did tiny Iggy-Figgy-Piggy waves to herself.

I was the one who had to be the teacher for an hour or more, after a long day at school forced to be a pupil. I couldn't prepare what I was going to do because it so much depended on Dad's mood. I tried drawing a whole series of everyday objects familiar to him: a shelf of books, a shirt, trousers, a cup of tea, a plate of fish and chips, with the word carefully printed underneath. The first time I produced them Dad was tired after a tussle with the physiotherapist. He barely glanced at each card and shook his head lethargically whenever I asked him to say a word.

'Poor dear, he's not up to it,' Mum murmured.

I felt Dad simply couldn't be bothered. I was tempted to draw pink and black lace underwear to see if that got any response.

I tried again the next evening and this time Dad *over*reacted. When I showed him the cards his good hand whipped out and smacked them away.

'Damn-fool, damn-fool, damn-fool,' he growled. 'Not blooming *baby*.'

At least he was saying words, even though they were unprompted ones. I gave up the cards after that, although lovely Nurse Ray collected them up and asked if she could use them for some of her other patients.

I was so pleased I did her a set for all the old lady stroke victims, drawing a lipstick, a hairbrush, a nightie, a photo of grandchildren and a television. The nurse gave me a kiss and said I was an inventive little angel.

I decided I wouldn't bother trying to teach Dad any more. It was clearly a waste of time.

The next visit Dad was lying prone on his pillows, grey with fatigue, purple circles under his eyes. I thought he'd be extra irritable, but he grabbed hold of my wrist and tears ran down his face, dribbling sideways into his ears. I didn't know if his eyes were watering from exhaustion or whether he was really crying. I felt awkward and embarrassed, but tender too. I sat down beside him on the edge of his bed, trying to reassure him that he'd soon get better, he'd be out of hospital right as rain, ready to teach us and take us out on trips. I reminded him of all the places we'd visited, and Dad made a stab at repeating 'National Gallery', 'Hampton Court', 'Windsor Castle', 'Box Hill' and 'Hastings'. Most of the words sounded weird, but when prompted he could tell me which one had paintings, which was once owned by a Tudor king, which was owned by our current Queen, which was a high hill with a perilous chalk path and which was famous for a long-ago battle.

It was hard putting all this effort into teaching Dad, and then having to go home and do my own homework. I learned which teachers would simply moan a bit but not pursue it if you failed to hand it in, and which would harass and hound you. Mrs Godfrey was Queen Harasser and Hounder. I drew a picture of her like a one-breasted Amazon driving her wheel-spiked chariot while bloodied pupils wailed in her wake.

111

I didn't have an Iggy-Figgy back-up system like Grace. I had to struggle by myself. Sometimes the English homework seemed ridiculously easy, and the French and history and religious education and PSHE seemed a total doddle most of the time, but I floundered hopelessly with the science and ICT and maths. I *wished* we got art homework. I only had two double lessons of art each week, nowhere near enough.

I worked hard on my still life. I added a few extra favourite books – *The Bell Jar*, *The Catcher in the Rye*, *Tess of the D'Urbervilles*, *Frankenstein* and *The Chrysalids*, shamelessly trying to impress Mr Raxberry.

He nodded at each title, giving me his little smile. 'Mrs Godfrey would be proud of you,' he said.

'Mrs Godfrey *hates* me,' I said.

'No she doesn't!'

'She does, she finds me fantastically irritating. She's forever putting me down and punishing me. I don't know why, because I try really hard in English. Well, I did. I can't be bothered now.'

'Keep bothering, Prue. Maybe you disconcert her. She's not used to girls like you.'

'I'm not used to women like her,' I said. I paused. 'I wish all the teachers were like you, Mr Raxberry.'

'Shameless flattery will probably make you teacher's pet,' he said, laughing. Then he looked at me more seriously. 'Are you finding it all a bit of a struggle?'

'A bit,' I said carefully. Understatement of the century!

'And someone in the staff room said your dad's not well at the moment?'

'He's had a stroke. He's getting a bit better now, but still can't move much, or say many words.' My voice went wobbly as I said it.

Mr Raxberry looked at me, his eyes warm and concerned. 'It must be horrible for you,' he said. 'If it gets too much any time, use the art room as a bolt hole. Painting is excellent therapy. Here, this should help you find your way around.'

He tucked a roll of paper into my school bag. I didn't look at it there and then in front of everyone. I waited until I got home, and Grace was in the kitchen having a snack with Mum. The rolled-up paper was fastened with scarlet ribbon. I untied it, smoothed it out against my hot cheek, and then wound it round my finger like a fat silk ring. Then I carefully smoothed out the long rectangle of paper.

It was the map he'd promised me. He'd drawn the school in three dimensions, with the appropriate teacher in their classroom – each a wicked caricature. He'd drawn strange alien creatures lurking in the cloakroom and gnawing pizzas in the canteen. A great tribe of these two-headed claw-footed horned and tailed beings ran amok in the playground. He'd drawn me cowering away from them in my red-and-white tablecloth dress. I was standing at the start of a tiny scarlet pathway. I followed it with my finger, all the way past the playing fields, straight to the art block, where Mr Raxberry was painting at an easel.

I kissed the tip of my finger and then very carefully pressed it down on the tiny figure.

I didn't take my map back to school. I looked at it so often I could still see it written in the air after I'd rolled it up. I tucked it carefully in my drawer with the underwear set I never wanted to wear again.

Oh God, that underwear! The girls must have told the boys. They all seemed incredibly interested in it.

'Come on, Prue, show us your slaggy underwear,' they yelled after me.

They crept up behind me and pinged the elastic of my bra through my dress and tried to pull up my skirt. I hated the feel of their hot scrabbly hands. I knew I should stay calm and disdainful, but I shrieked and slapped at them, making a spectacle of myself. Then they'd mimic me and say stupid things until I was nearly in tears. Rita and her little gang, Aimee, Megan and Jess, would watch, smiling.

Mr Raxberry came along the corridor in the midst of one of these episodes.

'Hey, guys, make room for a member of the hallowed staff,' he said, waving them out the way.

They sauntered off, not too bothered whether he'd seen or not, because he was only old Rax.

Mr Raxberry paused, pretending to be looking at messages on the notice board. His back was to me, but when I started creeping away he turned and came over. 'Were they giving you a hard time?' he said.

'No, no!' I said, scarlet.

I couldn't bear the idea of telling him, maybe having to bring my underwear into the conversation. Mr Raxberry knew I was lying, of course, but he simply nodded. He walked along the corridor beside me, changing the subject, talking about an arts programme that evening.

'It's on cable telly. Do you get it? If not, I could maybe video it for you,' he suggested.

'That's very kind, Mr Raxberry, but actually. I don't have any kind of television, or a video either,' I said.

I waited for him to shake his head in astonishment and act like I was a creature from a different planet, but he just nodded again.

'So that's how you find the time to read so much,' he said. 'I should get rid of our television. My little boy watches endless horrible cartoons. I'm sure it's not good for him. Maybe that's why he keeps trying to beat up his baby sister.'

'You've got children,' I said. My voice sounded odd. I felt as if someone was squeezing my throat. It was such a shock. I knew he was probably in his mid-twenties, plenty old enough to have children. I knew he probably had a partner. Well . . . I hadn't actually thought about it too much. He was Mr Raxberry, my art teacher, not Mr

Raxberry, family man, with wife and two kids.

'My little boy's three. He's called Harry. And Lily's six months old. Hang on.' He felt in the back pocket of his jeans for his wallet. 'Here they are,' he said, showing me a photo.

I looked at the dark little boy clasping a roly-poly baby a little too tightly. They seemed surprisingly uninteresting, nondescript children, nothing like their father.

'They're lovely.' I tried to sound enthusiastic. I wondered what his wife looked like. Did I dare ask? 'Do you have a photo of your wife too?'

He paused a moment. 'Yes. Yes, there's one of all of us in here *somewhere*.' He fumbled amongst five-pound notes and travel cards and bunched-up stamps, and eventually found a crumpled holiday snapshot.

It was of the whole family, walking along an esplanade, squinting in the strong sunshine. Mr Raxberry was in denim shorts, a black sleeveless T-shirt and canvas shoes. He looked less like a teacher than ever. He was pushing a little baby Lily in a buggy. Her sunhat had fallen sideways, almost totally obscuring her face, but she was kicking her fat little legs contentedly. The little boy was scowling under his baseball cap, hanging on to his mother's hand, looking as if he was whining to be carried.

I looked at her. She wasn't as pretty as I'd thought she'd be. She was wearing shorts too, baggy ones down to her knees, with a big T-shirt over the top. She was obviously self-conscious about her figure. She wasn't fat, not like Grace, certainly not like poor Mum, but she was a little too curvy, big breasts but also a big tummy and a big bottom. Maybe she simply hadn't got her figure back after having the baby.

I looked at her face. It was difficult to tell what she was really like because she was frowning in the sunlight. The little boy was pestering her too. She wouldn't look happy and relaxed in these circumstances. Her hair was lovely though, soft and shining and fair, in a pageboy bob just brushing her shoulders. So Mr Raxberry liked big, curvy blondes. I wished I wasn't small and thin and dark.

I tried hard to think of something to say. There were a hundred questions I wanted to ask. Why *her* out of all the hundreds of women you must have met? What makes her so special? Do you tell her all your secrets? Does she put her arms round you and soothe you when you're tired or worried? Does she paint too? Does she read? Do you both sketch on holiday and then sit cosily at either end of the sofa, toes touching, reading your books? Do you go shopping together? Do you have the children in bed for a big family cuddle on Sunday mornings? Is she your childhood sweetheart, your one true love?

'What's her name?' I asked out loud.

'Marianne.'

'Oh. That's nice,' I said lamely. 'I wish I had a pretty name like that.'

'What's wrong with Prudence?'

'What's *right* with it? It's an awful Victorian virtue name. My dad used to be very religious. He really went overboard. I'm Prudence Charity and my sister's Grace Patience, can you believe it?'

'I've got a terrible name too. Keith. How naff is that, especially as I used to have a bit of a lisp as a child. Imagine! "My name's Keef." Thank God most people called me Rax. No, you're lucky, Prudence and Grace are quaintly beautiful names. They make me think of little Victorian girls in pinafores and button boots.'

'Exactly,' I said. 'My clothes are almost as old-fashioned!'

I was still rotating my hideous dresses. Mum had sent me to school with ten pounds. She thought we could be kitted out in second-hand uniform for a fiver each. But the school shop didn't charge jumble-sale prices. Each garment cost a fortune, even the old threadbare stuff. I bought us a shabby blazer which we wore in turns. It was too tight for Grace and it absolutely swamped me, but I was past caring.

Mum was appalled that it was going to be so expensive acquiring a whole uniform. She did question me several times on the exact price of the blouses and skirts and school ties. I heard her asking Grace too, as if she didn't believe me. I suppose she felt she couldn't trust me after I'd spent the maths tuition money.

'I think your clothes kind of suit you, Prudence,' said Mr Raxberry.

'I hate them,' I said. 'I can't wait to get the proper school uniform, but it's going to take ages before we can afford it all.'

Mr Raxberry paused. 'Perhaps . . . perhaps you could earn a bit yourself?'

'I don't know how. I can't get a Saturday job because I have to help in our bookshop and I don't get paid for that. I'd do a paper round but the shop down our street doesn't do deliveries any more. I can't think of anything else I could do.'

'Babysitting?'

'I don't know anyone with babies.'

'You know me,' said Mr Raxberry.

I stared at him. 'Do you really mean it?'

'Why not? Marianne and I need to get out more. I don't think we've had one proper evening out since Lily was born. How about it? Maybe Friday? Say seven thirty? We'll be back by eleven and I'll drive you home of course. Do you think your mother would mind?'

'Of course she won't mind!' I said.

Mum *did* mind, terribly.

'What do you *mean*, this teacher has asked you to babysit, Prudence? He barely knows you. You've only been at the school five minutes.'

It felt as if I'd known Mr Raxberry all my life, but I knew it might not be wise to say this to Mum.

'It's Mr Raxberry, Mum,' I said.

'Oh, Rax,' said Grace.

She called him by his nickname, even though he didn't even teach her year. I'd never been able to psych myself up to calling him Rax. It seemed too intimate and personal, even though the whole school, teachers, pupils, even the dinner ladies, called him Rax too.

'I don't care who he is, you're not going to a strange man's house,' said Mum.

'He's *not* a strange man, Mum. You've met him, remember? The teacher with the little beard and the earring.'

'Oh. Him! So he's got a *baby*? He didn't look old enough.'

'He's got a little boy, Harry, and a baby, Lily. And I'm babysitting for them on Friday night.'

'You are *lucky*, Prue. Can I come too?' Grace begged.

'No, it's just me. It will look as if we're asking for double the money if you come too, Grace,' I said quickly. 'He only asked me because I was moaning about not being able to afford the school uniform.'

I didn't want Grace tagging along too. I wanted to keep Mr Raxberry and his family all to myself.

'How dare you tell a teacher we can't afford the uniform!' said Mum.

'But it's true, we can't.'

'That's *our* business. You shouldn't go round blabbing about our finances,' said Mum, red with mortification.

'I don't *blab*,' I said. 'This was a private

conversation with my art teacher. And do you have any idea how awful it is to be the only girl in the school – well, apart from Grace – not to be wearing a proper uniform? I can't stand wearing this awful dress—'

Grace gasped. Mum looked stricken. I had always pretended I liked my terrible outfits so as not to hurt Mum's feelings. But what about *my* feelings?

'I'm sorry, I don't want to be rude—'

'Then *don't*,' said Grace.

'But it *is* awful, having to wear little girly dresses. They were fine when we were small, Mum, but now we just look eccentric and old-fashioned.'

'Well, I can't kit you out in a whole new set of clothing just because you feel embarrassed to be wearing my home-made clothes,' Mum said. She tried to sound cool and dignified, but there were tears in her eyes.

'I know, I know. That's why I want to earn some money babysitting,' I persisted.

'You don't know anything about babies.'

'It's not a *tiny* baby. She's sitting up, probably crawling around. And the little boy's three going on four. Anyway, they'll be in *bed*. All I have to do is be there, just in case they wake up and want a drink or whatever.'

'You might have to change a nappy,' said Grace. 'You won't like that. You practically throw up if you step in dog poo.'

'Shut up!' I said, my stomach heaving. I'd even

manage dirty nappies if it meant being at Mr Raxberry's house.

'How will you get home?' said Mum. 'I'm not having you walking the streets at night, but we can't afford a taxi.'

'Mr Raxberry is going to drive me home.' I said it calmly, though my blood fizzed at the thought. Mr Raxberry and me, alone in the car, driving home in the dark . . .

'I still don't like the idea. And goodness knows what your dad will say,' said Mum. She suddenly nodded triumphantly. 'What are we thinking of? You can't go, Prue, you'll be visiting your father at the hospital.'

'I can take one evening off,' I said. 'Just *one*.'

'He'll wonder where you are.'

'You can tell him I'm babysitting.'

'I can't say it's for your *teacher*. Your dad will have another stroke if he knows you're going to school.'

'He'll have to know *some*time, Mum.'

'I know, I know. But not yet, when he's still so poorly,' she said.

'Well, I'm still going babysitting on Friday, Mum, no matter what you say. I'll see Dad tonight; I'll see him every single night except Friday.'

'He'll fret about it.'

'I can't help it. I'm the one who has to sort him out and teach him and go over stuff. It's OK for you and Grace, you just sit there.'

'I know, dear. I'd be happy to take my turn,

but I just don't seem to have the knack for it.'

'I *certainly* don't,' said Grace.

'It's so hard, and I keep getting behind with my homework and getting into trouble at school,' I whined.

'You could try explaining that you're having to help out with your dad,' said Mum guiltily.

'I don't want to talk to them about Dad,' I said, sensing Mum was weakening. 'I just want to help out, Mum. I want to help Dad. I want to earn a bit of spare money. I know we're horribly in debt, I've seen all the bills.' I paused. 'I feel especially bad about that sixty pounds. I just didn't realize. I'd take the underwear back but I've already worn it. I've *got* to earn it back, then I won't feel quite so bad.'

'Oh lovie, all right, all right. I understand,' said Mum, patting my shoulder.

Grace understood more fully. She waited until we were in bed.

'What's this thing with old Rax, Prue?' she whispered. 'Why do you really want to babysit?'

'I *said*, I want to earn some money.'

'Yeah, but you're so *keen*.' She thought about it. 'Are you keen on *Rax*, Prue?'

'Of course not,' I said hurriedly.

'You're always hanging round the art block. And you always go pink when he says hello to you.'

'I do not!'

'Yes you do. Yeah, you've got a thing about him, haven't you?'

'No, I haven't. For goodness' sake, he's a boring old *teacher*.'

'Yes, but he's not really like the others. He's much more laid back and casual. Of course he's not really good looking—'

'Yes he is!' I said.

'What, with that weird little beard? Iggy and Figgy and me think beards are so gross. And then he's got this earring. Iggy says it means you're gay if you just wear one earring, though I suppose he can't be if he's got a wife and two children.'

'I don't care if he's got a boyfriend, a girlfriend, or a beard like Father Christmas. I just want to do some babysitting to earn a bit of extra cash, that's all,' I declared. 'Now shut up and go to sleep.'

She did shut up. I thought I had her convinced. But later, when she turned over, she mumbled, 'You *do* so fancy him. You can't fool me, Prudence King.'

I told Mr Raxberry I could babysit on Friday. I announced it as casually as I could, leaving it right to the end of the art lesson, acting like I'd almost forgotten about it.

'Oh, thanks,' he said, equally casual, as if it was the most ordinary everyday thing in the world. Maybe it was. Maybe half the class already babysat for the Raxberry household.

He told me his address and told me his road was on the number 37 bus route.

'Fine, no problem,' I said.

I wondered if he expected me to bus home after all? He *had* said he'd drive me home, hadn't he? Or had I just made that bit up? I couldn't help imagining Mr Raxberry in my head, the way I'd always imagined Jane and Tobias – but I didn't get muddled with them, because they weren't real.

Tobias insisted he *was* real, materializing as I walked across the playground.

I was supposed to be on my way to the Success Maker centre for an hour's maths coaching, but I was wondering whether to skip the class. I'd discovered that the special tutors there didn't always follow it up if you failed to put in an appearance. In fact they always greeted you with extreme enthusiasm, as if you'd passed a difficult exam simply by setting foot inside their glorified Portakabin.

I looked longingly in the opposite direction, towards Mr Raxberry's art block. I imagined myself on his map, running along the little red road.

'You can't go there. He's busy teaching,' said Tobias, pulling me back. 'Talk to *me*. We haven't spent any time together for ages. Please, Prue.'

'Oh go away. I'm not in the mood,' I muttered.

'You be careful. If you keep ignoring me I'll go away altogether, and then where will you be when you're lonely?' said Tobias. 'Watch out. I'm fading a little already.'

I looked at him. His beautiful face was blurred, his golden curls tarnishing to fawn, his blue eyes barely there.

I felt a pang, knowing that he was right. All my imaginary friends had faded away as I'd gradually grown out of them. I could barely remember the strange companions of my little girlhood: the white rabbit as tall as my waist, the flock of flower fairies, the tame green dragon with crimson claws, the black and white jumping cow who flew me over the moon . . .

Even Jane was fading now, though she had been my constant friend for years. I tried to conjure her up in a panic, but she pressed herself against the corridor walls, her back to me, refusing to show me her face.

'You see,' said Tobias. 'Watch out, Prue, or you'll lose me too. I'll go for good, I'm warning you.'

His attitude was starting to irritate me. He was a figment of my imagination. What made him think he could threaten me like this?

'Go then,' I said rashly. 'See if I care. I can always make someone else up.'

I turned away from him – and the Success Maker. I started marching back across the playground. I decided to hide in the girls' cloakrooms until the bell went. I had a book in my school bag. I'd be fine. I didn't need Tobias.

'Hey, Prue,' he called after me.

I heard him running – and then he caught hold of me. His hand was on my shoulder, clutching it. I turned. There he was, his fair hair tousled, a smile on his face, a real boy, so real I could see the freckles on his nose, smell his shampoo, feel the warmth of his body.

'Tobias!' I blurted, like an idiot.

'Tobias? No, I'm Toby,' he said.

Of course it was only that Toby from my class, Rita's boyfriend, the one most of the girls fancied.

'Oh, sorry,' I mumbled.

'Tobias!' he said, in a pseudo-posh voice, mocking me.

'Yeah, right, I know,' I said. I tried to act cool and casual, but sounded like a sad member of the Iggy-Figgy-Piggy club.

'You're going the wrong way,' he said. 'The Success Maker's that way.' He gestured over his shoulder.

'Yes, I know.'

'Aren't you supposed to be going for the maths session?'

'I don't feel like it right now, OK?'

He raised his eyebrows. 'Can't say I blame you. I've just been for an English session and it's doing my head in. Tell you what, let's skip everything and go for a smoke.'

I stared at him. I didn't want to go with him at all. I wasn't even sure what 'going for a smoke' really meant. Was it some sort of euphemism? But Rita had been particularly mean to me that morning, making stupid remarks, and when I'd tried to ignore her by reading my book she'd snatched it from me and thrown it in a corner, tearing the dust wrapper and crumpling several pages. I'd felt like slapping her, but she was bigger than me, and Aimee and Megan and Jess would start on me too. Going for a smoke with Rita's precious boyfriend seemed an easier way of getting my revenge.

'Sure,' I said. 'So. Where are your cigarettes, then?'

'Not *here*. Behind the bike sheds,' Toby hissed.

In every school story I'd ever read the rebellious children got up to mischief *behind the bike sheds*. I looked at him sharply, wondering if this was some elaborate wind-up. He was certainly behaving theatrically, putting his finger to his lips as we walked stealthily past the classroom windows.

I followed him, walking normally. I hummed under my breath to show him he couldn't boss me about. He shook his head at me, but waited until we were away from the classrooms, approaching these infamous bike sheds. I thought he'd tell me off, but he seemed impressed.

'You are so cool, Prue. You just don't care, do you?'

I shrugged.

'Is that why you're here? Did you get expelled from your old school?'

'I've not been to school, not for years. I went when I was little, but then my dad kept me and my sister at home.'

I peered at all the bikes in the banal little shed. It didn't really seem like a Den of Iniquity. Toby leaned against the ripples of the corrugated iron wall and fished a squashed packet of cigarettes and a box of matches out of his back pocket. I felt hugely relieved.

I'd never smoked before and inhaled warily when he lit one for me.

'You smoke then?' Toby said.

'Yeah,' I said, blinking because my eyes were

starting to water. I held my chest muscles rigid, determined not to cough.

'Rita's always nagging me to give up,' said Toby.

'Well. Rita's always nagging, full stop,' I said.

'Yeah, I can't stick that in a girl. They go on about how they're mad about you and then they end up mad *with* you, bossing you about all the time, trying to get you to change.' He paused. 'Have you got a boyfriend, Prue?'

I felt my face getting hot.

'You're blushing! Come on, who is he?'

'There's no one, really.'

'Yes there is!'

'No. Well, there's someone I *like*.'

'Ah!' said Toby. He inhaled deeply and then blew expert smoke rings.

I tried to copy but couldn't quite get the hang of it, though he did his best to show me how to shape my lips and tongue. I started feeling dizzy from inhaling. I leaned back against the wall myself, shutting my eyes for a second.

When I opened them Toby's face was alarmingly close to mine, making me start. His eyes were half-closed, his lips puckered, almost as if he was about to kiss me.

I moved sideways sharply.

'Hey, don't run away,' he said. He reached out for me but I ducked away.

'Prue, come on. I'm just trying to be friendly.'

'Yeah. And what would Rita have to say about that?'

'Rita doesn't own me. Sometimes I wonder what I ever saw in her.'

'Oh come on, she's the prettiest girl in the class.'

'You're prettier than she is. Listen, I've been thinking. You're not so great at maths and IT, right?'

'That's putting it mildly.'

'Well, I'm a whiz at it, honest. It's just I'm rubbish, at reading.'

'What, you don't like it?'

'I can't *do* it,' said Toby, shuffling. 'It's not that I'm *thick*. I'm severely dyslexic – that's what they say.'

'You mean you can't read at all?' I said, wondering how he could bear a world where books were meaningless.

'Yeah, I can *read*,' he said, flushing. 'I know all the words and stuff, it's just that I get them all mixed up. Plus at my old school they used to make fun of me, so I just stopped trying and messed around. *Anyway*, what I was thinking, you're obviously the hotshot at English. You talk like you've swallowed the dictionary and you can run rings round Mrs Godfrey, so how about you giving me a bit of extra coaching? Then I can help you with maths and IT in return. OK?'

'I don't know.' I stubbed out my cigarette, thinking about it. 'When would we do this coaching?'

'We could get together at lunch time.'

'Oh yes, Rita will be thrilled.'

'I told you, Rita doesn't own me. I'm sick of her telling me what to do.' He was obviously worrying about it all the same. 'Tell you what!' he said, smiling. 'We could go round each other's houses once or twice a week. What are you doing tonight after school?'

'I've got to go and visit my dad in hospital.'

'Well, tomorrow then. Friday?'

'Not Friday. I definitely can't make Friday.'

'Why? What are you doing then? Seeing your boyfriend?'

'I *said*, I don't have one. No, I'm babysitting.'

'Oh, right.' He didn't pursue it. He offered me another cigarette. I refused, feeling dizzy enough with just one. He edged up close again, so I started walking away smartly.

'Hey, come back. You can't just stalk off like that – someone will see you're not in class.'

'I don't care.'

'You really don't, do you?' he said. 'You're so different from all the other girls, Prue.'

'I wish I wasn't.'

'Are they giving you a hard time?' he asked. 'You come and tell me if they get at you too much. I'll sort them out for you.'

'Yeah, they'll relish that,' I said sarcastically.

'So, when are we going to get it together for these coaching sessions?'

'Sometime,' I said. I wouldn't commit myself any more.

'And are you going to give me a kiss sometime soon?' he asked.

132

'This year, next year, *sometime* . . . or maybe never,' I said, running off.

He ran after me, trying to grab hold of my hand, but I kept snatching it away. We must have run past Grace's class because she was all agog when we went home from school.

'You were holding hands with Toby Baker!' she said.

'How do you know Toby Baker?'

'*Everyone* knows him. Iggy and Figgy think he's dead cool.'

'Well, they're easily impressed. And I wasn't holding hands with him. I wouldn't.'

'*I* would,' said Grace. 'He's just, like, drop-dead gorgeous.'

I sighed at her. 'Shut up! You sound so vacant. You don't really think that at all – you don't like boys any more than I do. You're just saying stuff to impress Iggy and Figgy but they're not here, right, it's just you and me, so stop *pretending*.'

Grace blinked at me, looking wounded. 'I thought you were all in *favour* of pretending,' she said. 'Why do you have to be so horrid about Iggy and Figgy, they're my *friends*. I'm not talking to you now, see!'

I laughed at her. I knew Grace couldn't keep quiet for more than five minutes. Only *one* minute later she said, 'What were you doing with Toby Baker anyway? Is he your boyfriend?'

'No. Though I think he'd like it if he was. He kept pestering me,' I said.

I wasn't interested in Toby, but I couldn't help

enjoying the fact that he liked me, especially as so many girls seemed crazy about him. I knew he was the golden boy of our class, but I hadn't realized he was an icon throughout the school, with worshippers as small and silly as Iggy and Figgy.

'I wish you would go out with him. Iggy and Figgy would be seriously impressed if they knew Toby Baker was going out with my sister. Then you could invite him round to tea and I could invite them and they could actually meet him.'

'He wants to come round to our place so we can help each other with stuff.'

'Oh Prue!' Grace started skipping, her pink panda dress wafting alarmingly high up her large legs.

'For heaven's sake, Grace, stop acting like a toddler.'

'Don't be mean again.'

'Well, don't be so babyish. And there's no need to get excited anyway – I'm not having him round.'

'Oh!'

'Can you just imagine it, with Mum flapping round and asking him all sorts?'

'Yes, I suppose. And Dad would go bonkers if he found out you had a boyfriend.'

'Dad *is* bonkers now,' I said, sighing.

I didn't really mean it. I knew my father wasn't intellectually impaired. But he couldn't help sounding weird as he parroted key words and phrases after me. He sounded demented whenever he threw a tantrum and repeated the same swearword over and over again, like a satanic version of a Buddhist chant.

He was in a foul mood that night because the physiotherapist had made him wear someone else's shorts for his exercise session. Dad was outraged, utterly refusing to co-operate, hissing with rage whenever he looked down at his sad, skinny legs. He'd always loathed shorts on anyone, male or female. Grace and I weren't even allowed to wear them as little girls.

Mum helped him into his pyjamas while we lurked outside his room, but Dad stayed infuriated, even decently covered in his blue and white stripes. He kept pointing at the baggy black shorts hanging from the end of his bed. He acted as if a giant black bat was flapping from his bedpost.

'Yes, Dad. Shorts,' I said meanly. 'Say the word "shorts".'

Dad said a much more graphic word.

'They just want to help you, Bernard,' Mum said. 'The physiotherapist says she's sure you could get the use of your leg back if you'd just try to co-operate.'

'I know you don't like doing the exercises, Dad, but they're good for you,' I said.

'I hate exercises too. PE's my worst thing at school,' said Grace.

There was a sudden silence. Grace sat very still, her eyes bulging as she realized what she'd said. Mum looked agonized. Dad shook his head irritably.

'What?' he said. 'What? *What?*'

'She said she hated exercise, dear. So do I. Now, where's the girl gone with the tea trolley? Isn't it time you had a nice cup of tea?'

Dad looked at her scornfully. He could see through her diversionary tactics in two seconds. He turned to me. 'What?' he repeated.

'Grace and I have started a school game, Dad,' I said. 'We're teaching each other, setting each other tasks, as you're ill and can't do it for us just at the moment. The rule is, we have to do absolutely everything the other one asks. So I get a bit mean to poor Gracie sometimes, and make her do all these exercises for PE.'

Dad's eyes were narrowed. I stared innocently back at him. Then he suddenly started laughing, wheezing away as if he was about to break in two.

'*More* PE. More more more. Grace fat!'

I forced myself to laugh too. Mum laughed. Grace laughed the loudest.

It was OK. We'd got away with it.

I walked along Laurel Grove, peering at all the neat 1930s houses. I looked at the bay trees in ornamental blue pots outside front doors, the carriage lamps, the pebbles and spiky plants in mock Japanese gardens. I couldn't imagine Mr Raxberry living there. Surely anyone with an earring and artistic tendencies would be considered deeply suspect?

I checked the address, written in his own lovely italic writing on the back of my school jotter in my bag, though I knew I'd got it right. My bag was full of things to do: my sketchpad and crayons, patchwork, two novels and an old shop copy of Penelope Leach's baby book in case of emergencies.

Number 28, 30, 32 – and there was number 34 Laurel Grove. At first glance it didn't look any different from the other houses in the road, a black and white semi-detached house with a sloping roof and a green front door. At *second* glance, as I walked up the garden path, it stayed an ordinary, slightly shabby house with an abandoned Thomas the Tank Engine shunted into a cotoneaster bush and muddy frog wellingtons lolling on the porch. Mr Raxberry didn't belong here. He should be living in an urban warehouse flat, large and airy and white, with huge canvases on the wall and a large easel in the centre of the room. I saw him there, painting, his face tense with concentration, his earring catching the sunlight. I was sitting on a black leather sofa, talking to him while he painted my portrait. *That's* the way it should be.

I rang the doorbell and waited. I could see into the living room, glimpse the cream canvas chairs and the beige sofa and the bleak square shelving. I *must* have come to the wrong address.

Then the door opened. There was Mr Raxberry in black jeans, soft blue shirt and bare feet, but he was holding a baby, a little girl with tufty black hair and a cross expression. She was wearing a small navy jumper and nothing else. Her little pink bottom perched neatly on Mr Raxberry's hand.

'Hi, Prue. Sorry, we're in the middle of a nappy change, aren't we, Lily?'

Lily grizzled irritably. I held out my hand to her uncertainly and she reared away from me, butting her head against Mr Raxberry's shoulder. She started crying in earnest.

'Take no notice, she's tired,' said Mr Raxberry. 'Come in, come in.'

I stepped into the hall and followed him towards the beige living room. The carpet was strewn with wooden blocks and wax crayons and limp teddy bears.

'Sorry! We'll get cleared up in a jiffy. I'll just shove a nappy on Lily. Marianne's upstairs giving Harry his bath. She'll be down in a minute. Would you like a coffee or a Coke or something? And I'd better show you how the television works.' He said all this boring ordinary stuff, the baby still balanced in his hand, but his eyes were looking at me. *They* were saying, 'Hark at me, bleating all this suburban daddy stuff. What am I *like?*'

'It's OK,' I said. 'I'll clear up the living room if you want to go and do the baby.' I wondered if I ought to fix the nappy myself but I didn't want him to see me struggling, doubtless snapping the wrong bits together.

He smiled at me gratefully and went upstairs with his grizzly little girl. I got down on my hands and knees and started gathering toys. The carpet was a bit gritty and could have done with a good going over with a hoover. Mum would have been ashamed to have a visitor see her house in such a state. Maybe Mrs Raxberry simply couldn't be bothered? I imagined her sprawling on the sofa, stuffing chocolates and watching television while the baby wailed and the little boy created havoc.

Why would Mr Raxberry want a wife like that? Why didn't he want a wife who was artistic and creative? He was so chic and stylish himself. Why not go for a complementary partner?

Mrs Raxberry came into the room at that moment. I stared at her, startled. I'd been imagining her as this great wobbly jelly woman when she was just an ordinary fair-haired mum, thinner now than the photo in his wallet, though the woollen dress she was wearing was clinging a little too closely.

'Hello! You must be Prudence. I'm Marianne. Oh God, I'm sorry, let me do that. I meant to get everything cleared up before you came but it's just been one of those days, and the kids have been driving me crazy.'

I must have looked alarmed. She laughed at me. 'Don't worry, they'll be fine. They'll both sleep like logs now. Harry's putting up a *bit* of a fight about going to bed, but it's not like it's a major strop.'

With perfect timing Harry started screaming upstairs: 'Mum! You come back now! I need you *now*! I want a story NOW!'

Mrs Raxberry raised her eyebrows and sighed. 'Can't you see to him, Keith?' she called up the stairs. She turned to me. 'Harry's a bit unsettled because we haven't been out for ages. He'll calm down soon, I promise. Keith will just read him one more story so he doesn't get too worked up, and then I'm sure he'll drop off. If he gets *really* upset, though, you can always ring us at the restaurant, I've left my mobile number by the telephone. I don't really know why we're going out for a meal. I had some fish fingers with Harry at tea time to keep him company even though I'm supposed to be on a diet. Does this dress look much too tight still? It looks really awful, doesn't it?'

'No, no, it looks lovely on you,' I lied.

I was disarmed by the way she talked to me like a friend she'd known for years. I didn't want to be her friend. I didn't want her to be so nice.

She wasn't so nice to Mr Raxberry though. Harry was still shrieking.

'For God's *sake*, Keith, can't you read Harry his story?'

'I'm changing Lily's nappy at this exact moment in time,' he called back.

'Can't you do both? Haven't you heard of multi-tasking?' She sighed, raising her eyebrows at me. 'Men! Why do they have to make changing a nappy into such a big deal? It's like he wants a medal pinned to his chest every time he does it.'

I wriggled uncomfortably, not knowing what to say.

'Oops! I keep forgetting he's your teacher. What's he like at school, eh? Is he pretty hopeless?'

'He's a brilliant teacher,' I said stiffly. 'He's taught me so much already.'

'Yes, I know you like art. Keith's told me all about you.'

I wanted to ask exactly what he'd said, getting her to repeat it word for word, but I was too shy.

'Art's my favourite subject,' I said. 'I want to go to art school.'

'Ah. Well, try not to end up an art teacher, Prudence.'

I made some non-committal noise. She was standing on tiptoe, peering at herself in the mirror above the mantelpiece.

'This dress *is* too tight, especially if I'm going to be having a big meal. I wanted to go to see a film tonight but there doesn't seem to be much on. I think I'll change into my navy top and my white trousers, yeah?' She looked at me. 'You're so lucky to be so skinny. Mind you, I wasn't much bigger than you before I had Harry. Dire warning: don't have kids! Come on, you'd better come and meet them. You can get them sorted out while I change. Keith's probably put a nappy on Harry and is reading *The Gruffalo* to Lily.'

I found Mr Raxberry sitting up on Harry's bed, with Lily on his lap and Harry cuddled against his chest. Lily was still nappyless. Harry was muttering in an ungrateful monotone, 'Don't want you reading, Daddy, I want *Mum.*'

I decided I didn't much care for either child. Harry was one of those bullet-headed little boys, wriggling and squirming and grumbling. Lily seemed sweeter, but her pink prawn limbs and bare bottom made me feel a bit squeamish. I put on a false smile nevertheless.

'What lovely children,' I said, practically clapping my hands and applauding them.

'Who's that big girl? I don't like her,' said Harry.

'That's Prudence. She's going to look after you and Lily tonight,' said Mr Raxberry.

I knew this was a silly thing to say. Harry reacted predictably, insisting he didn't want to be looked after by me, he didn't like me, he didn't like his dad either, he wanted *Mum*. Mrs Raxberry came running, half in, half out of her navy top.

'I'm here, Harry. It's OK, sweetie.' She took a deep breath. 'For God's sake, Keith! *I'll* sort the kids. You go and get changed.'

'Changed?'

'You're not going to wear those awful jeans to La Terrazza?'

'OK, OK.'

I couldn't understand her. Mr Raxberry looked wonderful in his jeans. Why did she treat him like an idiot all the time?

She picked Lily up. 'There now, come to Mummy. Who needs a nappy to cover her little pink bot?' she cooed in a silly voice.

Lily kicked her little legs like a frog and then weed all down Mrs Raxberry's white trousers. She squealed, and told Mr Raxberry it was all his fault. She stamped off to get changed again, a wet, squirmy Lily under one arm.

I looked at Mr Raxberry. He looked at me. We were both trying not to burst out laughing. He raised his eyebrows at me and then went off to get changed himself.

'OK, I'll read you your Gruffalo book, Harry,' I said, in a nice-bright-cheerful-nanny voice.

Harry pushed the book away peevishly and slid down the bed, half-hidden under the sheets. 'Stupid smelly big girl,' he said, entirely disappearing under the duvet.

I ducked my head under too. 'Don't mess with me, little boy,' I hissed. 'You come out and I'll tell you your story and if you're very very good I'll give you some chocolate when your mum and dad have gone out.'

'A whole big bar?' said Harry.

'Well, that depends on how good you are.'

He was positively angelic, especially when it mattered, saying goodbye to his mum and dad. I decided childcare was a piece of cake – well, bar of chocolate. If I ever had children they'd be impeccably behaved, though they'd probably be little dumplings with no teeth.

Lily was too little for bribery, but she seemed contented enough. She looked like a very tiny snowman in her small white sleeping suit. I held her on my lap as I sat on Harry's bed and made her wave her little arm to Mr and Mrs Raxberry.

'You're sure you're going to be all right, Prudence?' said Mrs Raxberry. 'You look very *young.*'

'I'm fifteen,' I said. Well, I would be next year.

'Oh dear, is that all?' she said doubtfully, pulling down her skirt. She was back in her skin-tight dress. 'You have done lots of babysitting before, haven't you?'

'I've been babysitting my little sister for years,' I said truthfully. 'Don't worry, we'll be fine.'

I produced the chocolate as soon as they'd gone out the front door. Harry drooled his way through the entire bar. I had to keep wiping his mouth so he wouldn't get chocolate slurp on his sheets, and when his eyelids started drooping I got his toothbrush and whisked it round his teeth as he sprawled, half asleep. He grumbled at me, but turned over on his side and rubbed his nose into the soft tummy of his teddy bear.

Lily cried a little when I carefully slid her into her wicker cot, but she calmed down when I stroked her feathery curls.

'There now,' I whispered.

I watched over the two of them for a few minutes. They'd stopped being irritating now they were asleep. They were just two sweet little children. I'd always thought I couldn't stand to have children myself but now I wasn't so sure. I imagined being Mrs Raxberry. This was my house, these were my children, he was my husband.

My heart started thumping at the thought. I tiptoed out of the children's bedroom and hovered on the landing. I peered inside the bathroom, still wet and steamy. I felt the two large, damp, navy towels, wondering which one was his. I looked at the toothbrushes in the jar and thought of his even white teeth, and the way he smiled.

I looked at the razor and imagined it gliding down his soapy cheeks, carefully stopping short of his neat beard. I looked at the hairbrush and thought of it tugging through his dark shiny hair. I looked at the two navy towelling dressing gowns hanging on the peg. They seemed identical in size. I sniffed them cautiously. One smelled faintly of face cream and hairspray.

I held the other one, his one. I fitted my arms into the sleeves and wrapped the gown round me, tying it tightly. It felt as if he was holding me, wrapping his arms round me. I closed my eyes for a moment, imagining it. When I looked in the misty mirror I almost expected him to be looking over my shoulder, smiling at me.

I took his dressing gown off reluctantly and hung it carefully back on the hook, suddenly worried that they'd been arranged in a special way.

My face was flushed, my hands were trembling. I told myself to go downstairs and start reading my book, do my homework. *I could watch television!* I knew Grace – and Mum – would want a second-by-second account of every programme I'd watched, even the adverts.

I couldn't help it. My feet were creeping along the carpet to the next door, their bedroom. I pushed the door open, holding my breath. I'm not sure what I'd imagined. It wasn't this ordinary, untidy room with discarded clothes scattered over the daffodil duvet and grubby make-up spilling across the dressing table. I fingered each item curiously, opening her face cream and trying a tiny bit, dabbing her powder on my nose, daubing her pink lipstick on my lips. It tasted sickly sweet. I wondered if he liked the taste when he kissed her. *Did* he still kiss her? Of course he must do. They had children, didn't they?

I looked at their bed, half the poppers missing on their yellow duvet, the machine-embroidered flowers unravelling on their pillows, their padded headboard faded. Mr Raxberry saw everything in such sharp focus. How could he bear to sleep in this messy room?

I went to the white fitted wardrobe and opened it. Her clothes were on one side, a little rumpled, some falling off their hangers, pinks and lilacs and primrose, beige and navy and tan. His clothes were the other side, mostly black, with some blue denim. I stroked them very gently and cautiously, as if they were thoroughbred horses. I even knelt down and examined his shoes, trying them on my hands, making them do a little tap dance. He had small neat feet. I set the shoes back carefully, side by side.

I peeped inside the chest of drawers. I wanted to find special secret things but I just found underwear, socks, her tights in a brown tangle like a nest of soft snakes.

I looked at the books on either side of the bed.

147

Hers were pastel coloured to match her clothes, romantic tales of single women looking for true love. His books were special – a battered Penguin *David Copperfield*, a John Updike, a Hanif Kureishi. I flicked through them, wondering which were his favourite passages. I knew we had *David Copperfield* in the shop and several Updikes, and I could search for the Kureishi paperback in boot fair boxes. I could read them all and then bring them casually into one of our conversations and he'd be amazed at the similarity of our literary taste.

No, he wouldn't be fooled. He'd guess I'd sneaked into his bedroom and fingered the books by his bed. I piled them up again quickly and then backed out of the room. I checked the children again, trying to justify my presence, and then went downstairs.

I made myself a cup of coffee, taking it black and strong because it seemed more sophisticated, though it made me shudder. Then I forgot all about trying to act like an adult, becoming transfixed by the chocolates and sweets in a big earthenware bowl. Mum made toffee and fudge and truffles, but we never had a whole bowlful, not even at Christmas. I didn't imagine Mr Raxberry tucking into all the goodies. *She* was the one who had secret nibbles all day. Maybe she bribed Harry into good behaviour too.

She'd told me to help myself to anything I fancied. My fingers hovered over this and that before I selected one creamy white truffle. I rolled it round and round my mouth while I switched on the television and flicked through all the channels. I couldn't settle to watch anything. It was as if I was acting in my own highly coloured romantic drama. I needed to savour it.

I sat on the sofa, tucking my legs up, imagining what it would be like to sit there every night, the children upstairs in bed and Mr Raxberry beside me. Would we watch television, would we read our books, would we talk? Would we stay at separate ends of the sofa or would we loll against each other, cuddling up together?

I felt something hard and flat under the cushion, some little book. No, it was a sketchpad, a little Rowney one. I had the same size sketchpad at home. I opened it, holding my breath. Mr Raxberry's own private drawing book! I turned each page carefully, terrified of smudging the charcoal and chalk. There were quick sketches of the children: Harry running, riding his toddler bike, watching television with his teddy under his chin. There were sketches of Lily too, lying on her back kicking, propped in her highchair nibbling toast, laughing uproariously, her eyes squeezed shut and her mouth wide open.

There were several sketches of Mrs Raxberry feeding Lily, telling Harry a story, and one of her on her own. She was lying stretched out on the sofa, one arm above her head, the pose smoothing out her thick waist and large stomach so that she just looked lush and womanly.

I frowned at the picture. It was so tender and intimate, even though she was fully dressed. I wanted to rip it out of the book. I forced myself to flip past it. There were plant studies, bowls of fruit, a tree, and several sketches of the school, as seen from the art-room window. There were sketches of some of the pupils – a lovely one of Sarah laughing as she daubed thick paint.

Then I turned the page and saw a portrait of a thin girl with thick curly hair, a girl with big dark eyes gazing intently into space, in her own imaginary world. The girl was wearing a dress, the check pattern lightly suggested.

It was me.

They came home just after eleven.

'How were the kids? Did they wake? Did you give Lily her bottle? Did Harry want you to read to him?' Mrs Raxberry said in a rush as she burst through the door.

'They've been fine,' I said. 'Lily cried around ten and I warmed her bottle, but she was asleep again before I could feed her. There hasn't been a peep out of Harry.'

'Great, great! I'd better go and wake him for a wee then, otherwise we'll have a wet bed. Here's your money, Prue. Thanks so much. I hope you can maybe babysit again some time?'

I took a deep breath. 'I'd love to.' I shrugged on my jacket and went into the hall. I didn't even make eye contact with Mr Raxberry. I felt as if I'd been snuggled up with him all evening.

If I so much as glanced at the real man I was sure I would blush.

'Hey, where are you going, Prue?' he called after me.

'Home.'

'Well, hang on, I'm giving you a lift.'

It was what I'd been thinking about ever since I agreed to babysit, but now I felt weirdly scared.

'No, no, it's OK. I'll get the bus. It's not far, I'll be fine, honestly. Bye!' I burbled.

'I'm taking you home in the car,' Mr Raxberry said firmly. 'Stop arguing.'

So I stopped. I called goodbye to his wife and then Mr Raxberry and I walked down his garden path together.

'Here we are,' he said, opening the car door for me. 'Oh God, excuse the kids' rubbish. We don't even notice it any more.'

I kicked several juice cartons, a little truck and a set of plastic keys out of my way and sat in the front seat. Mr Raxberry got in the driver's seat.

'Seat belt,' he said to me.

I stared at him, I looked at my lap, I dithered anxiously. I'd been driven in a car so rarely I didn't know how to use a seat belt. Dad had once run a van for book-buying expeditions, but had rarely taken us out as a family. When the van needed a new gearbox several years ago he'd had to scrap it.

Mr Raxberry leaned towards me. For one mad magical moment I thought he was going to kiss me. Then he reached past me and pulled on a strap. He was simply fixing my seat belt for me.

'There now, safely strapped in,' he said, starting up the car. 'What did you do with yourself this evening, then?'

I blushed, but it was mercifully dark in the car. 'Oh, I read a bit, did a little homework. Whatever,' I said vaguely.

'I hope it wasn't too lonely for you. You can always bring a friend with you another time, or maybe your sister?' he said lightly.

'No! No, I'm fine by myself, I don't mind a bit,' I said quickly.

He looked over at me, nodding. 'I know. I liked my own company as a kid too. I used to go fishing most weekends. It wasn't to catch the fish; I used to feel sick and sorry if I ever *caught* anything. I just wanted to be by myself for a bit.'

'Do you still go fishing now?'

'Chance would be a fine thing! At the weekends we do the Sainsbury's run, and then I look after the kids while Marianne sees her girlfriends, and then on Sunday we drive all the way to Basingstoke to see her parents for a Sunday roast, and often Marianne's sister's there with *her* husband and kids, so we're all very busy playing Happy Families.' He kept his voice very light and even. I didn't know whether he was happy or bitter or bored, and I couldn't really ask.

We only had about ten minutes together and

there was so much I wanted to ask him. But everything I wanted to know was too direct, too personal.

Do you think I'm really any good at art?

Do you like me?

Why did you draw me in your secret sketchbook?

Instead, I chattered childishly about fishing, asking about lines and hooks and bait, as if I *cared*. I felt as helpless as a fish on the end of a line myself. He was reeling me in tighter and tighter until I was out of my element.

We turned into my street and I gave him directions to the shop.

'Oh, it's *this* shop! I've been here. I've had a good browse in the art section, but someone gave me a sarcastic ticking off for using the shop like a library.' He paused. 'Would that have been your dad?'

'That would *definitely* have been my dad,' I said. 'No wonder we have hardly any customers. He's always so rude to them.'

'How *is* your dad?'

'Well, he can't talk much still, and he can't really walk either.' I sniffed, suddenly near tears, feeling guilty because he'd have given Mum and Grace such a hard time at the hospital tonight.

Mr Raxberry didn't quite understand. 'Oh Prue, I'm so sorry,' he said. His hand reached out and covered mine.

The car took off like a rocket, soaring into space,

whirling up and over the moon, his hand on mine, his hand on mine, his hand on mine . . .

He gave my hand a gentle squeeze, and then put his own hand back on the steering wheel. The car hurtled back into the earthly atmosphere. He drummed his fingers on the wheel. We sat still, neither of us saying anything, staring straight ahead.

'Well,' he said. I heard him swallow. 'Perhaps you'd better go in now.'

'Yes. Thank you for taking me home, Mr Raxberry.'

That made him look at me. 'Hey, what's with this formal Mr Raxberry thing? Everyone at school calls me Rax – you know that.'

'OK then. Rax.' I giggled. 'It sounds funny.'

'Better than Keith.'

'Why doesn't your wife call you Rax?'

'Oh. She's known me too long. We were childhood sweethearts.'

I wasn't sure whether this was a good thing or not. 'You knew each other when you were at school?'

'From when we were fourteen.'

'*My* age?'

'Yep.'

'Goodness.'

'I take it you haven't got a sweetheart?'

'No!'

'I'm glad to hear it. Off you go then. See you at school.'

'Yes. Thank you. Goodbye . . . Rax.' I giggled

again and then undid my seat belt and jumped out of the car. He waited until I let myself in the shop door. I turned and waved and he waved back and then drove off.

I wanted to stay in the dark shop, breathing in the musty smell of old books, going over our car ride again and again, remembering every word, every gesture, every touch. I could hear Mum calling me from her bedroom, fearful at first in case I might be a burglar, though what self-respecting thief would want crumpled Catherine Cookson paperbacks, battered Ladybirds, leatherette Reader's Digest compilations and £4.99 in the till?

'Prudence? Is that you?'

No, Mum, I'm not me any more. I'm this new girl flying above the dusty floor. I want to stay up up up in the air.

I heard the creak of her bed, then the stomp stomp of her slippered feet. There was a patter from Grace too, and the bang of our bedroom door as she flung it open. I sighed and started up the stairs.

I told them all about the house and the furniture and the children and the wife and the television programmes. Then I pressed the five-pound notes into Mum's hand.

'But it's *your* money, Prue!'

'I want to pay you back for the maths tuition money.'

'You're such a good girl,' she said, making me feel *bad*.

I kissed her goodnight and went to bed. Grace started asking me all sorts of questions, but I told her I was too tired to start answering anything. I lay flat on my back, staring at the ceiling in the dark. I wondered if he was lying likewise, or whether he slept curled round his wife.

'Prue! *Please* tell me how you got on with Rax,' Grace whispered.

I pretended to be asleep.

'Prue!'

I still didn't answer. She got out of her own bed and tried to clamber into mine.

'Prue, tell me, what did he say on the way home?' she whispered, her hair in my face, her big soft body pressed against mine.

'You're squashing me! Move *over*. I was asleep.'

'No you weren't. You can't fool me, Prue. You're nuts about him, aren't you?'

'Of course I'm not. He's a boring old *teacher*, years and years older than me, and he's married with two children.'

'Yes, but you still fancy him.'

'No, I *don't*,' I said, and I pushed her out of bed.

'You do,' she said, sprawled on the floor. 'Ouch! I think you're nuts. You could have any boy you want. You could even have Toby Baker, yet you want old Rax!'

I pulled the covers over my head. I couldn't hear her any more. I just heard my own thoughts, drumming in my head like the blood at my temple.

I hardly slept but I got up early and cleaned and swept the shop. I carefully dusted Dad's Magnum Opus, and then spent ages copying out the first few sentences in large print, wondering if Dad might be able to read it and then say the words out loud – words he'd been composing half his life, chanting them under his breath as if they were a holy mantra.

'That's your dad's book! Careful with it. What are you doing?' Mum fussed.

I sighed and explained.

'Oh Prue! What a good idea! Why didn't I think of that. You're *so* clever.'

'Tell that to my teachers,' I said. 'They all think I'm thick thick thick.'

'Well, this Mr Raxberry can't think that or he'd never leave you in charge of his kiddies,' said Mum.

I ducked my head so she couldn't see I was blushing. I worked on Dad's book while Mum stood downstairs in the empty shop and Grace spent hours on the phone chatting to Iggy and Figgy. I flipped through Dad's various notebooks and stray pieces of paper and scrapbooks and journals, trying to pick out key passages. I stared at his small, cramped, backward-sloping scribble until my eyes blurred.

I still didn't really *understand* it. I'd thought it way above my head. Now I read it carefully, page after page, and I realized something so sad. It wasn't really difficult at all. There was no extraordinary philosophical theory, no dynamic take on the human condition, no overriding theme, no new angle. It was just Dad rambling and ranting. It held no meaning for anyone but himself. Maybe it didn't even hold any meaning for him now.

I closed his book, wanting to hide it away. It exposed Dad too painfully. It was like looking at him in his baggy underwear.

'Prue? Can you come down a minute?' Mum was shouting at me from the shop.

I didn't take any notice.

'*Prue!* Will you come down here? There's someone asking for you!'

I leaped up and went flying down the stairs, combing my hair with my fingers, tugging at my awful dress, wishing I had some decent clothes, wanting to check myself in the mirror but terrified he'd give up and go if I kept him waiting any longer.

I stumbled into the shop, cheeks burning, scarcely able to breathe. I looked all round. He wasn't there. I blinked. Mum came into focus, gesturing at some stupid boy standing by the door. Not some boy, any old boy. It was Toby Baker.

I sighed. 'Oh, it's you,' I said ungraciously.

'Hi, Prue,' he said, not at all put out. 'How are you doing?'

I stared at him as if he was mad.

'Your mum says she doesn't need you to work in the shop this morning, so I thought we could maybe do that tuition thing. You know, me help you with your maths and you could hear me do

159

a bit of reading. I've got my books with me.' He patted his rucksack.

'Isn't that lovely!' said Mum. 'Well, where would you two like to work? I suppose you could always sit at your dad's desk, Prue.'

'No, I thought we could go out somewhere in the town, McDonald's maybe, and have a cup of coffee first. We'd kind of relax then, so it wouldn't be like a school situation,' Toby said.

Mum nodded, mesmerized by his blond good looks and sweet manners. I heard a little gasp behind me. Grace had come running downstairs after me and was gawping at him. Her fingers twitched to start dialling Iggy and Figgy on the phone.

'Sorry, Toby, I can't,' I said. 'I've got stuff to do.'

'No you *haven't*,' Grace said.

'You've been a lovely helpful girl. You can go and relax a bit now,' said Mum. She looked worried, but she added determinedly, 'I think it's an excellent idea you two getting together and helping each other with your lessons.'

I didn't want to at all, but I couldn't say so right to Toby's face. I mumbled my way through several more excuses, none of which held up – and ended up being dispatched towards the town with Toby.

'I can't stay long though,' I said.

I'd got it into my head that Rax *might* just come by the shop, maybe while his wife was trailing round Sainsbury's. I'd die if I missed him.

I rather hoped all this tuition nonsense was a ploy and that Toby would try to drag me somewhere quiet to kiss me. Then I could simply shove him off me and run back to the shop. But to my irritation he seemed determined to behave perfectly, keeping a little distance between us as we walked into town, talking earnestly about his dyslexia and how he'd felt so humiliated as a little kid and he'd hated books so much he'd scribbled all over his sister's paperbacks.

I made all the right responses but it was such an effort I started to get a headache. However, there was a little bit of me that was pleased a boy like Toby seemed to like me. As we got nearer the town centre little gangs of girls going shopping looked round and stared enviously. They raised their eyebrows at my Saturday outfit. I was wearing last year's dreadful blue cord dress, which was way too short for me, and a shapeless hand-knitted purple sweater that had stretched in the wash. I'd threaded blue and purple glass beads into a strand of my hair and painted a blue cornflower on one of my old black shoes and a purple daisy on the other. I was worried that these homespun embellishments made me look weirder than ever.

Toby had made a serious effort. His shirt was always hanging out at school, his tie undone, his shoes unlaced, but now he was wearing a hooded jacket with a coveted logo, black sweater and black jeans so obviously new he could barely bend his legs. He'd just washed his famously floppy blond hair. It fell silkily over his forehead into his eyes, so he had to keep shaking his head every so often. I knew all the girls at Wentworth thought this a fabulously sexy gesture, but I was starting to find it intensely irritating.

We went to the McDonald's in the shopping centre. Toby insisted on buying us two Cokes, plus two portions of french fries. I thought of Grace and how she'd die for a chance to sample McDonald's chips.

Toby manoeuvred us to a table right at the back and then opened his rucksack. He really did have half a dozen textbooks and two pads of paper tucked inside.

'OK, I thought I could maybe talk you through some basic maths. Not that I'm any great shakes, mind, but I'll help if I can.'

'Please don't,' I said. 'I mean, it's very nice of you, but I *hate* maths. I don't want to do it.'

'But you'll have to master it sometime.'

'No I won't. I can do enough. How many people are sitting at this table? Two. How many Cokes have they got? Two. How many chips have they got left?' I helped myself to a handful. 'Not many at this rate.'

'You're so different from all the other girls, Prue. I really reckon you, you know that.'

'Don't start all that. Look, I'll help you with your reading if that's what you really want. Get your book out.'

He brought out this grim little reader in big

print with cartoon pictures of teenagers and a lot of stilted phrases and dated slang.

'Oh God,' I said.

'It's not *my* fault. It's better than some of the others – Peter and Jane and Pat the flipping dog.'

'OK then, get cracking. *The Big Match*. Start!'

'I feel a fool. OK, OK. *The – Big – Match*. Why does match have a "t" in it anyway? It's stupid. Right. *The – Big – Match*.'

'You've *said* that. And I've said it too. Now start on the rest.'

He started. I realized how bad he really was at reading. I thought he'd just trip up on a few of the longer words, maybe mix up the odd *were* or *where*, the way Grace used to when she was five or six. But Toby was still way back at the beginning stage, stumbling through each and every word. It was as if the letters grew into tall trees and he was blundering through a dense forest, unable to find his way out.

I sat and listened. I helped him out, prompting him, sometimes taking over and reading out a whole phrase. I kept my voice gentle, neutral, encouraging, the voice I used for coaching Dad. Toby was much sweeter natured. He kept apologizing, thanking me over and over, telling me I was a born teacher. He thought I was being so kind because I really cared, when inside my head I was hot, angry, bored. I listened to him stuttering away and I had to press my lips together to stop myself screaming at him.

When he eventually made it all the way through the story and Bil-ly had fi-nal-ly got tick-ets for the Big Match we both cheered as if Toby had scored a goal.

'Wow! That's the first book I've ever read all the way through!' he said.

He was flushed with pride at his achievement, even though *The Big Match* wasn't really a *book* and I'd told him three-quarters of the words.

'It's all down to you,' he said, and he squeezed my hand.

I snatched it away quickly. I didn't want anyone else holding my hand now. I stuck it into the empty french fries packet, pretending to be looking for a last chip.

'We'll get some more! And a burger? Or are you more an ice-cream kind of girl?'

'No, no, I don't want anything, really,' I said. 'I've got to get going. Mum will need me to help in the shop.'

'She said it was fine. I'm sure you can stay out longer. We really ought to give you a bit of maths tuition now.'

'I *said*. No!'

'Well then, we could go round the shopping centre if you want. Anywhere you like, I don't mind. Even clothes shops.'

'There's not much point my going round any clothes shops. I haven't got any money for any decent clothes.'

'I thought girls just liked to look. Rita always wants to spend *hours* in New Look and TopShop.'

I fingered my awful sweater defensively. 'I know I look a freak,' I mumbled.

'You don't. I love the way you look. You're not boring like all the other girls, you've got your *own* style.'

'Yeah, part jumble sale, part botched home-made,' I said.

I was pleased all the same. I hoped Rax felt like that about me too. I wondered if he ever took his wife and kids to McDonald's on their Saturday morning shopping trips. I wanted to see him so much. If he spotted me with Toby he'd realize I wasn't completely a sad little Prudence-No-Friends.

I supposed I counted Toby as a friend now, just so long as he didn't try to be anything more.

I wandered round the shopping centre with him for half an hour, but I couldn't really say I enjoyed myself. Toby was very eager to please, shuffling along one pace behind me so I had to keep choosing where we were going. I didn't know which shops to amble in and out of, how long to take admiring different outfits, which racks to spin with interest. It all seemed so false and uncomfortable and awkward. I tried hard to keep up a steady stream of chatter. His answers were mostly monosyllabic. Maybe he was used to small simple words, like the ones in his reading book.

I seemed to be fated to help people with their reading. It had been tedious with Toby but it was far worse with Dad. He was clearly furious with me for not turning up on Friday. He wanted to interrogate me but couldn't find the words. He came out with a long semi-comprehensible splutter: 'Baby? – No! – *Not!*' I knew he was expressly forbidding me to do such a thing again but I chose to misunderstand.

'Yes, Dad, I simply wanted to start earning some money of my own. I'm so glad you think it's a good idea,' I said.

Dad reached boiling point, straining to say what he meant. He thumped the bed with his left arm. He even did a feeble mini thump with his right.

'Oh Arthur, you're really getting lots of

movement back now!' Mum said, clutching his bad hand and stroking it.

Dad snatched it away from her, not wanting to be distracted. 'Baby – no-no-no!' he repeated.

'Yes, Dad. Lily's the baby, and Harry's the little boy. They can be a bit of a handful, but I can get them sorted out. Just call me Mary Poppins, eh?'

Dad looked as if he wanted to call me all sorts of names, though Mary Poppins wasn't one of them. But then I took out the compilation I'd made of extracts from his Magnum Opus. The moment I read out the first line Dad lay still. He listened, his head cocked to one side, his mouth snapped back into a straight line. He looked almost his old self.

'Now you try to read a little, Dad,' I said.

He reached for the book. He cleared his throat. He pronounced the first four words clearly, with proper expression. I thought a miracle had happened. Dad had recovered all his faculties and I could stop feeling chewed up with guilt. But then he stumbled, he repeated himself, he couldn't get any further though he strained to the utmost. His entire Magnum Opus was reduced to four words: *I, Bernard King, think . . .*

Dad's eyes filled with tears.

'Oh Prue, don't upset him! Maybe you should put it away,' Mum whispered.

'Don't worry, Dad. I'm sure you'll be able to read it all soon. Meanwhile, I'll read it, shall I?'

Dad nodded, and so I read to him. He twitched

and sniffled for a minute or two and then he became absorbed. Grace yawned and twiddled her thumbs and did mini Iggy-Figgy waves to herself. Mum frowned at her as if she was fidgeting in church. She had an expression of pious concentration on her face but her eyes were darting all round the room. I knew she was thinking about Dad's washing and cooking our tea and all the final demands and bailiff's threats at home.

I read on, my voice starting to mimic Dad's old intonations and accent as I worked my way through his convoluted sentences. I started to ham it up just a little, inserting a Dad-cough here and a Dad-sniff there. Mum glared. Grace snorted. Dad snorted too, regularly, again and again. He was fast asleep and snoring. His Magnum Opus had worked like a bedtime story for a tired toddler.

I left my cut-price annotated version on his bedside locker. I hoped Dad might enjoy glancing at it, but when we visited on Sunday it was missing. I asked him about it but Dad looked blank and shook his head. So much for my labour of love. One of the cleaners had obviously chucked it in the rubbish bin. Dad had forgotten all about it.

I'd been going to copy out more of it, maybe even do a couple of watercolour illustrations, but now I decided not to bother.

I hid myself away on Sunday evening, constructing a surreal sculpture based on our old doll's house. I made a papier-mâché man, deliberately too big for the house. His arms reached out of the windows, his feet stuck out of the door, his head was halfway out of the chimney, but he couldn't escape, try as he might. I fashioned a fat fur mouse out of an old pair of mittens, and made two tiny mice from each thumb. The man had a collar round his neck. The fat mouse had the lead tightly clasped in her paws. The two tiny mice scrabbled on his shoulders, shrieking in his ears.

Grace crept up on me and peered over my shoulder. 'That's good – but *weird*,' she said. 'It's like that Alice book. *Is* it Alice?'

Dad had once discovered what he thought was a first edition of *Alice in Wonderland* at a jumble sale and thought it would make our fortune, but of course it wasn't a *real* first edition, just an illustrated edition from much later that was hardly worth a bean. Dad couldn't bear to see it on the shelf in the shop and gave it to me as a colouring book.

'Yes, it's Alice,' I said to Grace.

How could she be idiotic enough to think I'd give Alice a *beard*?

'Is it for homework?'

'Sort of.'

'Have you done all your other homework?'

'Nope.'

'Hadn't you better get cracking?'

'I'm not doing it.'

'You'll get into trouble.'

169

'See if I care.'

I *did* get into trouble on Monday, but it wasn't over homework. I got to school early, wandered across the playground, walked over to the playing field and hovered near the art block. I hoped that Rax might be at school early too, but his art room was in darkness and there was no sign of him. I sighed and started trailing back towards the main building. We didn't have art on Monday. I had a dreaded maths session in the Success Maker.

I looked longingly at the school gate, wondering whether to make a run for it. Rita was flouncing through the gate into school, tossing her head, obviously sounding off about something to her friends, Aimee, Megan and Jess. Then she looked up and saw someone. She started running forwards, her pretty face contorted. I looked round. There was no one behind me. She was angry with *me*.

'You cow! You scheming lying cheating little *cow!*' she screamed right in my face.

I stepped back, because she was spraying me with spit.

'Don't you *dare* back away from me!' she yelled. She seized a handful of my hair and tugged hard.

'Stop it! Get off!' I said. 'Have you gone mad?'

'You're the mad girl, thinking you can mess around with me by stealing my boyfriend!'

'I *haven't* stolen your stupid boyfriend,' I said, jerking my head to make her let go.

'You liar! I saw you with him in McDonald's,' said Aimee. 'You were right at the back, cuddling up to him, practically sitting on his lap, hanging on his every word.'

'I was listening to him *read*,' I said.

'Oh yeah, and I can read *you* like a book,' cried Rita. 'You set out to get him away from me the moment you came barging into our school in your stupid sad dresses and your slag's underwear. How *dare* you! Me and Toby have had a thing going ever since Year Eight. He's *mine*, everyone knows that.'

'OK, OK. He's yours. *I* don't want him,' I said. 'I don't even like him.'

'*What?* Toby's the only decent boy in our year. Everyone reckons him!'

'Well, not me. So I don't know why you're making such a stupid fuss. You can keep him.'

'You *know* he's broken up with me!' Rita said, and she started crying.

Aimee and Megan and Jess had all been egging her on, enjoying the fight, but now they clucked round her like mother hens.

'He told me it's all over. He says he still wants to be my friend but he doesn't love me any more. He tried to smooth his way out of things but I soon got the whole story out of him. It's all because of *you*, Prudence King!'

They all looked at me accusingly.

'I haven't done anything!' I said.

'He says you talk together, that you say all sorts of stuff. What have you been telling him?'

'Nothing! Well, nothing special. Look, Rita, I swear I didn't know he was going to break up with you. It's not *my* fault.' I tried to say it calmly and reasonably but my heart was thumping hard. Maybe it *was* my fault, just a little bit? It was awful seeing Rita crying like that, tears dribbling down her face, her nose running, with everyone staring at her.

I held out my hand. 'I'm sorry,' I said.

She stared at me, her face all screwed up, almost ugly. 'Don't you *dare* feel sorry for me!' she said, and she flew at me and slapped my face.

I slapped her back, just as hard.

'Fight, fight, fight!' the girls yelled.

Rita and I hit out at each other, slapping, scratching, tugging hair, tearing at each other's clothes, toppling over and rolling on the floor.

'Prudence King, Rita Rogers, stop scrapping this *instant!*'

It was Miss Wilmott. She grabbed Rita by one wrist, me by the other, and pulled us both up. 'Whatever's got into you! Fighting like gutter children and yet you're both in Year Ten! What sort of behaviour *is* this?'

'Prue stole Rita's boyfriend, miss,' said Aimee. 'It's all Prue's fault.'

'I don't care whose fault it is. I'm not having any pupils of Wentworth behaving like animals, especially not over boyfriends!' said Miss Wilmott. 'Go and tidy yourselves up, girls, and then come and stand outside my office. You're both in very serious trouble.'

We ended up having to spend the entire morning outside her office, me standing on one side of the door, Rita the other, in public disgrace. We weren't supposed to look at each other, but whenever I glanced Rita's way she seemed to be in tears.

I didn't particularly mind standing there. It was certainly preferable to maths. I'd have liked to be able to read, but that couldn't be helped. I held long conversations in my head with Jane instead. I didn't want to talk to Tobias. I wanted to steer clear of all boys, even imaginary ones.

Every now and then the bell went and pupils charged past us, rushing up and down the corridor. They stared at Rita, they stared at me. Rita's friends had obviously been talking. It was clear from the black looks directed at me whose side everyone was on.

Form 10 EL ambled past on their way to a music lesson in the hall. There was a lot of nudging, a lot of shoving. The girls hissed 'Slag slag slag' at me, like an incantation. The boys whooped and laughed and strutted, thrilled that two girls had been fighting over one of them. The only boy who shuffled past, head down, was Toby.

He looked at me anxiously and mouthed 'I'm sorry'.

I put my head down and stared at the scuffed wooden floor, not wanting to respond. He hovered in front of me a moment or two, but then moved on. I kept my eyes on the floor as if I was learning the pattern of the parquet by

173

heart. He paused in front of Rita too. Her sniffles increased.

I stared down resolutely. There were further footsteps. They stopped in front of me. I saw black canvas boots, black jeans. I looked up. There was Rax, his head tilted, one eyebrow raised.

'Are you in disgrace?' he said.

I nodded. He made little tutting noises, showing he wasn't taking it at all seriously. I longed to talk to him but I didn't want Rita to listen. Rax understood. He gave me a sympathetic smile and then walked on. He tutted at Rita in a friendly fashion too, but not in the same way.

I looked up to watch him walk the length of the corridor. He turned round at the end and gave me a quick wave.

I couldn't wait to talk to him properly in the art class on Tuesday. I worked hard on my still life, adding shadows and highlights. Rita kept out of my way, but Aimee and Megan and Jess kept barging past, trying to jog me. I learned not to paint when they were anywhere near me.

Even Daisy turned on me. She came and peered over my shoulder. 'You think you're so great, Prudence Slag, but that painting's rubbish.'

Sarah didn't say anything nasty but she didn't smile at me any more. They'd all decided to hate me. Even Toby kept his distance, right at the other end of the classroom, but I'd made it clear enough I didn't want to talk to him.

Rax didn't seem to notice. He didn't really seem

174

to notice *me*, just giving me the occasional nod or brief tip: 'Try a glimmer of white there . . .'; 'Is that shadow really black? What other colours is it made of?'; 'Maybe you want to suggest the book titles, rather than actually print them out?'

I listened, I nodded, I did what he said, but inside I was dying. Why wasn't he talking *properly*? He spent ages chatting to all the others. He didn't just say arty stuff, he talked football with the boys and rock bands with the girls. He stood beside Rita and Aimee and talked for a full ten minutes. I couldn't hear what he was saying. It must have been amazing because they kept giggling. Rita stopped looking mean and miserable and laughed and joked with him, batting her long black eyelashes.

Maybe Rax had decided he was on Rita's side. Perhaps he thought I'd deliberately lured Toby away from her. Maybe he hated me now like everyone else.

I hunched over my still life, blinking hard, finding it difficult to focus. I concentrated on not crying for the rest of the lesson. As soon as the bell went I flung my brush down, not even bothering to clean it, grabbed my bag and bolted for the door.

I was right out in the playground when I heard him shouting my name.

'Prue! Prue King, come back!'

I wondered about making a bolt for it, but I trudged slowly back.

'You don't just throw your brushes down all

clogged up with paint!' said Rax. 'Come on, you know better than that. You can help me clear up all the paint pots too.'

'Serves you right, slag,' said Rita, and Aimee and Megan and Jess all made faces at me.

I started washing out brushes at the sink, my back to everyone. I couldn't stop a tear dribbling down my cheek.

'Hey, you're not crying, are you?' Rax said. 'Oh Prue, you didn't think I was cross with you, did you?'

I nodded, the tears spurting now.

'Don't!' He picked up a cloth and gently dabbed at my eyes. 'Whoops! Now you've got black paint on your eyes. You'll look like Lovely Rita if you don't watch out.'

'*Lovely* Rita?'

'Like the Beatles song.' He sang a line or two about a meter maid. 'So, what on earth's been going on between you two? Why is everyone treating you as if you've got bubonic plague?'

'They think I stole Toby away from Rita.'

'And did you?'

'*No!* Well, not really. I did go to McDonald's with him, but just to help him with his reading. It was all his idea.'

'I bet it was. So you're in the doghouse with everyone now?'

'They didn't like me much before but now they positively hate me. And I thought you did too, because you hardly talked to me at all and yet you spent ages with Rita.'

'Yes, because if I'd made a big fuss of you and your wonderful painting it wouldn't really have increased your popularity. What would you like me to do, Prue? Shall I have a word with Miss Wilmott?'

'No!'

'What about your form teacher?'

'Absolutely not.'

'There's meant to be a student counselling service now, one of Miss Wilmott's new ideas for Wentworth. You could have a chat with them.'

'I don't want to have a chat with *anyone*, thank you,' I said, swilling out the sink. 'I'm fine. I don't care about them.'

'You were crying.'

'I was crying because I thought *you* were cross with me.'

'I'm not cross with you.' There was a little pause. 'Anything but.'

Then he started putting the paint jars away with unnecessary fuss and clatter, not looking at me.

'So, are you able to babysit again this Friday?' he said.

'Yes please.'

'Then it's a date.'

Fridays started to feel like *real* dates. I'd rush home from school to put the immersion on for a bath. Mum always moaned about the waste of hot water, but I took no notice. I wished I had proper bath oil, scented soap, special shampoo.

Mum bought bumper packs of the cheapest brands of soap, and until I protested bitterly she expected us to do our hair with washing-up liquid.

I longed for decent clothes to wear once I was scrubbed and shampooed. I'd saved up enough babysitting money for a green skirt and sweater, and Mum had found a boy's white shirt at a jumble sale so I was in an approximation of school uniform now. (Grace got lucky too. Figgy had a large lumpy cousin in Year Eleven and she passed her entire old uniform on to Grace.)

I generally wore my school skirt to Rax's, with a black jumble jumper, weird black and green striped tights (seconds) from the one pound shop, and my customized painted black shoes. I tried different hairstyles: beaded plaits; odd bunches tied with black velvet ribbon; scraped back with little butterfly slides. I didn't have proper make-up but I experimented with my watercolours, shadowing my eyes with purple. Once I painted tiny blue stars on my earlobes; another time a daisy bracelet in china-white and emerald all round my left wrist.

'For heaven's sake, it looks as if you've got a tattoo!' Mum fussed. 'Whatever will your teacher *think*!'

He seemed to like the way I looked. He always noticed and admired each new improvisation, although one evening he said he still had a soft spot for the red-checked tablecloth dress.

I wore it the next time, with the red cardigan,

a red rose plastic slide, and my lips painted carmine. I tried painting my cheeks too but I looked like a Dutch doll so I scrubbed them clean again. I didn't need anything to act as rouge. I blushed enough naturally whenever I was with Rax.

The children had got used to me now. I didn't have to bribe Harry any more. I played Gruffalo games with him, making up my own extra adventures, sometimes drawing his favourite bits for him. Lily was too little for stories, but she liked a special Peepo game, chuckling again and again whenever I bobbed out behind a cushion.

'You've really got a way with the kids,' said Marianne. 'They like you so much, Prue.'

Marianne seemed to like me too. She'd chat to me as she was getting ready, discussing diets and hairstyles and clothes. I switched off while she rattled on, but whenever she mentioned Rax she had my full attention. She always seemed to put him down, sighing about him as if he was an exceptionally stupid child.

'It would make much more sense if he took over the childcare while I went back to my accountancy work, but he's so hopeless he'd never cope. The kids play him up anyway, especially Harry. I don't know how he manages at school.'

'He's a brilliant teacher. Everyone loves him,' I said.

'Oh, come on, Prue, I bet everyone takes the mickey. He's so *stupid* wasting his time teaching, and it's crap money anyway. He earned double

179

that amount when he worked at the advertising agency – no, *triple*. But of course he didn't find that *creative* enough, though it beats me what's creative about giving out pots of paint to a lot of bored teenagers. Sorry, I don't mean *you*, Prue, I know you're very talented – Keith keeps telling me.'

'Does he?' I said eagerly.

'You must know he thinks the world of you,' said Marianne.

I hoped he did, but I wanted her to keep on telling me. It made me feel strange though, horribly guilty. She seemed to have no idea how I felt about Rax. She started treating me as if I was her *friend*.

'It's so good of you to babysit on a regular basis like this, Prue. Keith and I had got out of the habit of going out together. We don't really *do* much, but it does us both good. It gives me a chance to dress up a bit and feel like a human being again – and it's cheered Keith up too. I know he keeps up a smiley front at school, but he's been really down the last few months. Well, since before Lily was born. He's never said as much, even to me, but he gets these moods. But now he's much cheerier, more like the *old* Keith.' She sighed. 'Make the most of being young and having your freedom, Prue.'

I nodded politely, though I didn't want to be young, I didn't want to be free.

Rax scarcely said anything to me in front of Marianne and the children. He waited until we

180

were alone, in the car driving home. We had ten minutes together, twenty if we stayed chatting in the car outside the shop.

We talked about art, we talked about books. Rax kept scribbling down recommendations and I kept all his notes tucked inside my copy of *Jane Eyre*, treasuring old Sainsbury's receipts and Cadbury's wrappers because they bore a few words of his beautiful italic writing. But the best conversations were when he stopped acting like my teacher and I got him to talk about himself. He shied away from talking about the way he felt *now*, but he talked easily enough about his childhood.

He told me about his first big box of felt-tip pens and how he'd spent hours kneeling up at the kitchen table, colouring the seaside with big white-tipped waves and little red boats and v-shaped seagulls flying round and round the rays of his yellow sun. He drew himself standing on a rock licking a giant strawberry ice cream with chocolate flakes sticking out like horns. His mother had entered it for a children's art competition and it had come second.

'Another boy at my school came first, and I couldn't help minding dreadfully. I managed not to show it in front of him, but I cried at home – how pathetic is that!'

'But very understandable.'

'My mum understood too, and had my picture specially framed. I think she's still got it hanging in her kitchen.'

'Has she got any of your later work, things you did at art school or afterwards?'

'No, I think she feels I went off dreadfully after the age of seven. She may well be right.'

'And do you still like strawberry ice cream with chocolate flakes?'

'You bet I do!'

Then we got onto our favourite foods. Rax couldn't believe I'd never eaten a pizza or a chop suey or a chicken tandoori.

'I'll have to treat you sometime,' he said.

'Yes please!'

I kept hoping that he'd suggest a *specific* time, but he was probably just playing a game. Sometimes he treated me like a little kid, as if I wasn't much older than Harry. I tried to behave in a sophisticated manner, but sometimes he teased me when I used an elaborate phrase or struck a pose.

'Don't laugh at me,' I said, stung.

'I'm not laughing. Well. Just a little bit,' he said.

'I'm simply trying to impress you,' I said.

'You don't have to try, Prue. You do that already,' he said.

'Really?'

'You're a funny kid.'

'I'm not funny. And I'm *not* a kid,' I said, flouncing out of the car.

'Hey! Don't go off in a huff!' he said, winding down his window.

I stuck my head back inside. 'Who's huffy? Not me!' I said. Then I blew him a little kiss goodbye.

I didn't touch him. It was just a silly little gesture. He didn't need to take it seriously – though I wanted him to.

He wasn't quite so chatty this last time, driving me home. I tried hard to introduce interesting topics of conversation, but nothing really seemed to spark with him. We got home much too soon.

'Perhaps you could park the car up the road a bit instead of just outside the shop?' I suggested. 'If Mum hears the car she'll wonder why I'm not coming in straight away.'

'And why *aren't* you coming in straight away?' said Rax.

'Because I want to talk to you!'

'I know, I know. And I want to talk to you too, Prue. But . . . but we're starting to act as if . . . as if there's something between us.'

'There is,' I said.

'Well, yes, I know we get on really well, and it's a privilege for me to help you with your art, but that's all it can be, Prue. You do know that, don't you?'

'I know. But what do you *really* want inside? What if you weren't my teacher?'

'It doesn't matter what I feel inside.'

'It matters to me. *You* matter to me.'

'Don't, Prue. Look, this is all my fault. I should have kept my distance. You're going through a difficult time, you're feeling very vulnerable, your dad's not well. It's not surprising you've got overly attached to me.'

'I'm not *attached*.' I took a deep breath. 'I love you, you know I do.'

'Prue. Look, you're a very sweet girl—'

'Don't treat me like Sarah.'

'Oh dear God.' He put his head in his hands, resting against the steering wheel.

'It's all right,' I said. 'I won't make things difficult for you. I won't tell anyone else the way I feel. I won't do anything at all. But please, won't you tell me if you love me just a little bit?'

'I'm married, I've got two small children. I'm a teacher, you're my pupil – you're fourteen years old, for God's sake.'

'Do you love me?'

'Prue, please, stop this. Go indoors now, your mother will be wondering where you are. Off you go.'

He waited until I was safely out of the car, standing on the pavement. Then he whispered one word as he drove away. I couldn't hear him, of course, but I saw his face clearly in the lamplight. He said yes.

Yes yes yes yes yes yes yes yes yes yes yes yes.

14

Rax seemed to be avoiding me at school. He barely nodded when we passed in the corridor. When I started a new project in art he didn't even comment. We'd started working on aspects of Christmas. I found his postcard of a Botticelli Nativity and I made a fair stab at copying it, using gouache for the first time. I did a little replica Mary, Jesus and Joseph, I painted all their visitors, rural and exotic, and the holy livestock, and used up a lot of pink and gold on the host of heavenly angels circling the cattle shed.

There was a strange graveyard in the foreground with dead people springing forth from the earth, resurrected, embracing each other joyfully. I copied each one, but I deliberately embellished the couple in the corner enjoying the warmest embrace. I gave the girl long dark curly hair. I gave the man a little beard with a hint of sparkly highlight on his earlobe.

I wanted Rax to look at it closely but he only gave it a quick glance every time he went to have a chat with Sarah. I hoped he'd look at it more carefully after the lesson. I was sure I understood. He was being particularly cautious. It would look strange, even suspicious, if he singled me out.

I didn't like it all the same. School was so lonely now. Rita and the other girls hissed slag at me whenever I passed. The boys made crude remarks. Toby did his best to shut them up. Then he hung back, trying to talk to me.

'I'm so sorry, Prue. I didn't mean for it to end up like this. I never thought Rita would be so mean to you. I've tried talking to her, telling her to cut it out, but she just told me to get lost.'

'Well, she would do, wouldn't she?' I said. 'And if she sees you talking to me now she'll get even meaner. You shouldn't have broken up with her, Toby.'

'But I don't reckon her any more. You're the only girl I want.'

'Oh Toby. I told you. I like you ever so much, but I don't want to be your girlfriend,' I said.

'Maybe you'll change your mind,' Toby said cheerfully.

'I don't think so,' I said, but obviously I couldn't explain why.

Rax didn't mention babysitting at all in the last art lesson of the week, but then, right at the end, when everyone else was clattering out, he asked if he could have a word with me.

'Look at her!' Rita said to her friend Aimee. 'Look at the smug little smile on the slag's face, just because old Rax wants her.'

My heart started beating fast. Rax had heard too. He paused and stood still.

'Yeah, talk about teacher's pet. *I* don't think she's that good at art, she just copies stuff,' said Aimee.

I breathed out, happy for them to carry on rubbishing my art. Toby irritatingly took it into his head to interfere.

'You shut up, you lot. You're just jealous of Prue's talent,' he said.

This naturally encouraged them to be far more vitriolic.

'Hey, you guys, how about conducting your slanging match outside in the playground?' said Rax.

'Prue *is* talented, isn't she, Rax?' Toby persisted. 'That Christmas Jesus scene is brilliant, don't you think so?'

'Yes I do,' said Rax. 'But perhaps we shouldn't keep telling Prue that or she'll get big-headed.'

'Her head's as big as an elephant's bum already,' Rita said, and flounced off, circled by Aimee, Megan and Jess.

Toby hung back, waiting for me.

'You go *on*, Toby,' I said.

He sloped off, looking miserable. I sighed. Then I looked at Rax.

'Do you really think I'm talented?' I asked.

'Yes, you're brilliant,' said Rax, but he said it flatly, as if he wasn't really engaging with the subject.

'Shall I come round usual time tonight?' I asked.

'Well. That's why I wanted a word. We won't need you to do any babysitting tonight,' he said.

He was standing at the sink, the taps full on, washing out paint pots and palettes. I wondered if I'd actually heard him properly.

'You won't need me?' I whispered. 'You've not got someone *else* to babysit, have you?'

'No, no. We're just not going out, that's all.' He stayed at the sink, splashing the palettes around, although they were all pristine.

'Why?'

'We fancied a quiet night in, watching *The West Wing* with a takeaway pizza,' said Rax.

'Oh.' I waited. He wouldn't look round. 'So. *Next* Friday then?'

Rax stood still a moment. Then he squared his shoulders. 'Maybe not, Prue,' he said. He turned round properly. His face was so tense there were lines all round his mouth. He licked his lips, wiping his hands on his jeans. 'I don't think the babysitting is really a good idea.'

'But the children *like* me. Harry loves me reading him stories, and I can always make Lily laugh. Marianne likes me too – we have all these chats together while you're getting ready.'

'I know, I know, you're great at babysitting

and my whole family adores you. But I just don't think it's a very good idea any more.'

'Why?'

'You *know* why, Prue,' he said impatiently.

'Because I love you?' I said.

'Don't!' he said, looking round anxiously, as if there were children eavesdropping in the cupboard and Miss Wilmott tape-recording at the door. He took a deep breath. 'That's why we have to stop this. It's dangerous for both of us.'

'Dangerous for you,' I said. 'You're scared you'll lose your job if anyone finds out.'

'Well, of course I am. I've got a family to support. But it's not just the job. I don't want to upset you – you're only fourteen, and you're taking our friendship so seriously.'

'Are you still trying to pretend that's all it is?'

'Yes. It's a close friendship, nothing more,' said Rax.

I started to cry.

'For heaven's sake, Prue, stop that. It's true. We haven't *done* anything.'

'Is it because I look so weird?'

'Stop it!'

'Well, *you* stop it,' I sobbed. 'I *have* to babysit, I *have* to see you. It's not the same at school, *you're* not the same. You keep on and on about my age.'

'Well, you're still a *child*.'

'If you start saying all that only-fourteen stuff again I'll start screaming.'

'Don't!' He looked alarmed, as if he thought I

189

was really going to start shrieking my head off.

'The only real time we have together is our time in the car,' I said. 'Ten minutes, once a week. That's not too much to ask, is it?'

'Twenty minutes. Sometimes half an hour.'

'What have you been doing, timing us to the exact second? "Uh-oh, I've given this girl ten and a half minutes, warning bells, she'll misinterpret my innocent caring teacherly concern as something much more serious and scary so shove her out the car quick."'

'You're being silly now,' he said, but his mouth twitched. He started laughing, shaking his head at me. 'You're a terrible girl, Prue,' he went on. 'You won't ever act the way you're supposed to. You just say whatever you think, act in the rashest way possible. Dear God, your dad must have been having a joke calling you Prudence. You're the exact opposite!'

'Well, I'm glad he didn't call me Rash. Imagine, especially if I went through a spotty stage,' I said, wiping my face with the sleeve of my sweater.

'Don't *do* that. You're worse than Harry sometimes,' he said, finding me a paper towel.

I hoped he'd wipe my eyes for me but he kept me carefully at arm's length.

'Please let me babysit tonight,' I said. 'Marianne said she was going to look out some of her clothes that are too small for her. It will look so rude of me if I don't turn up. And I told Harry I'd read him my own *Wild Things* book.

190

I was going to act it all out for him – I promised.'

'And I suppose you promised Lily you'd read her the whole of *Alice in Wonderland* and then you'd act out the Mad Hatter and the March Hare and Tweedledum and Tweedledee?' said Rax.

'Tweedledum and Tweedledee are in *Alice Through the Looking Glass*,' I said. 'There! We can have ten minutes tonight demurely discussing our favourite nursery classics. I swear I won't cry or make a scene or try to make you stay later.'

He didn't say anything.

'Don't you trust me?'

'I don't trust either of us,' he said. 'OK, OK, come round tonight. But it must be the last time. This is getting too worrying. God knows what could happen if we carry on like this. I want you to tell Marianne that you can't babysit for a while. Say you've got too much homework – any old excuse. Will you do that?'

'If you make me,' I said.

I left it at that, scared he might change his mind again. Grace was standing forlornly at the school gate. I'd forgotten all about her.

'Where have you *been*? Iggy and Figgy went home ages ago.'

'You should have gone home too, silly. I don't see why you always have to tag on to me all the time.'

'I don't see why you have to keep being so *mean* to me. I'm your *sister*. I'm not nasty to you. I keep sticking up for you when Iggy and

191

Figgy say stuff about you. If you must know, we've even had a little row, because they said you took Toby away from Rita on purpose, even though you didn't want him yourself – although how mad is that? – and *I* said—'

'I don't care what they said, what you said, whatever. Why can't you all just mind your own business?' I snapped, marching off.

'There you are, you're being mean again,' Grace said, hobbling after me. 'Why won't you tell me stuff, Prue? We never used to have any secrets.'

'I haven't got any secrets,' I said.

'Yes, you *have*. You act all weird and moody most of the time. You're not just playing your pretend games now, something's going on. I can tell. I think you're in love.'

'Don't be silly,' I snapped, starting to run.

'I *know* you, Prue.'

'You don't know anything,' I said, running hard.

'It's Rax!' Grace yelled after me.

Some of the kids in the street turned round and tittered.

I stood still, waiting for her to catch me up. Then I grabbed her by the shoulders, digging my fingers into her marshmallow flesh. 'Shut *up*!' I said.

'It *is* Rax,' Grace said triumphantly. 'You love him.'

'I'm warning you, Grace.'

'It's OK. Lots of girls get crushes on teachers, even funny ones like Rax,' said Grace.

'It's not a *crush*,' I said. I hated the word, with all its silly girly giggly connotations. 'It's reciprocal.'

'It's what?' said Grace.

'He loves me too.'

'Don't be daft,' said Grace, giggling.

'Don't you dare laugh at me! He *does* love me. He does, he does. He feels bad about it, he's worried about his family and his job and all that, but he can't help himself. It's as if we're made for each other, soul mates.'

Grace stared, her eyes round as marbles. Then she laughed again. 'I'm sorry! Don't – you're hurting!' she said. 'I'm not *really* laughing, Prue, it's just it's so weird. He's a teacher, he's years and years too old for you.'

'Age doesn't matter, not when you fall in love.'

'But what's going to happen?'

'Well.' I thought hard. 'Well, we'll go on seeing each other when I babysit, and then . . . and then . . .'

Grace looked at me. 'And then?' she repeated.

'We'll just have to wait and see,' I said lamely. 'I'm not going to talk about it any more. And if you breathe a word to anyone – especially Iggy and Figgy – I'll kill you, do you understand?'

I said it with such vehemence that she backed away and trailed along several paces behind me all the way home.

I knew I was treating her very badly. Part of me wanted to stop and put my arms round her and beg her to forgive me, but I still felt too angry. I couldn't bear her laughing at me, behaving as if I was making half of it up. Rax and I *were* made for each other. Fate had brought us together. We were an unlikely couple, like Jane Eyre and Mr Rochester. They belonged together. They had to wait years but their story had a happy ending.

I tried hard to look older when I got ready to go out. I wore my black sweater, and hitched my school skirt up like a miniskirt. I stuffed my feet into a pair of ancient strappy high-heeled sandals from our dressing-up box. They'd been a ten-pence jumble-sale find long ago. Grace and I used to shuffle about happily, pretending to be big ladies. They were still several sizes too big for me, but I strapped them up as tightly as they would go, determined to make myself look as sophisticated as possible. I still had to walk with a hop-skip-shuffle to keep them on my feet, but I hoped Rax wouldn't notice when he drove me home. I didn't care how many times I twisted my ankle on my way there.

Mum created a scene about the shoes. She was shocked by my painted face too. I took no notice of her.

'I don't know what to do with you, Prudence,' she wailed. 'You're getting so wilful. Just you wait till your father gets home! He'll give you such a talking to.'

I held my tongue. It was starting to look as if Dad might never recover his speech. He had abruptly lost all interest in repeating words after me. He refused to make any attempt to say anything to us, though he still swore when especially irritated. This was a great deal of the time. However, the nurses said he was improving dramatically. He had supposedly started to walk during his physiotherapy sessions but he barely turned over in bed while we were there.

Someone had put a television in his room, thinking it an act of kindness. Dad behaved as if a miniature Kingdom of Hell was flaming at the end of his bed. Whenever the nurses switched it on he pulled the sheets up over his head, as if in fear of being scorched. But as the days passed he gradually peeped at several programmes, watching with one eye. Now he gazed avidly at the screen and shushed us if we spoke during his favourite shows.

'Do you think Dad will let us have a telly when he comes home?' Grace asked eagerly.

'What are you going to buy it with, Monopoly money?' said Mum.

She was still sifting through the bills and final demands every day. She got in such a state that she plucked up the courage to ask Dad what we should do.

Dad ignored her. Mum asked again, louder, though she went pink, terrified a passing nurse might hear about our money problems.

Dad still took no notice whatsoever, though we knew there wasn't anything wrong with his hearing.

Mum didn't pursue it. She managed to make small talk and gave Dad her usual kiss on his forehead, but on the bus going home her lip started quivering.

'It's all very well for your father, tucked up safe in the hospital,' she said. 'But what are we going to do when these bailiffs come and bash down the door?'

'Can't we sell the shop, Mum?' I asked.

'It would kill your father, Prue. He loves the shop so, you know he does. And anyway, *I* can't put it on the market, it's your dad's property. I doubt if anyone would buy it now anyway. It needs so much work doing to it – and the whole parade's gone to seed.'

'So what will happen to us?' Grace asked.

'We'll manage somehow,' I said. 'If we get slung out of the shop then they'll have to rehouse us *somewhere*.'

'On the Wentworth estate!' Mum said. 'And what would we have to live on, anyway?'

'You'd get . . . I don't know, unemployment benefit?'

'Your dad's never forked out for his proper national insurance payments, or mine either,' said Mum.

'Then you'll just have to put Grace and me on the streets,' I said, joking.

'You're starting to *look* like a street girl!' Mum shouted after me now, as I went out the door. 'Whatever will your teacher think, going babysitting looking like that!'

196

'I look fine. You're just hopelessly old-fashioned,' I said, but I kept glancing at my reflection anxiously all the way to Laurel Grove.

Marianne answered the door to me. I saw her initial bemused expression. Then she smiled, rubbing her forehead above her nose.

'I look funny, don't I?' I said.

'What? No, no, of course not. Come on, Prue. You look very original, as always – and enviably *skinny*. No, I've just got a bit of a headache, that's all. You know, time of the month and everything.' She peered at me in the light of the hall. 'You've gone a bit mad on your make-up tonight, haven't you?'

'I *knew* I looked awful.'

'Just a bit . . . bright. Why don't you try slightly subtler shades? Which lipstick do you use?'

'I haven't *got* any lipstick, or any other make-up. I just have to use my paints.'

'I *see*. Yeah, that's a bit of a problem. Here, come up to my room, let's see if I can find you anything.'

I had to follow her upstairs and into her bedroom. She rummaged through her messy cosmetic bag.

'Hang on, I know I've got a dusky pink lipstick somewhere.'

I couldn't tell her that I'd experimented with it several times, that every time I came to babysit I couldn't stop myself creeping into their bedroom and examining everything in it. I'd even taken to lying on her pillow and pretending that Rax was lying right next to me.

I averted my eyes from their bed now and let Marianne wipe off all the paint with her make-up remover cream. She started applying her own make-up on my face.

I could hear chuckles and shouts from the children in the bathroom. I thought Rax was giving both of them a bath. I was alarmed to open my eyes after Marianne had finished shadowing them to see Rax reflected in the mirror, watching us.

'Oh, sorry!' I said foolishly. 'Shall I go and see to the children now?'

'We're not finished yet!' said Marianne. 'What about eyeliner? Just a very subtle grey shade? Keith, you haven't left the kids in the bath, have you?'

'No, no, they're in their jim-jams. I'm just looking for Harry's Honeybear, but I got distracted by the make-up session. It looks great.'

'Just call me the makeover queen,' said Marianne. She gathered my long wild hair in her hands. 'Hey, let's see what your hair looks like pinned up.'

I could feel myself blushing. I felt horribly self-conscious in front of Rax. I didn't want Marianne dabbing at me any longer, even if she was good at it.

'No, it looks silly up. I don't like it,' I said.

I liked my hair springing over my face and bouncing round my shoulders. I felt too exposed with it pinned up. But Marianne twirled it round her finger, and fixed it in a little chignon on top.

'There!' she said. 'Oh, that looks so *good*! You've got such a lovely neck, Prue, just like a little ballet dancer.'

I pulled a face, fidgeting.

'Doesn't she look lovely, Keith?' said Marianne.

'Yes, she does,' said Rax. 'But maybe you should be getting on with *your* hair and make-up, Marianne, or we'll never get out. The film starts at half past eight.'

Marianne sighed. 'We can always get it out later on DVD. I'm not sure I can be bothered, not with this headache. I don't really feel like going out at all.'

'I think we should try to make the most of tonight. It might be our last chance for a while,' said Rax.

He looked at me. I stared into the mirror at my own reflection, pretending to admire my new hairstyle.

Rax waited a moment. 'Prue isn't sure she can keep on babysitting on a regular basis,' he said.

I swallowed. 'Yes I can.'

I didn't dare look at him.

'Didn't you tell me at school that your mum isn't too happy about it?' Rax said sternly.

'Oh, she's had second thoughts.'

'Are you sure?' said Marianne. 'We've been a bit cheeky, simply commandeering you and taking you totally for granted.'

'I'm quite sure,' I said.

'Well, that's good,' said Marianne. 'Isn't it, Keith?'

Rax said nothing. I knew he was probably furious with me but I couldn't help it. He walked out of the room, ignoring both of us.

Marianne raised her eyebrows at me. 'Take no notice. He's been a bit edgy all week. Oh well, I suppose I'd better show willing and get ready. I'd much sooner stay home and play hairdressers!'

She smiled at me. I watched myself in the mirror, smiling straight back at her. I felt so wicked. I waited for the mirror to crack, for the walls to close in on me, for the carpet to slide down into a dark pit, taking me with it.

I stayed sitting on Marianne's padded stool, the two of us smiling into the mirror, as if we were posing for our portrait.

I still felt wicked when Rax and Marianne had gone out.

I made a special fuss of the children, bending over Lily's cot, holding her little chubby fist while I sang to her. I had to struggle to set my fingers free after she'd fallen fast asleep.

Harry was in a surprisingly sweet clingy mode too. I read him my old copy of *Where the Wild Things Are*. He pretended to be a little frightened so he could sit on my lap and have a cuddle. I drew him a big, stripy, wickedly-clawed Wild Thing with his children's wax crayons.

Then I made up a new *Wild Things* story about a little boy called Harry who sailed to the land where the Wild Things are, only there was no one roaring or showing their claws this time. The Wild Things bowed low to King Harry and bought him lots of presents and lay on their backs so he could tickle their fat furry tummies.

'Like this,' I said, upending Harry and tickling him.

I had to do it again and again, but he was getting sleepy now, rubbing his eyes. I began another story about the Wild Things in the dead of winter, when the snow came right up to their snouts and they all snuggled down in their cosy burrows.

'Like this,' I said, tucking Harry under his duvet. 'There you are, Baby Wild Thing. Shut your eyes and suck your claws.'

Harry giggled and sucked his fingers and fell asleep in seconds.

I stood there in the dark nursery, listening to the faint snuffle of the children sleeping. They were both treating me like their fairy godmother but I was worse than any wicked witch, intent on working my black magic on their father.

I crept into the main bedroom again and switched on the light. I looked in the mirror and a ghost image of Marianne peered back at me accusingly.

'I'm sorry,' I whispered. 'I wish you weren't so *nice* to me. I don't want to hurt you. I just can't help it. I love him so.'

I went to their double bed and buried my face in his pillow. I imagined him there beside me, his arms round me . . .

Then I heard a door, noises, Rax's voice!

I sat up, heart thudding, not sure whether I

was still daydreaming. No, there really were voices downstairs! Oh God, how could they be back already? Had I fallen asleep? I leaped off the bed, plumping Rax's pillow, smoothing the daffodil-yellow duvet, racing across the carpet. As I came out of the door Marianne was coming up the stairs and she saw me.

She frowned. 'Prue? What were you doing in our bedroom?'

'Oh Marianne, I'm sorry. I just wanted to look in your mirror again, to see my new hairstyle and make-up,' I said.

'Oh, I see! Yes, you look lovely.'

Poor Marianne looked *awful*, greasy and greeny-white.

'I've been sick,' she said, seeing me staring. 'Keith had to stop the car.'

'You poor *thing*. Do you think you've got a bug or something?'

'No, it's just the time of the month. It sometimes hits me like this. I'll be all right once I've had a good night's sleep. I was stupid to try to go out. Oh God, my *head*.' She leaned against the banisters, her eyes closed.

'Would you like me to help you into bed?' I asked timidly.

'No, no, I'll manage. Get Keith to give you your money, eh?'

'But I haven't earned it.'

'That's not your fault, love. Oh well, I'd better lie down or I'll *fall* down. See you next week then?'

'I hope so,' I said.

She waved her fingers at me and then trudged into her bedroom, sighing. I heard the springs creak on her bed within seconds.

I went downstairs slowly, my mouth dry, my tummy tense. Rax was standing in the hallway, still in his jacket.

'Marianne's gone to bed,' I said.

'Yes. Right. I'll take you home then.'

'All right.'

I followed him out of the front door, down the path, through the gate, into the car. I looked at Rax as he drove off.

'Are you cross with me?' I asked, in a very small voice.

'Yes,' he said.

I didn't dare say any more. We drove in silence. I tried to think of some way I could make everything all right again. This was our precious ten minutes together and it was ticking away. We were wasting it all.

The silence in the car was becoming unbearable. Rax seemed to think so too, because he reached out and switched on the radio. Loud pop music filled the car. Lyrics of lost love, broken promises, betrayals. Every line seemed to have significant meaning.

Rax stared straight ahead, frowning. He seemed to be concentrating hard on the traffic, although the back roads were nearly empty. We got to my street in just over five minutes. He drew up right outside the shop and switched off the engine. The love song stopped abruptly. The car was silent.

'Right,' said Rax. 'How much do we usually pay you then?'

'I don't want any money,' I said.

'Don't be silly. Let me pay you for a full night's babysitting. Here, take this.'

He took several notes from his wallet and thrust them at me.

'No!'

'Take it. It's a bit extra, to thank you for being such a good babysitter.'

'Will you let me keep coming?'

'No. I told you. This has got to stop. It's getting out of hand. I think Marianne senses something. That's maybe why she was ill.'

'No it isn't! She *likes* me, Rax, she wants me to keep coming. It's just that you won't let me.'

'Yes.' There was a very long pause. 'Well. Off you go then.'

'Is that it? You're not even going to say goodbye properly?'

'For heaven's sake, Prue, you'll see me at school often enough.'

'But it's different there. We can't talk properly. You're the teacher and I'm the pupil.'

'We *are* teacher and pupil.'

'What about if we weren't? If I didn't even go to Wentworth? How would you feel about me then?'

'I'd feel exactly the same as I do now. You're a child of fourteen.'

'The same age as Marianne when you started going out together. What if Marianne and I were both girls in your class at school? Would you like her best – or me?'

'Will you *stop* this! You're distorting everything, playing silly games. Look, Prue, I don't want to hurt you, but you must understand. I'm your schoolteacher. We could both get into such huge trouble. I took an interest in you because you were new to the school and finding it hard going and I sympathized. I tried to help you and then I made the big mistake of asking you to babysit for me and now somehow it's all become too intense, too worrying. I feel so guilty, which is mad, because nothing's actually *happened*.'

'It has now,' I said, and I reached over and kissed him on the lips.

I'd never kissed anyone properly before but I'd imagined it enough times and I'd practised how to do it on the inside of my arm. It was a timid, dry-lipped kiss – but it was a real kiss all the same.

'For God's sake!' Rax said, trying to pull away.

I kissed him again, sliding my arms round his neck and holding him tight so that he couldn't pull away from me. After a few seconds he stopped trying. He kissed me back, deeply and passionately. I was so happy I didn't care about anything or anyone any more. I just wanted to freeze time and stay inside the car, kissing Rax for ever.

'Prue, we're right outside your shop,' Rax said. 'Your mother—'

'She's not expecting me back for ages, you know that.'

But there were people coming out of the Chinese takeaway, looking in our direction.

'Oh God,' said Rax. He started up the car and we drove off.

'Where are we going?'

'I don't know. Round the block. I just need to think what to do,' he said.

I kept quiet then, peering out at the dark streets. We circled the block, but Rax didn't stop. We drove on to the outskirts of the town. We were only a mile or so away from the hospital and my dad's stroke unit. I wondered what he would say if he knew his elder daughter was driving in the dark with her schoolteacher sweetheart.

We drove down a dark lane with fields on either side, and then Rax drew up beside a clump of trees.

'Where are we?' I whispered.

'Oh, this is just . . . somewhere I used to come,' Rax said. He was whispering too.

I wondered if it was somewhere he came with Marianne. I didn't want to ask. I didn't want him to think about her. I didn't want him to think about anyone but me.

I reached over to kiss him again.

'No! No, listen, Prue, we've got to talk,' he said, trying to turn his head.

'I don't want to talk. You'll just say sensible things and I won't want to listen. Let's just do this.'

I kissed him and he kissed me back. This time I couldn't even think what it was like, or wonder who he'd kissed before. There was no one else in the world. We were whirling in our own starlit space.

'I love you,' I said breathlessly. 'I love you, I love you, I love you.'

I waited.

'Tell me you love me just a little tiny bit,' I begged.

'Prue—'

'Go on. You said it before, when you drove off that time. You said it then because you weren't sure I could see, and you could pretend it didn't really count. Say it now, Rax. Say it properly.'

'I love you.'

'Oh!'

'But this is crazy. We're both mad. You're still so young.'

'Shut *up*.'

'And I'm married, I love my family, I don't want to do anything to hurt them. I don't want to do anything to hurt *you*. You're enjoying this now because it's so exciting and romantic and dangerous. It's the best game in all the world. It's *my* imaginary game too. Don't you think I haven't lain awake at night thinking about you, wishing we could be together, fantasizing all sorts of things.'

'Really?'

'Of course.'

'Then why have you been trying to stop seeing me?'

'Because there is no way we can ever be together. You know that, don't you?'

'Maybe . . . maybe sometime—?'

'It's not going to happen.'

'But we love each other so much.'

'You think you love me—'

'I *do*!'

'And next year you'll fall in love with another teacher, or maybe an artist, whoever – and then at art college you'll fall passionately for the scruffiest student—'

'You really think I could go to art college?'

'And then another student, and then another, and then *eventually* you'll meet the man of your dreams and you'll live with him and have his children and then one night you'll be kissing each other and he'll ask you about your past loves and you'll say, "Oh yes, I remember when I was fourteen. I fell in love with my art teacher," and I bet you'll have a struggle to even remember my name.'

'Will you always remember *my* name?'

'Oh yes. There'll be no forgetting you, Prudence King.'

'You haven't kissed any of the other girls at school?'

'For God's sake, what do you think I am? Of course not.'

'But you're glad now that you kissed me?'

'I'm very happy, very unhappy, very confused,' he said. 'I don't know what to do now.' He let out his breath in a long sigh. 'I really don't know.'

I couldn't see his face properly in the dark. I felt it very gently with my fingers.

'I think you're looking sad. *Please* don't be sad, Rax. Be happy. *I'm* happy, the happiest I've ever been in my whole life. I never dreamed I could feel like this. I've read all sorts of books, I've pretended stuff, but I had no idea it would feel so wonderful.'

'Oh Prue. Come here.' He pulled me nearer, his arms right round me, holding me tight, my head on his chest. I was stretched sideways, bits of the car sticking into my waist and hip and leg, but I'd have happily let someone saw right through me just to stay in his arms. He very gently kissed the top of my head, nuzzling into my hair.

'It's starting to escape from the topknot already,' he said. 'Ouch, there's a hairpin! Do you mind if I take the pins out and let it hang free again? Your new hairstyle's very sophisticated, but I like it better the old way.'

I shook it free at once, combing it with my hands. Rax played with it too, winding strands round his fingers.

'I love your hair,' he said.

'It's *horrible*! I wish I had straight silky hair.'

'Your hair's like you.'

'Yes, wild and mad and untidy.'

'OK, wild, but also springy and full of life. And utterly uncontrollable. What am I going to do with you, Prue? What are we going to do?'

'I know,' I said. 'We're going to start driving and keep on driving, all through the night, until we get somewhere we've never been before, where no one knows us, and we'll start our new life together, Prue and Rax. We'll find some old cottage or beach shack, we'll live very frugally on bread and cheese – maybe chips! – and you won't go to work and I won't go to school. We'll paint all day. You'll teach me lots of things. We'll go for long walks hand in hand and in the evenings we'll curl up together and then we'll read. Maybe you'll read to me – would you like that?'

'I'd like that. I'd like all of it,' said Rax. 'If only!'

'Let's make a wish that it will come true some day,' I said. I reached up and pulled out one of my spiralling hairs.

'What are you doing?'

I found his left hand and wrapped my hair round and round his ring finger. 'There! That means that *one* day you'll be mine. I'm wishing it. You wish it too, Rax. Come on, close your eyes and *wish*.'

'Sometimes you're more like four than fourteen,' said Rax. But then he went quiet, holding onto his own hand. I knew he was wishing too.

'OK. That's the future taken care of,' he said. 'But we're still in the present now. I've got two little children and a sick wife at home. If she wakes up she'll be wondering what the hell has happened to me. *I'm* wondering. Maybe I've gone crazy. Come on, let's get you back home again.'

'It's still quite early. We could stay another half hour, easily.'

'No, it's time to go, Prue,' he said, gently pushing me back into my seat.

We drove off down the lane.

'We *could* drive up to Scotland, down to Cornwall, across to Wales—' I said.

'We could. But we're not going to. We're going to take you straight back home, OK?'

'*This* time.'

'This time,' Rax said.

'But *one* day—'

'Yes, one day,' he repeated wearily.

'Are you just humouring me?' I asked.

'Yes. And humouring myself too.'

'We'll work it all out, Rax, you'll see. I swear I won't make things difficult for you at school. I'll be the total soul of discretion. Don't laugh at me, I *will*. I'll do whatever you say, I promise, just so long as I can still see you in secret just a little bit.'

I went on burbling, fearful now because Rax had gone so quiet. But when we came to my street he parked a little way up the road, glanced round quickly and then gave me one last long wondrous kiss.

'Out you get, right now, or I really will drive off with you,' he said.

'Then I'm staying!'

'Prue. Please. Go now.'

'One more kiss?'

'What happened to your doing whatever I say?'

'OK, OK. Goodnight, darling Rax. See you at school.'

'Ssh! Yes, right. Off you go now, there's a good girl. No hanging about or waving or blowing kisses, OK?'

I got out of the car and walked obediently to the shop door without even turning round. I unlocked the door and stepped inside, into the stale, musty world of sad old books that no one wanted to read any more.

Mum was upstairs in the kitchen with all our bank statements and bills spread all over the table.

'Oh Mum, put them *away*. They'll just stop you sleeping,' I said.

Mum looked at me, red-eyed. 'I'm not sleeping whether I look at them or not,' she said. She paused, glancing at some of the crumpled bills.

'I had no idea,' she said. 'I can't work out your dad's system. I know I don't have a head for business but even I can see you need to pay your bills, you can't just let them *slide*.'

I didn't want to slide down this familiar dreary slope with Mum. I wanted to stay soaring above the stars with Rax.

'I tried to tackle your dad about it, but he was in one of his moods. He really doesn't like it when you're babysitting, Prudence. I think it worries him. Well, it worries *me*, dear. It's too much responsibility for a girl your age.'

'Mum, *please*. Look, I'm tired, I'm going to bed.'

Grace was waiting for me too, asking endless questions. I took no notice, humming under my breath as I got ready for bed.

'Do you really love Rax?' she asked. 'You *do*? You are weird, Prue. What's the point? I mean, obviously he doesn't love you.'

'How do you know?' I said, before I could stop myself.

'He's married, he's got children!' said Grace.

'I know. But that doesn't stop you falling in love if the right person comes along.'

'You are so nuts!' said Grace. Then she paused. 'You don't *mean* it, do you? Prue, has he said anything? Has he told you stuff? Has he kissed you?' She started spluttering with laughter, lying back on her bed and drumming her legs in idiotic fashion.

'Stop it!' I said. 'Stop being so ridiculous!'

'Imagine kissing *Rax*!' Grace chortled. 'Oh yuck yuck yuck! That stupid beard mustn't half scratch and tickle!'

'Just shut *up*, you fat lump. I don't know why you find it so funny. No one's ever going to want to kiss *you*. You're pathetic.'

Grace stopped, as if I'd thrown a bucket of water over her. 'You're the one who's pathetic,' she said. 'You're the one everyone laughs about at school. You're the one who gets a stupid crush

214

on a manky old teacher. You're the one who pretends all sorts of stupid stuff, making out you're having this big grown-up affair when all the time I bet he's just feeling sorry for you!'

I flew at her, putting my hand over her mouth to stop her saying it. She struggled and then bit my fingers hard. I slapped her; she pulled my hair. I tried to bang her head, she kicked at me, and then we rolled off the bed with a thump.

'Girls, girls! Whatever's happening!' Mum shouted, rushing in.

We were still kicking and slapping there on the floor.

'Just you *stop* that, both of you! What are you playing at? Have you both gone demented? I need you to be grown-up sensible girls, yet here you are behaving appallingly! It's that school, isn't it? You've only been there five minutes and yet you've both changed so dreadfully. You talk so badly now, Grace, and you just giggle giggle giggle with those friends of yours on the phone. As for you, Prudence, you've become so wilful, doing exactly as you please, and you go out of here painted like a street girl. I can't bear it! I wish your father was here. Oh dear God, why can't he hurry up and get better and come *home*?'

16

I wouldn't make friends with Grace. I wouldn't even talk to Mum properly, but I did mind the shop for her on Saturday morning while she went to Tesco. For a long time we had no customers whatsoever. I roamed round and round the shelves, picking up odd volumes here and there, sifting one pile of books and shunting others into corners.

Dad had always had his own idiosyncratic display system. He divided his stock into categories – fiction, biography, art, general paperbacks, juvenile, etc. – but his cheap shelving wasn't flexible, so large art books and children's picture books were over on the big shelves near his desk and little Everymans were crammed willy-nilly into odd corners. For years now newly-bought stock had simply been stuffed wherever he could find a space.

There was a special locking cabinet of supposedly precious books but he'd lost the key long ago and so he'd had to jemmy the door open. We were supposed to sit at the desk in front of the cabinet, on guard, but this was pointless. No serious collector wanted Dad's precious books. There were a couple of illustrated Rackhams but some of the colour plates were missing; then there were several sets of Dickens and the Brontës, but very faded and foxed; there were various first edition modern novels but mostly without their dust wrappers. All our books were as faded and out of fashion as our family. No wonder we had fewer and fewer customers.

I dealt with one old lady looking for a book she'd loved as a little girl, and a middle-aged man came in looking for Rupert annuals. Then a whole hour went by with no one. I flicked through an old water-stained book of favourite artists through the ages. I wanted to find someone who painted Rax-style men but didn't have much luck. He was long and lean and soulful like an El Greco, but the men were too effeminate and pop-eyed. He was pale with a pointy beard like a Veronese or a Titian, but their men were too square-shouldered and muscular. He was dark and pensive like Picasso's Blue Period men, but they were too angst-ridden and melancholy. I flicked through the book to the end and then started sketching my own Rax on the back page. I knew every feature so well it was as if he was posing in front of me. I was lovingly shading in the hollow under his cheekbones and highlighting the sweet curve of his mouth when the shop bell rang. I looked up, wondering if I could possibly have conjured him up out of sheer longing.

It was Toby.

I slammed the book shut. 'Not you again!'

'That's not very welcoming,' said Toby. He came over to the desk and touched the art book. 'Let's see.'

'No,' I said, hands tight over the edge of the pages so he couldn't open it.

'You're not supposed to draw in books,' said Toby.

'It's not worth anything, and it's my book anyway,' I said, shoving it under the desk. 'Just go *away*, Toby. I don't want to see you.'

'I'm a customer,' he said, pretending to look at the books.

'Yeah, a customer who can't read,' I muttered, but not loud enough for him to hear.

'Seriously, I want to buy a book. I'm really getting into reading now. What would you recommend?'

'Oh Toby, you've got us both into enough trouble with your wretched reading.'

'I'm sorry about Rita and the other girls. I thought they'd have stopped giving you a hard time by now.'

'I don't care.'

218

'I don't know what I ever saw in her. She came round to my house last night and said she was prepared to take me back.'

'Well then!'

'But I said I wasn't interested.'

'Then she'll *really* have it in for me on Monday morning.'

'We could have fun together, you and me, Prue. Just as friends, like. I could help you out in the shop, clear up all this stuff on the floor. You just tell me where you want all these boxes to go, I'll shift them for you.' He seized one as he spoke, lifting it a little too recklessly. The soft cardboard sagged and twenty-odd volumes fell out all over the dusty floor.

'Whoops!' he said.

'Careful! Honestly, Toby, will you leave them *alone*.'

'Hey, look at these!'

Toby was looking through the old volumes of Victorian pornography, his mouth an O of astonishment as he pored over the colour plates of the Reverend Knightly and his cavorting congregation.

'Where did you get these dirty books?' he said.

'They're not "dirty" books. It's Victorian erotica,' I said haughtily, though I couldn't help blushing.

'Fancy your dad selling porn!'

'It's not. All sorts of highly respectable people collect it.'

'Yeah, and you and I know why. You're such

a *weird* girl, Prue. Here's you looking at hot stuff like this as cool as a cucumber, and yet you get all fussed when I simply try to kiss you.'

I wondered what he'd think if he saw the way I kissed Rax. It all seemed so sad. There was Rita wanting Toby and Toby wanting me and me wanting Rax – but Rax wanted me back. He *did* want me, I knew he did. Though why had he seemed so unhappy last night, in spite of everything?

'Prue?' said Toby.

'What?'

'Are you all right? You look as if you've got a pain.'

'No. No, I'm fine. I just want to be on my own for a bit, Toby. You go now. Look, take one of the naughty vicar books. If anything will encourage you to read, he will. And if it gets too much of a struggle you can always look at the pictures.'

'Are you sure? I'll buy it. How much is it?'

'I haven't a clue. It isn't priced. Just take it.'

'Well, I'll just borrow it if you don't mind. Can I have a bag or something? I don't want my mum or my sisters to see it!'

Mum and Grace came into the shop while Toby was leaving. Mum looked disappointed.

'Can't you stay a bit, lad? We're just going to have a cup of tea and some shortbread. And if you can wait half an hour or so, I'm making a batch of rock cakes to take to the hospital this afternoon.'

'Do stay, Toby,' said Grace. 'Mum's rock cakes taste so yummy when they're hot out of the oven.'

So Toby stayed, holding his book bag very gingerly, as if it was burning his hands.

'What have you got there, then, Toby?' Mum asked.

Toby went scarlet. 'Oh, nothing,' he said foolishly.

'Nothing?' said Mum. 'It's one of our books, isn't it? What have you been buying?'

I waited to see what he'd say. He seemed at a total loss for words.

'Toby's a bit embarrassed about it,' I said, teasing him.

Toby looked agonized.

'It's actually an old Rupert annual. He used to love them when he was little, but he feels silly wanting a kid's comic book.'

'Oh, *sweet*,' said Grace. 'I always loved Rupert, Toby. Hey, my friend Figgy told me this great joke. What's Rupert's middle name? Can't you guess? It's "The". You know, Rupert *the* Bear.' She went into peals of laughter.

Toby laughed too, relieved. He was very kind to Grace, chuckling at joke after stupid joke. He was very polite to Mum, chomping up the last of her shortcake and then eating *three* rock cakes, rolling his eyes and kissing his fingers in a pantomime of appreciation.

I was grateful to him but irritated too. My sister's silly jokes were excruciating. My mum had simply made a batch of boring old rock cakes, for goodness' sake.

'I wish my mum made cakes,' said Toby.

'Rock cakes are very simple, lad. I'll write you out the recipe. Your mum could whip you up a batch in a jiffy.'

'My mum isn't a whipper-upper. She's a shove-it-in-the-microwave lady,' said Toby. He nodded at Grace and me. 'You're so lucky! It must be wonderful to have real home baking.'

'We *are* lucky,' said Grace, giving Mum a hug.

I felt such a pang. Why couldn't I be nice like them? Why did I always have to be so prickly and grudging and difficult?

Oh God, did I take after Dad?

'Tell you what, you ought to sell your shortbread and rock cakes in the bookshop,' said Toby. 'Yes, serve coffee and home-made cakes. They do that in bookshops now – the one down the shopping centre's got a coffee shop; it would be very popular with your customers.'

'*What* customers?' I said.

'Oh dear,' said Mum. 'Prue's right. We really don't seem to get many customers nowadays.'

'You want to advertise your books on the Internet. That's how everyone does business nowadays,' said Toby. 'I could help you set it all up. I can't really type it all out for you, I'd get the words mixed up, but Prue could do that.'

'But we haven't got a computer, Toby. They cost hundreds of pounds.'

'No probs! My eldest sister's going out with a

guy who works in this fancy office and they're forever upgrading their equipment and chucking the old stuff out. He could get hold of a perfectly good PC for you for next to nothing. Then you could surf the Net, look at e-bay, see what sort of book bargains people were offering. I bet it would make all the difference to your business.'

'Do you really think so?' Mum said, leaning forward eagerly.

'I *know* so,' said Toby, swaggering a little. 'That's how most businesses are run now. You can trade on the Internet and send the books off by post. Grace could package them all up for you, couldn't you, Grace?'

'Ooh yes, I could do. I'm good at doing parcels. And I *love* bubble wrap, it's such fun to pop,' said Grace.

'That way you'd attract a new type of customer. Then if we also tidied up the shop a bit, gave it a lick of paint, advertised your coffee and cakes, it would appeal to your traditional book buyer too.'

They were staring at him as if he was a second Moses and he had Ten Business Commandments straight from God. They *were* good ideas too. This boy who could barely read had far better ideas than I'd ever had.

'Toby's right, Mum,' I said.

Toby flicked his hair out of his eyes and gave me a huge, dazzling grin. Grace sighed. Mum sighed too.

'I know Toby's got some very good ideas,' she said. 'But what would your dad say? You know what he thinks about computers. He'd never agree to have one in the shop. I'm sure he wouldn't like the coffee and cake idea either. He'd think I was trying to turn the shop into a café.'

'You could do it while Dad's still in hospital,' I said.

'Oh Prue, I wouldn't dare,' said Mum. She paused. 'Would I?'

She went on about it after Toby went off, clutching his Victorian volume in his carrier bag. She talked about it on the bus all the way to the hospital.

'Perhaps now he'll see we have to change with the times,' she muttered. 'We could try out this computer idea, especially if we got it for almost nothing. And I could maybe ask one or two customers if they'd fancy a cup of coffee. I could try it out for free first, to see if they liked the idea. What would be the harm in that?'

'That's it, Mum, you tell Dad,' I said.

But when we got to the stroke unit Dad had something to tell *us*.

He wasn't in bed as usual. He wasn't even in his pyjamas and dressing gown. He was sitting bolt upright on one of the plastic chairs, dressed in his old suit, the one he'd been wearing when he'd had his stroke. He even had his tie neatly knotted. He clutched a notebook on his lap.

'Oh Bernard, you look wonderful, dear! Quite your old self!' said Mum.

'You look ever so smart, Dad,' said Grace.

'Hello, Dad. You really do look great,' I said.

He nodded at us all, taking his time, like a king on his throne waiting for his unruly courtiers to settle down. Mum wedged herself into another plastic chair and Grace and I perched uncomfortably on the end of the bed.

Dad cleared his throat. We sat expectantly. He raised the notebook lopsidedly, his good hand doing most of the work. He fumbled with the pages, trying to get it open at the beginning. Mum leaped up to help but he glared at her furiously, so she subsided again. Dad fiddled with the flimsy paper. I saw my own careful printing. It was my truncated version of his Magnum Opus! It hadn't got lost at all.

Dad cleared his throat once more. 'I – Bernard King – think – think – think – my – home-town – of – Kingtown – reflects – the – moral – degeneracy – of – our – current – unstable – and – unsatisfactory – age.'

He said it very slowly, without expression, struggling at each word, his mouth working as if he was chewing toffee, his eyebrows going up and down with the effort. But he *said* it, the entire sentence.

'Bravo!' said Mum, clapping him, tears pouring down her cheeks.

'Brill, Dad! Like, wow!' said Grace.

Dad winced at each word but for once let it ride. He looked at me triumphantly.

'I thought you'd thrown it away, Dad!' I said.

'Aha!' said Dad.

'You seemed totally fed up with the whole idea of reading aloud,' I said.

'With – you,' said Dad.

'So you've been secretly practising all by yourself?'

Nurse Ray put her head round the door. 'I should say so! He's been at it night and day for weeks, head in that book, mutter mutter mutter. I offered to help him but he wouldn't be having it. Wanted to teach himself, bless him.'

Dad huffed, irritated by her tone.

'Ooh, don't get shirty with me now, Bernard,' Nurse Ray said. 'You know you love me really, don't you, darling?'

Dad rocked backwards and forwards at her presumption, and she laughed at him.

'Have you told them your good news?' said Nurse Ray.

'Good news,' Dad agreed.

'It's splendid news, Bernard, seeing you reading your own book!' said Mum. 'Can you manage a bit more?'

Dad shook his head. 'Good news – going home!'

'Yes, dear, you carry on making progress like this and you'll soon be better and able to come home,' said Mum.

Dad tutted at her. 'Going home *now*,' he said. 'Today. *Now!*'

'Well, not just yet, dear. When the doctors say so,' Mum said, flustered.

Nurse Ray was nodding at her. 'He's right!

That's why we've got him all dressed up a treat in his suit. Dear God, I had to tie that tie for him three times and he still wasn't satisfied. Like I said, Bernard, you need a nice comfy sweatshirt and a pair of trackie bottoms, then you can whip them on and off in seconds.'

Dad said a very rude word to show what he thought of sweatshirts and trackies.

'He can come home right this minute?' said Mum.

'*Now!*' Dad said impatiently.

'We had a case conference yesterday and we all agreed that Bernard's more than ready to leave us,' said Nurse Ray. 'He's made that perfectly clear!'

'But he can't walk!' said Mum.

'He can stand, and shuffle a few paces with his Zimmer if he puts his mind to it. We're willing to arrange some out-patient physio-therapy – *if* His Lordship co-operates!'

Dad shook his head at this.

'But how will he get about?' Mum said weakly.

'We'll let you borrow a wheelchair from the unit, and if you get in touch with this phone number here someone will come out and assess the sort of chair Bernard will need for the future. They'll install hand supports in the bathroom and give you a commode if necessary.'

'*Not!*' said Dad. 'Right. Home. Now.'

He looked at us. His eyes swivelled from Mum to Grace to me. He breathed more quickly, his mouth working. 'Not want me?' he said.

'Oh Bernard, of *course* we want you back! It's just such a shock. But it's lovely, a lovely surprise,' Mum burbled.

Grace and I were still so stunned we couldn't say a word.

'I've got Bernard's bag all packed, and he's got all the medication he needs for the next few weeks. Make sure he takes his Warfarin.'

'Rat poison!' said Dad.

'Yes, but you're not a rat, darling, and it's thinning your blood nicely so you don't have another stroke,' said Nurse Ray, putting her arm round him. 'I shall miss your grumpy little ways, Sugar Lump!' She gave him a big kiss on his whiskery cheek.

Dad huffed again, but he patted her with his good hand.

Then we had to get him home.

'Will the ambulance men come and collect us?' said Mum.

'No dear, we can't spare an ambulance. Can't you take him in your car?'

'We haven't *got* a car,' said Mum. 'We can't take my husband on the *bus*!'

We had to call a minicab and manoeuvre Dad into the front, Mum and me heaving him onto the seat and tucking his legs in, while he snapped at us impatiently. Then Mum squeezed into the back seat, Grace and me squashed in beside her, with the wheelchair collapsed in the boot.

It cost £11.50 to get home. Mum could only

just scrape up enough money from her purse, and the cab driver had to do without a tip.

We sat Dad in the wheelchair and then struggled to get him up the step and into the shop. Dad snuffled up the stale smell of book as if the room was full of roses.

'Home now,' he said.

It was a terrible struggle getting Dad upstairs. The physiotherapist had taught him how to do it. He had to put his good foot up on the first stair, steady it, then somehow swing the bad one up beside it, balance, get his breath back, start again with his good foot up . . . Taking things one step at a time had a whole new meaning. We laboured over each step with Dad, Grace calling encouragement from the banisters, me walking backwards leading Dad up, Mum behind, her arms outstretched, ready to catch him whenever he faltered.

Dad was drenched in sweat by the time he got to the top. He insisted that he wasn't ready for bed though – he'd had enough of lying in a bed in that extremely-rude-word hospital. He was out of breath and his words were going again, but we certainly caught the gist of his meaning.

We helped him into his armchair. He sat propped up on all the cushions we could find, his feet sticking out on the leather pouffe. He looked horribly stiff and uncomfortable in his suit but he wouldn't let Mum loosen his collar and tie or even put his slippers on. He clutched my mini version of his Magnum Opus like a Bible. Every now and then he fumbled the pages open and read out a further line or two. Sometimes he simply repeated the first paragraph. Each time Mum reacted with awe and astonishment, and Grace and I clapped and commented too.

Mum made Dad a scratch supper of egg and bacon and sausage and beans and chips.

'If only I'd known you were coming home today I'd have made a special steak and kidney pud for you,' Mum said, though she had no money left in her purse. The fridge was nearly empty. The three of us went without the fry-up, making do with beans on toast.

Dad only picked at his meal, negotiating his way shakily round the plate with a fork. When he put it down he smiled at Mum. 'Lovely grub!' he said.

Mum looked so happy she made me want to cry. Dad was now so tired he could barely hold his head up. He conceded that he might be ready for a lie-down now.

It took almost an hour for Mum to help him

to the bathroom, get him undressed and into his pyjamas and lying down with a hot-water bottle. Grace and I weren't allowed to help during most of this performance, but we were summoned into the bedroom to say goodnight to Dad.

He looked much smaller in bed. Even his pyjamas seemed too big for him now, the sleeves flapping round his bony wrists. He nodded at Grace and me, and then held his cheek sideways in an oddly stiff way. We stood still for a moment, puzzled. Then Grace realized. She rushed forward and gave Dad a big kiss on the proffered cheek.

'Welcome home, Dad,' she said.

'Good girl, good girl,' he said.

I pecked at his cheek too.

'Good girl, good girl,' he repeated. 'Good – to – be – home,' he added, and then he closed his eyes.

We tiptoed back into the living room. The three of us slumped in silence, wondering what on earth was going to happen now.

Dad's docile good humour didn't last. He woke early on Sunday and had the three of us running round all day long. He insisted that we help him all the way downstairs to the shop and then got in a state because a few books had been moved around. He imagined some were missing, remembering books from years ago, insisting that someone had stolen them out of the cabinet. He bashed at the broken lock as if it had happened yesterday and swore at Mum as if she was personally responsible.

'Useless! Useless!' he screeched at her.

She cooked him another fry-up for his lunch but this time he frowned at his plate, his good hand tipping it.

'What's this?' he said.

'It's one of my special mixed grills, Bernard,' said Mum.

Dad sighed. 'Sunday! Where's . . . where's . . . ?' It took him two minutes of struggling and thumping, the egg and bacon congealing on his plate. 'My – roast – beef – and – Yorkshire!' he said in a rush.

Mum sighed too. 'Bernard, we haven't been able to afford roast beef for years, you know that. I'm sorry, I wish I could have made you a pie or a casserole, but I'm a bit short of housekeeping money just now.'

'Useless! Useless!' said Dad, as if poor Mum had been frittering it away on champagne and caviar.

'Mum *isn't* useless, Dad,' I said. 'She's done her very best since you've been ill, but we've got hardly any money left. There are all these scary letters saying they're going to send the bailiffs in. We're going to have to do something, work out a plan.'

'Rubbish!' said Dad.

'I'll show you the letters, Dad.'

'Let your dad eat his dinner first, Prudence,' said Mum.

'Don't want it,' Dad said petulantly, pushing his plate away.

'Then let *us* eat it. We're all starving hungry,' I said.

Dad glared at my impudence. I showed him the sheaf of threatening letters. He held them at arm's length, barely glancing at them.

'Rubbish,' he repeated, and then he tried to tear them up. Luckily he was too fumbly to do more than rip the edge and crumple them. Mum gathered them all up anxiously.

'We can't just tear them up, Bernard,' she said. 'Prue's right, we can't just ignore things. We need a plan.'

'Rubbish!' said Dad. He said it again and again, embellishing it with his favourite swearword. Mum tried to soothe him but he told her she was useless.

When we'd finally got him to bed that evening we were all exhausted. We hadn't dared bring up the most important thing of all – school.

'You should have let me tell him, Mum,' I said.

'But he was in such a dreadful state. He simply couldn't have borne it. I wonder if he's in a lot of pain with his bad arm and leg. Maybe that's why he's been so bad-tempered,' said Mum.

'You don't get pain if you have a stroke. His affected limbs just feel heavy, I'm sure.'

'Still, it must be awful for him,' Mum said.

'It's awful for *us*,' I said.

'What do you think he's going to say about school?' Grace said anxiously.

The phone had gone twice today, one call from Figgy, one call from Iggy, but Mum had run to the phone and said Grace was too busy to talk.

'He's not going to like it, not at all, especially when he realizes it's Wentworth. He'll be so angry with me,' Mum said. 'But what was I to do? I couldn't risk getting prosecuted. What if they'd taken you girls into care? I never wanted you to end up at Wentworth, I tried going to Kingtown High, but they've got two hundred already on their waiting lists. Oh Prue, help me make your dad understand. Maybe you could say it was all your idea? Then he might accept it more willingly.'

'OK. But I don't think he's going to accept it at all,' I said.

'But we will keep going, won't we?' said Grace. She pushed her hair back behind her ears, her chin jutting in the air. 'We *have* to keep going to Wentworth, Mum.'

'Do you really like it there, chickie?' said Mum.

'Well . . . it's OK. The lessons aren't quite as hard as I thought, and some of the teachers are kind. But it's Iggy and Figgy. They're my *friends*.' Grace's blue eyes filled with tears. 'I've never had *proper* friends before. They're just like the bestest friends in all the world. I couldn't bear it if I couldn't see them any more.'

Mum patted her hand comfortingly. 'What about you, Prudence? I expect you feel the same way about Toby.'

'Well . . .' I couldn't stop Mum thinking Toby

was my boyfriend. 'I *have* to stay at Wentworth too, Mum. I know you think it's had a bad effect on me but I know I'd argue back anyway, whether I went to Wentworth or not.'

'I know you're very good at arguing,' said Mum. 'I worry about you, Prue. I've no idea what goes on in that head of yours. I just want you to be happy, dear. If staying at Wentworth makes you happy then let's hope your dad sees reason.'

We all hoped Dad would sleep late so that Grace and I could be off and out before he started shouting for attention. We'd heard poor Mum getting up with him to help him shuffle to the bathroom at least three times in the night. But at half past seven he demanded another trip to the bathroom – and then asked to be bathed.

'Can't it wait till later, dear? The girls will need to use the bathroom soon.'

'Girls – can – wait!'

Grace and I had to go and use the dank outside loo in the back yard and then wash ourselves as best we could at the kitchen sink.

'Let's make a dash for school now,' I said. 'We'll get ourselves a sandwich and just clear off.'

We weren't quick enough. There was a commotion from upstairs. Dad had slipped getting out of the bath, and Mum couldn't get him up by herself.

'Girls! Girls, come here quickly!' she called.

'Pretend we haven't heard. We can still make a run for it,' I said.

'But what if Mum can't budge Dad? He can't stay on the bathroom floor all day,' said Grace.

'OK, OK.'

We trudged upstairs. Mum was grappling with Dad. He'd wound a towel round himself like a nappy. He was trying to preserve his dignity but it made him look like a giant baby.

'Come on then, Dad,' I said, seizing him under the arms.

Mum hauled at his bottom half and Grace pushed and pulled at his midriff. Between us we got him to his feet, and then Mum wrapped his old plaid dressing gown round him.

'Phew! What a . . . what a . . . *performance*,' said Dad as if it was all our fault. He breathed heavily, trying to compose himself.

'Sit down a minute, Bernard,' said Mum, steering him to the loo. She closed the seat and pushed him onto it.

'I'm fine, I'm fine,' he said, but he slumped sideways, his chin on his chest.

I caught Grace by the wrist and started tugging her out of the bathroom as unobtrusively as possible. Dad looked up.

'You girls – early birds!' he said.

Then he focused on our clothes. He blinked. 'Green?' he said. He looked at me, he looked at Grace. 'Peas in pod!'

Grace giggled nervously. Mum sat down heavily on the edge of the bath. I stood still. We didn't say anything – but he suddenly got it.

'School!' he said. He said it softly first. Then

he drew breath. 'School? *School?* SCHOOL!' He was bellowing now, sweat standing out on his forehead.

'Oh Bernard, calm down! You know it's not good for you to get so worked up,' said Mum. She tried to mop his brow with a flannel but he batted her away. He was trembling with fury.

'School?'

'I had to send them, dear. They were threatening us with prosecution, you know that. I didn't have any alternative.'

'Rubbish!' said Dad. He was squinting at the motif on my blazer. 'Wentworth,' he read, rolling his eyes. *'Wentworth!'*

'I couldn't get them in anywhere else, Bernard. I tried, I really did. I went to see the head at Kingtown but there's a very long waiting list. Wentworth was the only school with vacancies. It's not as bad as you'd think. There's a new headmistress, she's making all sorts of improvements.'

'Wentworth!' said Dad in disgust. He struggled to get up from the toilet.

'Careful, dear,' said Mum, trying to help.

'No! No, *traitor!*' Dad said. 'Girls! *No* school! No no no school.'

I looked at Grace. She started sobbing.

'*Please*, Dad,' she said. 'I *love* school. I have these two friends Iggy and Figgy.'

'Stupid,' said Dad.

'No, they're not stupid, they're very special,' Grace said bravely.

238

'*You're* stupid! Useless, useless, useless,' said Dad.

Then he turned to me. 'Your fault! Liar! Thief! Tart! Useless. Rubbish daughters!'

'They're not rubbish daughters! Don't say such terrible things! They're dear good girls. I won't have you hurt them like this!' Mum cried. She turned to us. 'Take no notice of your father. Go to school, girls. Quick, off you go!'

We stared at Mum. We couldn't have been more shocked if the taps or the toilet had spoken. But there wasn't time to wonder. I grabbed Grace and we ran for it. We went on running right out of the house, down the road, all the way to Wentworth.

Grace saw Iggy and Figgy in the playground and shot across to them. I saw her talking to them, waving her arms wildly. Then they hugged her, first Figgy, then Iggy. I felt ashamed. They were sweet girls in spite of their silly nicknames. They obviously really liked my sister. I wished some of the girls in my class liked me.

I had to see Rax urgently. We didn't have art on Mondays. I couldn't possibly wait till Tuesday. I didn't even know if we'd be able to get away from Dad again. And what was going to happen about Friday nights?

I hurtled across the playground, making for the art block. I knew Rax generally didn't arrive at school until later, but I was so desperate to tell him that I went looking for him just in case.

I heard Toby call out to me as I ran but I took no notice.

'Toby wants you,' said Sarah, who was bouncing a red ball on a string. She had no idea what she was doing. The ball bounced wildly backwards and forwards. Sarah cackled with laughter, making no attempt to catch it or jump it or control it in any way. It was enough for her just to watch it.

'Yes, but I don't want Toby,' I said.

Sarah blinked at me, trying to work out my meaning. I hurried past her.

'Toby *wants* you,' she called after me.

'Well, tell Toby I'll catch up with him later,' I said, and rushed on.

I chanted inside my head. *Let Rax be there, please please let Rax be there. I'll do anything, but let Rax be in his art room, all alone, so I can talk to him.*

I got to the art room, I opened the door – and wonder of wonders, Rax was sitting on his desk, shoulders slumped, staring into space.

'Rax, Rax, Rax!' I called.

He stared at me and then jumped down from his desk. 'What's the matter, Prue?'

'Oh, Rax,' I said, starting to cry.

'What is it? What's happened? Tell me!' said Rax.

'It's Dad! He knows!' I sobbed.

'What?' said Rax. He looked horrified. 'What do you mean, he knows? You didn't *tell* him, did you, Prue? What did you *say*?'

'I didn't say anything! He came home this weekend, he's getting better, he can talk now, and he saw us in our Wentworth uniform, and he says we can't come to school any more!' I wailed.

'What about you and me? Did you tell him about us?'

'Of course I didn't!'

'Oh, thank Christ.'

'But don't you see, Rax, he hates the whole idea of Wentworth. He positively forbade Grace and me to come today. We just rushed out, but he's so fierce, he won't let us get away tomorrow, and he won't let me babysit, I know he won't.'

I looked at Rax, tears streaming down my cheeks. He breathed out, leaning against his desk. I saw the look of relief on his face. I saw it and I couldn't bear it. I sobbed harder.

'Prue! Prue, stop it. Come on, calm down. It'll be all right. Don't worry. Don't cry so. You're getting in such a state over nothing.'

'Nothing! Is that all our love means to you? *Nothing?*'

'Ssh now! Of course not. But there's no point getting hysterical. We'll get everything sorted out. I'm sure you'll be able to stay at school. Prue, *please* don't cry like that.' He took two steps forward, hands outstretched, and I fell into his arms.

I wept against his chest. He patted my back like a father. 'There there,' he murmured, as if I was Harry's age. I wept harder, hating him for not caring more, but loving him because he was still my true love and soul-mate.

'I *love* you, Rax,' I said – as the art-room door swung open behind us.

We wheeled round, Rax pushing me away from him. We looked at the door. It was only Sarah, smiling at us, her red ball dangling on the end of its elastic.

Rax rubbed his forehead with the palm of his hand. Then he forced a smile on his face. 'Hello, Sarah,' he said.

'Hello, Rax,' she said cheerfully. 'Look at my red ball!'

'Great,' he said.

'Prue, Toby wants you,' Sarah insisted.

'Never *mind*,' I said, scrubbing at my eyes with the back of my hand.

'You're crying,' said Sarah.

'No, no, she's just got something in her eye,' said Rax. 'Prue, you'd better go and find out what Toby wants.'

'But I have to talk to you!'

'*I* like talking to Rax,' said Sarah.

'And I like talking to you, Sarah,' said Rax.

Sarah smiled at me triumphantly. 'You go and find Toby,' she said.

'But I *must* talk to you, Rax!' I said desperately.

'Later,' said Rax. 'Off you go now.'

I was summarily dismissed. I floundered across the playground, still crying.

'Prue, *there* you are! What's the matter?

What's happened? Is it Rita? What's she done now?' Toby said, rushing up to me.

'Nothing,' I said. 'Just leave me be, Toby.'

'But I've got the most amazing thing to tell you!' said Toby. 'Didn't you hear me shouting at you? You know that book you lent me? You'll never guess what!'

I could guess, all right. He'd read a whole page himself, or maybe a whole chapter. I didn't care if he'd read the whole book.

'I'm sorry, Toby, not now. For God's sake, can't you leave me *alone*!'

I ran away from him into school. I hid in the girls' cloakrooms until the bell went for lessons. It was English first. Mrs Godfrey was irritably teaching the balcony scene from *Romeo and Juliet*. The class read out line after line, talking like metronomes, ruining the romance and the poetry.

I ached to read Juliet but I knew Mrs Godfrey would never pick me. She was talking about the concept of love now, getting impatient when some of the class started whistling and making crass remarks.

'For heaven's sake, stop all this nonsense!' she said. 'Romeo and Juliet are one of the most famous pairs of lovers in literature. Can anyone think of a modern equivalent?'

'Posh and Becks, miss?'

'Brad and Jennifer.'

'Richard and Judy.'

'Prue and Toby,' said Rita furiously.

'No,' said Sarah. 'Prue and Rax.'

I sat very still, praying that people would keep on shouting out stupid suggestions. But Sarah had a loud voice and silenced everyone else.

'Prue and *Rax*?' said Rita.

'Yes, they're dead romantic,' said Sarah.

'Don't be silly, Sarah,' said Mrs Godfrey, sighing.

'I'm not silly,' said Sarah, getting worked up.

'No, I know, I simply meant your *suggestion* was silly,' said Mrs Godfrey.

'Prue and Rax are lovers,' Sarah insisted.

Someone gasped, someone giggled.

'Will you stop staying that, please, Sarah,' said Mrs Godfrey.

'They are, they are. Rax was hugging Prue and she said "I love you" to him,' said Sarah. 'You *did*, didn't you, Prue?'

There were more gasps. Everyone stared at me. The kids in front swivelled right round. Mrs Godfrey stood still, shocked into silence.

The bones in my spine juddered all the way down my back, as if I'd fallen from a great height.

Mrs Godfrey said nothing at all to me, but she must have spoken to Miss Wilmott after the lesson. Sarah was sent for. Then me.

I'd rehearsed a dozen different excuses, stories, lies . . . but as soon as I saw Miss Wilmott's face I knew it was pointless. She looked at me with disdain, breathing shallowly as if I'd started to smell.

'I want you to tell me all about your friendship with Mr Raxberry,' she said.

My mouth dried. 'There's nothing to tell,' I mumbled. 'I know Sarah said stuff in the English lesson, but she's got it all wrong because – because she's simple.'

'Sarah might not be the brightest girl in the class, I know. That's the point. She's not the sort of girl who would fantasize. She says she saw you and Mr Raxberry together in the art room before school and you were embracing. She says you told Mr Raxberry you loved him and he held you in his arms and fondled you.'

'No!' I said. '*Fondle* sounds horrible. He was just being *kind* to me, like a good teacher.'

'I believe you've been babysitting for him on Friday evenings?'

'Yes, but I'm a friend of his family. There's nothing in it. We haven't done anything *wrong*.'

'I'm not sure that's entirely true, Prudence. I've already had a long conversation with Mr Raxberry himself. I feel that there are some aspects of your friendship that could be considered inappropriate.'

'No! No, he's done *nothing*. You mustn't blame him. All right, I *did* say I loved him, but he didn't encourage me in any way. He was just comforting me because I'm so unhappy. My father doesn't want me to come to Wentworth any more.'

Miss Wilmott leaned forward, propping her chin on her fingertips. 'Do you really *want* to stay at Wentworth, Prudence? I don't think you've made much of an effort to fit in. You are obviously gifted in certain areas, and I'm sure in good time you'll learn to cope with maths, but I haven't been at all happy with your attitude. You don't seem to understand how to behave in school. I've heard tales of unsuitable underwear and then a silly romance with one of the boys in your class. I feel that in the space of a few short weeks you've made rather a bad name for yourself.'

I felt my face flaming. 'That's incredibly unfair! I don't know who's been telling you tales, but you've got an entirely slanted viewpoint. You shouldn't be influenced by rumours and tattle-tales.'

'This is precisely what I mean, Prudence. I don't know whether you intend to be deliberately insolent but you certainly come across as an unpleasantly opinionated and arrogant girl. Your sister seems to be a sweet child and she's settled down well at Wentworth. I shall be happy to keep her here, but I can't help feeling that you'll be much better off elsewhere. I shall try hard to engineer a suitable transfer to another school.'

'But I *want* to stay here.'

'Why is that? Let me make myself clear. I can't risk having you and Mr Raxberry at the same school, whatever the ins and outs of your friendship. Things have to be nipped in the bud immediately. If you won't leave then I shall have to ensure Mr Raxberry finds another position.'

'No, you can't do that! He's a brilliant teacher.'

'You should have thought of that before you started acting in this ridiculous and precocious manner. If I were another kind of headteacher I would have Mr Raxberry instantly suspended. There could even be a court case. He would not only lose his job, he could find himself in very serious trouble. Did you ever stop to think about that?'

I couldn't help crying then, though I hated breaking down in front of her. 'Please don't get him into trouble, Miss Wilmott,' I begged. 'None of this was his fault.'

'I'm inclined to believe you, Prudence. So what are we going to do? Are you going to let me transfer you to another school?'

I sat there, agonized. I so wanted to save darling Rax – and yet why hadn't he wanted to save *me*? Had he told Miss Wilmott it was all my fault, that I'd got a ridiculous crush on him, that I'd made ludicrous advances to him? I burned at the thought. I wanted to tell this horrible, patronizing woman how hungrily he'd kissed me, but I couldn't do it. I loved him. I had to help him.

'All right. I'll leave Wentworth,' I whispered.

'That's very sensible of you, Prudence. Right. I'll send you to the Success Maker for the rest of the day. Make the most of your last maths tuition! The tutor in charge will tell you when you may go home. Before too long you should be notified about a new school. Off you go now. Of course I need hardly add that I'm strictly forbidding you to get in contact with Mr Raxberry from now on.'

I knew I couldn't risk running straight to Rax. I couldn't get him into any more trouble. I spent a terrible endless time in the Success Maker, in such a state of anxiety I was even more hopeless than usual, and the tutor despaired.

Sarah was part of our small dunce tuition

group. She blinked at me nervously. 'Did I get you into trouble?' she asked.

'Yes.'

'I didn't mean to. Miss Wilmott kept asking me stuff.' Sarah was nearly in tears. 'Why is it bad to love Rax, Prue? *I* love him.'

'It's not bad. Take no notice. Miss Wilmott's just being horrible.'

'Was she very cross with you?'

'Yes.'

'But you don't have to stand outside her door as a punishment?'

'She's not letting me come back to the school after today.'

Sarah blinked again, her blue eyes watering. 'Is it all my fault?' she asked.

'No,' I said, with an effort.

'It *is*,' Sarah said, her face crumpling.

'No. Don't cry, Sarah. It's OK. I don't *want* to come to this crummy old school. I hate it.'

I *did* hate it, but it felt dreadful to be excluded all the same. They kept me back an extra ten minutes by myself in the Success Maker. I realized it was so I couldn't see any of the others in my form. They were acting as if I might contaminate them. I couldn't even say goodbye to Toby.

When they eventually let me out I marched across the playground with my head held high in case Miss Wilmott or any of the staff were spying on me from their windows. Grace was hopping up and down at the gate.

249

'What's going on, Prue? I asked some of the girls in your class if they'd seen you and they said you were in dead serious trouble but they wouldn't say why.'

'I can't come back to Wentworth,' I said.

'Yes we can. Mum will maybe talk Dad round. Or we can just run out like we did today. We have to keep coming to school. I'd die if I couldn't stay friends with Iggy and Figgy.'

'No, Grace. You don't understand. You can keep coming to school if you can get past Dad. *I* can't. Miss Wilmott told me I can't come back.'

'What? For the whole week? What have you *done*?'

'I can't ever come back. Well, to hell with her, to hell with all of them.' I tore open my bag and pulled out all my school textbooks and exercise books. 'I won't need this – or this – or this!' I started hurling them over the wall, into the empty playground. They flew through the air like large awkward birds, pages flapping.

'Prue! Stop it! You've gone crazy. Tell me why you can't come back,' Grace said, tugging at me.

'Because I love Rax,' I said, running off down the road. I ran and ran, with Grace thudding along behind me. I rushed round the corner – and there was Rax's car. He was parked, waiting for me. He leaned out of his window. He looked very pale, but he nodded pleasantly to Grace.

'Hello, Grace. Do you think you could go home by yourself just this once? I need to talk to Prue.'

Grace stared, open-mouthed.

'Yes, you go home, Grace,' I said, and I got in the car with Rax.

We drove off quickly.

'We're not supposed to see each other any more,' I said.

'I know.'

'If Miss Wilmott saw—'

'She can't see round corners.'

'So where are we going?'

'I don't know. I don't care. I just had to see you. What's happening? Are they excluding you?'

'Miss Wilmott doesn't want me back at all.'

'Oh God. Prue, I'm so so sorry.'

'It's not your fault.'

'Yes it is. I hate myself. I let her think the worst of you, the best of me, just to save my own skin. I said it was ridiculous talking about a love affair between us. I said you simply had a crush on me, and that I was just trying to be kind.'

'Well. That's what you said before, to me.'

'And you were brave enough to stand up to me and force me to acknowledge the truth.'

'Which is?'

He hesitated. Then he said it, very softly. 'I love you.'

'You *really* do?'

'That's why I had to take a risk and see you this one last time. I didn't want you to think I didn't care.'

'Then let's keep driving. Let's really run away, you and me. I don't care where we go. We'll find a little seaside town with a harbour and boats, just like the one you painted when you were little, and we'll both eat ice creams every day.'

'I can't, Prue. You know I can't. I'm going to stay with my family, stick with my job, do all the safe sensible things. But every night when I close my eyes I'll think of us together in this car and how badly I *wanted* to drive off with you. I'll imagine us walking hand in hand at the water's edge—'

'I'll imagine it too. I'm good at pretending.'

'You've got your whole life in front of you. You won't have to pretend, you can live it for real.'

'Can we at least drive to that secret place where we kissed?'

'No. We can't go there, it would be crazy.'

'Please, Rax.'

'No. Stop it.'

'I can't bear the thought of not seeing you.'

'Listen. I told you, one day someone will ask you about the first time you fell in love and I bet you you'll struggle to remember my name.'

'I'll always remember you, and every little thing about you.'

'You wait and see. Now, I think I'd better take you home.'

'No!'

'If you arrive long after Grace your parents will think it strange.'

'I don't care. I'm in enough trouble as it is.'

'What do you think they'll say when you tell them you can't go back to Wentworth? I wish I

252

wasn't such a coward. I ought to go and meet them and try to explain.'

'To my *dad*? Don't be silly, Rax. Listen, couldn't we meet up sometimes, after you've finished school?'

'No.'

'We would be very careful.'

'We'd still be found out sooner or later.'

'Then can't I phone you? Or write to you? *Please*, Rax.'

'No. This is it, Prue. We have to say goodbye.'

He drove me home. He did park a few metres away from the shop, but there were people wandering up and down the pavement and it was still daylight. Even I could see we couldn't kiss properly. Rax reached for my hand instead, squeezed it gently and then whispered, 'Goodbye.'

I whispered it too, and then I got out of the car and watched as he drove off. I stayed staring down the road long after he'd gone round the corner. Then I turned and stared at the shop. I looked at the uninviting window display of yellowing books in bad bindings. I stared at the peeling olive paint on the shop door and the OPEN notice hanging lopsidedly in the window panel. I couldn't stand the thought of going through that door, back into my own life.

Maybe I could run away by myself? I could make for the seaside, lie about my age, get some sort of job in a shop or a café or a hotel. I could walk along the sands every day. It would be desperately lonely but I could think about Rax, pretend he was with me, imagine our life together . . .

I started to walk down the street. Then I stopped. I couldn't *really* run away. I couldn't do it to Grace or Mum. They would be frantic if I disappeared. I didn't know about Dad. He didn't seem to want me as his daughter any more.

I took a deep deep breath as if I was about to dive into a murky swimming pool, and then opened the shop door. Grace was sitting at the desk, building copper and silver and gold towers out of the money in the till. They were very *small* towers. She saw me, and the towers tumbled down, small change spilling off the desk and rolling all over the floor.

'Oh Prue, you're back! Thank goodness! I was scared you might run away with Rax,' said Grace, rushing over and hugging me.

'I wish,' I said sadly.

'I couldn't believe it when you just hopped in his car and drove off. So are you and Rax – you know – like, really in love?'

'Ssh, Grace,' I said, looking upwards.

I could hear Mum's heavy footsteps upstairs in the kitchen.

'It's OK. I told Mum you had to stay behind and see one of the teachers. I'd never tell on you. Prue, Mum and Dad are acting kind of *weird.*'

'So what's new?' I said.

I expected Mum to be tearful and repentant

after standing up to Dad this morning. I thought he would still be apoplectic, ranting and raving in his new staccato voice. But the kitchen seemed strangely silent, though a wonderful sweet syrupy smell started wafting downstairs.

'Oh yum! Mum's baking!' said Grace. 'What do you think she's making? Jam tarts? No, I think it's treacle tart! Oh, I've got to go and see.'

She went rushing upstairs. I stayed in the shop by myself. I found the big art book and looked at my portrait of Rax on the back page. I bent over it, my finger stroking every pencilled line.

'Prue!' Grace came galloping down again. 'It *is* treacle tart, yippee. Mum says we can shut the shop early and come and have some tea.'

The kitchen was warm from the oven and thick with the smell of the golden tart shining like a sun in the middle of the kitchen table.

Dad was pushed up to the table in his wheelchair. He was sitting painfully upright, head held high, as if he was attempting to show he wasn't permanently disabled, that he could leap out of the wheelchair in one bound if he put his mind to it. He saw me, he saw Grace, but his eyes slid straight past us, as if we were invisible. He had obviously decided we were no longer anything to do with him. He took no notice of his wife either. He sat in stony isolation, his amended Magnum Opus balanced on his bony knee.

Mum was making a pot of tea. She was very

pink in the face, wearing her red-and-white checked apron, a cousin of my dreaded dress. Her hair stood out in wisps, there was a smear of flour on her nose, and the sash of her apron emphasized her thick waist – but she looked better than usual. She didn't look defeated any more.

'Hello, girls.' She looked at me. 'Are you all right, Prudence?'

I shrugged.

'Come and have a nice cup of tea.'

'Can we have the treacle tart now, Mum?' Grace begged.

'Of course, dear.'

Mum cut her a generous slice. She cut one for me too.

'I'm not really hungry, Mum.'

'You're mad! I'll have Prue's slice too, Mum. Oh, you make such *superb* treacle tarts,' Grace said indistinctly, spraying crumbs everywhere.

'I'll have to show you how to make tarts yourself sometime.'

'I'd sooner just eat yours! Are you going to serve cakes in the shop, Mum, like Toby suggested?' said Grace. Then she looked anxiously at Dad.

Mum glanced at him too. 'I don't see why not,' she said. 'I think it's a very good idea.'

Dad muttered his favourite worst word, staring straight ahead.

'Please don't swear in front of the girls, Bernard. Or me, for that matter.'

Dad swore more forcefully.

'Your dad and I have had a little tiff, girls,' said Mum. 'Come on, Bernard, there's no point sulking. You'll have a piece of my treacle tart, won't you?'

Dad clamped his mouth together as if she was about to force-feed him.

'Don't be like that,' said Mum. She paused, standing behind him. She raised her eyebrows at us, her hands resting on the handles of his wheelchair. She looked at the corner, as if she was going to wheel Dad into it and leave him there.

Grace giggled nervously.

'Useless!' Dad muttered.

'Stop it!' said Mum. 'I told you, Bernard, I'm not standing for it. You're not going to say these dreadful things to the girls. I know you're their father – but I'm their *mother*. You're upset because they're going to school but there's simply no alternative. You can't teach them now, you know you can't. And they've settled down so happily at Wentworth. Well, Grace certainly has. It's not been so easy for Prue, though she's doing really well in art.'

That was it. That was my chance. I cleared my throat.

'Mum. Dad. I've got to tell you something.'

Grace stared at me, almost dropping her slice of treacle tart. 'Don't talk about Rax!' she mouthed at me.

I shook my head at her. 'I don't really want

to stay at Wentworth,' I said. 'I'm not going any more.'

'Oh Prudence! Make your mind up!' said Mum.

'I just don't fit in there,' I said. 'Grace has got her friends.'

'You've got Toby,' said Mum.

'He's about the only one that likes me. Maybe it's my fault, I don't know. But can't I just stay home now? I can help out in the shop. I can help look after Dad.'

'Don't need – blooming looking after!' Dad said, but he reached out with his good hand and took hold of mine, squeezing it awkwardly. He thought I was being loyal to him, doing what he wanted after all. 'We can work – on Magnum Opus,' he said.

Each word was like a hammer blow but I was past caring. I just nodded weakly. I hated Dad's dry clasp. I wanted to keep the feel of Rax's hand on mine. But Dad hung onto my hand, tugging a little.

'Who's – Toby?' he asked suspiciously.

'He's a lovely lad,' said Mum – and at that moment the shop bell rang downstairs. 'We're closed!' she said. 'Wouldn't you know it! No customers all day long, and then they come calling the minute you close. Run down and see who it is, Grace.'

Grace ran. She came back two minutes later with Toby. Mum looked a little anxiously at Dad, but smiled at Toby all the same.

'Why, Toby, what a lovely surprise! We were

just talking about you, dear. Bernard, this is Toby, Prue's friend.'

Dad glared at him, still hanging onto my hand. 'How – do – you – do?' he barked.

His hand grew hot and I could feel him shaking. I suddenly realized how much effort it took for him to say the simplest thing now.

'How do you do, Mr King,' said Toby politely.

'Would you like some treacle tart, dear?' said Mum.

'Yes please!' said Toby.

'What are you doing here?' I asked, frowning at him.

'I had to see you. You wouldn't listen to me at school! It's about the book.' Toby started delving into a carrier bag and unpeeling bubble wrap.

'Which book?' I said.

'This one!' said Toby, suddenly exposing *The Intimate Adventures of the Very Reverend Knightly*.

'Toby! Put it away!' I said sharply.

'What's this book?' said Mum.

Dad dropped my hand. He waved his good arm wildly. The sweat stood out on his forehead. 'Not! Not!' he said, his speech deserting him again.

'Let's have a look,' said Grace, opening it. 'Oooh! It's ever so rude!'

'*Not!*' Dad insisted.

'Toby, that's not a very nice book to bring into the house,' said Mum.

'It was in your shop, Mrs King,' said Toby. 'Prue showed it to me.'

Mum gasped. So did Dad.

'The thing is, did you know it's ever so valuable?' Toby persisted, taking a big bite of treacle tart. 'I looked it up on my computer. They've got lots of these special antiquarian dirty books on this website, you wouldn't believe it.'

'You shouldn't be looking, a young lad like you,' said Mum.

'Yes, but guess how much the exact same set of books is selling for! I had to check with my sister, just in case I'd got the wrong end of the stick. Go on, *guess*.'

'A hundred pounds?' said Mum.

'Fourteen thousand pounds!' said Toby. 'Yes, truly.'

'My Lord! Imagine! And I've never even set eyes on the book before!' said Mum. 'Well, bless you for finding it for us, Toby. By rights you deserve some of the money if we sell it.'

'Oh no, Mrs King, it's all yours. I haven't done anything,' said Toby.

'Right!' said Dad. '*I* knew. I knew – worth – thousands.'

I was pretty sure Dad had had no idea it was worth a fortune, but he couldn't help crowing. There were feverish pink patches on his cheeks. His hands were shaking so badly he spilled his cup of tea down his waistcoat, but we all pretended not to notice. He ate a slice of treacle tart too, and had the grace to nod at Mum. 'Not bad,' he said.

'You're a brilliant baker, Mrs King,' said Toby. 'Maybe you ought to close down the bookshop altogether and start up a cake shop?'

'Rubbish!' said Dad. 'Books. Books *best*.'

I went down to the shop and found the other volumes of the Reverend Knightly. I looked through them carefully, turning the pages at the very edge, checking they were all first editions. I counted every colour plate. All five volumes seemed in near-fine condition.

Dad very laboriously composed a detailed description of the books, dictating it at snail speed. I wrote it out for him and sent letters to several specialist book dealers. Dad asked fifteen thousand for the five volumes but they weren't interested. So I got Toby to help me type it all out on a special antiquarian book site on the Internet. We still didn't get fifteen thousand, but managed to sell the lot for £12,500, which still seemed a huge sum.

'It's enough to pay off all the debts,' said Mum. 'It's really all because of you, Prue. You were the one who let Toby borrow the book, though it was a very *odd* thing for you to do. Did you look inside it?'

'Not properly,' I said.

'Hmm!' said Mum. 'Still, I suppose it's a case of all's well that ends well.' She chucked me gently under the chin. 'Cheer up, chickie. I'm so glad that you and Toby are friends. He's such a lovely boy – and he has such good ideas! He's made such a difference, it's like he's already part of our family.' Mum looked anxious. 'You will stay friends with him, Prue, when you start at Kingtown High?'

I sighed. 'I'll stay friends with him, Mum. *Just* friends, though.'

'Well, whatever you say, dear.' Mum beamed at me. 'It's good that your dad doesn't mind too much about you going to Kingtown, as he went there himself.'

I was starting there at the beginning of the spring term. Miss Wilmott had pulled strings to get me a place there. My dad's old grammar school. I wasn't at all sure how I was going to get on there. If I was so hopeless at so many subjects at a school like Wentworth then surely I'd be floundering helplessly at a school with high academic standards.

When I went to see the headteacher I found her surprisingly reassuring.

'I understand your blind spot when it comes to maths, Prudence. I'm not too bright at maths myself. We'll see about some extra tutoring in various subjects, but obviously you're a girl who's going to excel at the arts. Miss Wilmott sent us your entrance papers for Wentworth, saying she thought you'd be an excellent student at our school, if we could possibly find a place for you. Your Shakespeare essay was outstanding.'

Mum was giving me the full Kingtown uniform for Christmas, with leftover Reverend Knightly money. 'You need to get off to the right start this time,' she said. 'I'm sure you're going to be really happy at Kingtown, dear. I wonder what the art teacher will be like? I know you thought very highly of that Mr Raxberry at Wentworth.'

I said nothing, bending my head, hiding behind my hair.

'I think you maybe had a little crush on him,' said Mum.

I swallowed.

'It's all right, dear. It's all part of growing up. But you'll get over it soon enough.'

I knew Mum meant well, but she simply didn't understand. I knew I'd never be really happy again. I missed Rax so so much. I couldn't bear to be without him. Sometimes it was so overwhelming that I had to shut myself away and cry and cry. I thought about him first thing in the morning and last thing at night. I dreamed about him. I painted him over and over again. I wrote very long letters to him, though I tore each one into tiny shreds.

I lived my ordinary life, I coached Dad with his speech, I helped Mum in the shop, I fooled around with Grace, I chatted to Toby – but it was just like a play. I was saying all the right words, going through all the motions, but none of it seemed *real*. I was pretending all the time. I just wanted to see Rax, to talk to him, to throw my arms around his neck, to kiss him, to tell him just how much I loved him, and that I would go on loving him for ever and ever.

I stayed right away from Wentworth — but several times I couldn't stop myself getting the bus and walking along Laurel Grove. I paused outside number 34, but then I walked on. I walked and walked and walked, slowly, dreamily, as if I was strolling along the seashore . . .